Aeroscopics

The publisher and the University of California Press Foundation gratefully acknowledge the generous support of the Richard and Harriett Gold Endowment Fund in Arts and Humanities.

Aeroscopics

Media of the Bird's-Eye View

PATRICK ELLIS

University of California Press

University of California Press
Oakland, California

© 2021 by Patrick Ellis

Library of Congress Cataloging-in-Publication Data

Names: Ellis, Patrick, 1980- author.
Title: Aeroscopics : media of the bird's-eye view / Patrick Ellis.
Description: Oakland, California : University of California Press, [2021] |
    Includes bibliographical references and index.
Identifiers: LCCN 2020051190 (print) | LCCN 2020051191 (ebook) |
    ISBN 9780520355484 (cloth) | ISBN 9780520355491 (paperback) |
    ISBN 9780520975934 (epub)
Subjects: LCSH: Paris (France)—Aerial views—History—20th century.
Classification: LCC DC707 .E39 2021 (print) | LCC DC707 (ebook) |
    DDC 914.4/36100222—dc23
LC record available at https://lccn.loc.gov/2020051190
LC ebook record available at https://lccn.loc.gov/2020051191

Manufactured in the United States of America

30 29 28 27 26 25 24 23 22 21
10 9 8 7 6 5 4 3 2 1

Contents

Acknowledgments

While writing this book, I obtained one habit of the nineteenth-century tourist: upon arrival in a new city, I aimed for the highest view one could access. Looking down from these perches now, in retrospect, I see below a map of gratitude.

From the campanile at the University of California, Berkeley, overlooking the campus where this project had its genesis: my great thanks to Mark Sandberg, who fundamentally changed the way that I look at spectacles past and present; to Kristen Whissel, for always having the mot juste; and to David Bates, guide to media and scientific arcana. Also to Barry Pateman, the anarchist authority on Bay Area archives; Gray Brechin, a marvelous coconspirator and host; Kathy Geritz, who shepherded ideas from this book into a film series at the Pacific Film Archive; Laura Horak, who offered sage advice from day one; and Linda Williams, who provided living proof that the study of film should be ebullient.

Berkeley is also where this manuscript, folded into a paper airplane, found its publishing house. There, I have received careful, animating editorial guidance from Raina Polivka and Madison Wetzell, along with crystalizing commentary from my reviewers. Elsewhere in the hills and streets of the East Bay, I had the good fortune to trade ideas with Nicholas Baer, Eliot Bessette, Jennifer Blaylock, Norman Gendelman, Jennifer Malkowski, Renée Pastel, and Justin Vaccaro.

In Atlanta, from the Westin Peachtree Plaza, I spy the Georgia Institute of Technology, where I finished this book. There was a supportive crew on the ground: thanks to Ben Bergholtz, Annika Orich, Nick Sturm, Anu Thapa, and Gregory Zinman. Rebecca Burnett and Andy Frazee showed me how to better tie my research to my teaching. I found ideal collaborators in Jerushia Graham, Wendy Hagenmaier, Virginia Howell, and Anna Westerståhl Stenport.

Atop the Glasgow Lighthouse, I owe a special thanks to my old friend and collaborator Jesse Olszynko-Gryn, who accompanied me over years of memorable *dérives* to some of the more important pinnacles of the continent. Other far-flung fellow travelers I must thank for their hospitality and insight: Tom Conley, Joe Culpepper, Oliver Gaycken, Nick Hopwood, and Isabelle McNeill. The late Ralph Hyde demonstrated an inspiring intellectual generosity.

The list of archives, museums, funding bodies, and speakers series that helped with this project could not be counted on any ordinary map. To single out a few: my thanks are owed to James Akerman at the Newberry Library, Patrick Deicher at the Bourbaki Panorama, Melissa Keiser at the Smithsonian National Air and Space Museum, Peter Kelly of the Douglas Victorian Society, and Jon Mogul at the Wolfsonian Museum. It has been a boon to have the support of various funding bodies, especially the American Council of Learned Societies, the J.B. Harley Research Trust, the National Endowment for the Humanities, and the Social Sciences and Humanities Research Council of Canada, without whose assistance I could not have performed my research. I was gratified to discuss ideas from this book with the David Rumsey Map Center at Stanford University, the George Washington Wilson Centre for Visual Culture at the University of Aberdeen, and the Centre for Film and Screen and the Twentieth Century Think Tank at the University of Cambridge.

Three final views, closer to home.

Looking down from a minaret in Plant Hall, I'm grateful to my new colleagues at the University of Tampa for such a generous welcome. Future collaborations are in store.

In Halifax, from Citadel Hill: thank you to the Ellises, to Ann and John Paul, for everything. The border is closed as I write, but we will fly over it again.

And from a hot air balloon, here or there, but always with Vanessa. More balloon rides to come. Next time we'll bring the kids.

Patrick Ellis
August 2020

Introduction

Spotting the Spot

Flying over Colorado, looking out of the window, I compare the topography below with the seatback screen map, trying to better understand what I am seeing. Such screens are dwindling, becoming an obsolete form of aerial vision. I remember the first time that I performed this cartographic cross-check. Thinking back over other aerial firsts that transpired during the years that went into this book, four scenes come to mind.

> Chicago, 2009: *A father and son take the elevator more than one thousand feet up to the top of the Hancock tower. There, the boy looks out of the window at the city below. He suggests to his father that the city they are looking at is a fake, a scaled miniature.*

> Oakland, 2013: *A consumer drone flies over the city. At first, it is assumed to be an airplane, but its unusual size and unfamiliar rotor buzz prompts many to look up and gaze at the new machine. Some stop in their tracks.*

> Lille, 2014: *A historic scale model of the city is on display. Locals examine the exhibit, and struggle to reconcile it with the digital maps on their phones. Even the cardinal directions are difficult to orient.*

> Stanford, 2016: *A student tries a virtual reality headset for the first time in the library. The immersive scene aims to replicate the experience of peering off of the open roof of a skyscraper. She becomes dizzy, and stumbles.*

The aerial view, and the media that offer this vision, is in the zeitgeist. People are having their first experiences with virtual reality simulations of flight; with drone's-eye views, both recreational and martial; and with the scalar play of Google Earth. This all seems new. But this impression of novelty is misplaced.

The aerial view was widely democratized in the nineteenth century, prior to commercial flight, prior even to widespread photographic circulation. There were devices—cartographic devices—that aimed to simulate this elevated view for a mass audience. Panorama paintings that reproduced a view from a great height; immense, miniature models of cities that circulated as proxies for a balloon view; filmic simulations of flight; observation rides that provided slow-moving aerial views of cities; and many others besides.

These media had many of the trappings and appeals of urban cartography (scaled, systemized, and symbolic representation), but none of a map's most common offering: wayfinding.[1] Instead, within these topsy-turvy aerial viewing apparatuses, new cartographic attributes emerged: scale shifted erratically, time seemed to slow, and the map's legend was rewritten. Over the long nineteenth century, these media toyed with the norms of cartography. A fundamental change in the connotations and appeals of the aerial view occurred, as a contemplative form of scrutiny (patient analyses of static urban scenes) gave way to a ludic glance (disorienting glimpses of moving urban scenes). From observation to intoxication: this was mechanical objectivity made giddy by height.

The aerial vignettes that began this introduction are contemporary examples, but typical of historical adaptations to new technologies. They include the human reactions of disbelief, surprise, disorientation, and giddiness. Such terms run contrary to the present understanding of the aerial view, around which floats a word cloud of menacing efficiency: rationalizing, clarifying, administrating, threatening. The aerial view is too simply understood as a transparently authoritarian viewpoint, one best made use of in planning and war, one that offers the information required to render massive change on the ground below, be it transformative or destructive. This has a certain historical credibility, especially if thinking of the aerial view from the First World War onward, as is the custom, and especially now, when the arrival of drone warfare has transformed the perception of the aerial view. The problem with the drone telos is that the history of aerial vision becomes only an index of bombing, death, and disruption, a record book of original sin. When taking a longer historical approach, the aerial view has altogether different qualities, and not at all clarifying ones. In this book, I turn the common assumption of the aerial view on its head, beginning with the historical public, joining them in their gaze, and trying to understand what they were seeing.

FIGURE 1.   The pictured location is the Crystal Palace. "Spotting the Spot,"
Ballooning and Aeronautics 1, no. 1 (January 1907), 132. Wolfsonian Collection.

What they were seeing was not at all clear; visibility was hazy. Writers in
the nineteenth century were under no illusions about the opacity of the aerial view. They recognized, for instance, that the interpretation and site recognition of bird's-eye-view photographs, even familiar ones, posed a challenge.
The journal *Ballooning and Aeronautics* even had, in the early 1900s, a
"Spotting the Spot" competition, in which it would publish an unidentified
"bird's eye view each month for the purpose of testing the geographical
knowledge of aeronauts, and of those who, although not yet as balloonists,
can form a mental picture of what certain localities would look like if seen
from above."[2] The editors recognized that such an image did not offer knowledge up to the viewer; that such views were seldom obvious; that they
required study; and that they were, per the premise of the game, opaque.

FIRST PRINCIPLES OF THE AERIAL VIEW

The opacity of the aerial view was likewise known to early balloonists and
balloon photographers. It is only after the World Wars, and with the immense
interpretative apparatus that was fundamentally conjoined to military aerials, that historians came to see the aerial view as per se clarifying, if not

menacing.[3] These decades marked a sea change in the understanding of the aerial view. There has since been a tendency to assume that all aerial views have the same type of utility. They do not. When such a view is not measuring anything—as most views, historically, have not—its utility is reduced. Other concepts were at work.

Here, I propose five forgotten *first principles of the aerial view*. Nonexhaustive, they nevertheless include the major thoroughfares of aerial thought in the nineteenth century. These principles will be mobilized throughout this book as tools for better understanding the aerial view.[4] They are drawn from the literature of the early balloonists, who were the first theoreticians of the aerial, although these emblematic principles will be located in many other sources in what is to come.

Doubling as treatise and manual, the "literary flight technology" of the early balloon account was a plentiful textual genre.[5] Beginning in the years immediately following the Montgolfiers' 1783 flight in Paris, a great number of books in this area were published, from *Details des deux voyages aérien d'apres la decouverte de MM Montgolfiere* (1783), to G.A. Kohlreif's *Abhandlung über die Luftbälle* (1784), to John Southern's *A Treatise upon Aerostatic Machines* (1785). This was a responsive and international scientific literature that aimed to distribute information regarding this most public but nonetheless inaccessible of sciences. It is difficult to overstate the unprecedented novelty of the aerial view, not merely in its ultimately transformative relation to archaeology, forestry, urban planning, and other fields, but in its disturbance of individual perception and attendant bodily response. Close attention was paid to the epistemology and physiology of this view. Lay readers were keen for accounts, and by the mid-1800s, there was sufficient volume of publication to warrant anthologizing and collection in popular editions; these editions are by and large what are referred to in the following.

1. The Aerial View Is Opaque

The aerial view customarily requires an appendix or instrument in order to be interpretable. Every object discussed in this book that provides the aerial view includes an informational accessory: narrative guides, legends, grids, rhumb and elevation lines, stereoscopic viewers, telescopes, and so on. To paraphrase the historian of cartography Christian Jacob, who was writing regarding maps: the aerial view is opaque like a cinema screen, not transparent like a window.[6] This opacity exists not only at the level of defamiliarization—in which a known landscape becomes unknown through a shift in perspective—but at the level of atmosphere. Weather and environmental effects can delimit the visible distance of the view (a wall of fog)

FIGURE 2. Aerial views are in practice often obscured in such a manner as this, but they are seldom preserved given their inutility. The Scottish Office Air Photographs Unit maintained many such images, including this, over Aberdeen. Joint Air Reconnaissance Intelligence Centre, Sortie Series 17, 1958.

as well as have significant aesthetic and hermeneutic effects. Think of the travelers who see Paris in a cloudy dusk from the Eiffel Tower, and then again, their home cities, clear at dawn, as an airplane lands; in each case, the atmosphere will translate (somehow) to the emotions.

No other view, save from a satellite, can be so simply obscured by the weather. Wrote one balloonist of the 1830s, describing an ascent: "The trees, the buildings, the spectators and their crowded equipages, and finally, the earth itself, at first distinctly seen, gradually became obscured by a thickening mist, and growing whiter in their forms, and fainter in their outlines, soon faded away 'like the baseless fabric of a vision.'"[7] One need not even rise so high as a balloon. Any long-planned trip up one of the great towers of the world, renowned for its views, can be made profitless by a cloudy day. The fight against this opacity leads the way to many of the objects outlined in this book. How can the aerial view be reproduced, routinely and clearly, so that it can be popularly understood?

2. The Aerial View Is Plastic

Connected to its opacity, the experience, interpretation, and understanding of the aerial view varies enough from site to site, time to time, and viewer to viewer as to be fundamentally ambivalent. Is the aerial view seized from the open-air vulnerability of the balloon, or the confines of the observation tower? From the geological timescale of the hilltop, or the engineering marvel of the skyscraper? Here is the difference between safety and alarm, between history and novelty: the site of the view matters. So, too, does the object of the view: is it of Paris, a city not designed on a grid, or Chicago, one that was? The former may naturalize the city and allow (as many have claimed) an appreciation of a spontaneous, organic formation; the latter, the opposite. The various elevated purchases addressed in what follows all impact the quality of the vista.

So, too, do the preoccupations or hobbyhorses of the viewer. Michel de Certeau, high above the city, spies rebellion in the pedestrians below; Paul Virilio notices only their vulnerability. Roland Barthes looks out from the Eiffel Tower as though he himself were the point of a symbolic, inverted exclamation mark; T. J. Clark looks back from Notre Dame and sees only the palimpsest of history.[8] Their views are in turn determined by the varying aerial ideologies of their time.[9]

This plasticity was certainly conspicuous to early balloonists. An anonymous poem of 1830 published on the occasion of a balloon ascent in Scotland (and so written in brogue) addresses the balloonists, and imagines the differing data that the balloon view may recover:

> Tell a' ye either see or hear,
> But no ae sentence less or mair:
> Remember, lad, we'll gar you swear
> To speak the truth;
> . . .
> Bring Horton plans o' emigration.

To Malthus state the population.
For Sinclair tak' an observation
O' agriculture:
He'll seize statistic information
Like ony vulture.[10]

Despite the appeal to the balloonists' objectivity, to "speak the truth" when they "tell a' ye either see or hear," an aerial report will nevertheless be understood differently according to the preoccupations of the dignitary listeners, ranging from emigration (Robert Wilmot-Horton, who advocated that the Irish emigrate to the New World), overpopulation (Thomas Malthus, the eponymous Malthusian), and the state of agriculture (John Sinclair, statistician and advocate for agricultural science). In sum—and to quote a line from Le Corbusier that has been a watchword for me, and will appear again in this project—"the bird can be dove or hawk."[11] The aerial can be pacific or martial. But it can also be a dodo, or a bluebird of happiness, a cockatrice, or a phoenix—that is to say, it can just as well be historical, intoxicating, calcifying, or renewing. The bird's-eye view, like the bird, is taxonomically a class, with many species. The same is true of bird's-eye *viewers*. Together, viewer and view vary enough so as to be plastic.

3. The Aerial View Is Slow

Hot air balloons move at the speed of wind, and they tend not to attempt a flight when that speed is much accelerated beyond the norm. A representative balloon ride that I took when researching this book traveled seven miles in an hour; this, combined with the lack of turbulence in a drifting balloon, is slow enough that lateral movement is almost imperceptible. The balloon era was slow moving.

Modern commercial flight paradoxically carries with it an analogous temporality. Traveling at speeds that sometimes approach a Mach number, the sense of acceleration is negligible (barring turbulence); moreover, looking out of the window, even the fastest objects on the ground, such as cars, appear to proceed at a snail's pace. Pedestrians, when visible, seem immobile. The perception of terrestrial slow motion is not a result of the airplane's speed, but rather its distance; when a mountaintop also allows an untrammeled view of a motorway, the cars likewise appear to move slowly. This is the effect of "motion parallax": nearer objects move quickly, farther objects move more slowly, and the observable difference in speed aids in our understanding of depth. This phenomenon and its physics—this fundamental quality of all elevated views—is almost never mentioned in contemporary literature.[12] It is, however, found in that of the balloon era.

A popular retelling of a biblical parable in the nineteenth century, for instance, used the phenomenon to explain the celestial view of God: "Some while ago two aeronauts, hanging in mid-air, looked down on the earth from their balloon, and wondered to see how . . . the long, rapid, flying train appeared but a black caterpillar slowly creeping over the surface of the ground."[13] The neglect that contemporary authors accord to this experience is attributable to the almost invisible ubiquity of motion parallax, which engenders a perceptual near-sightedness; we are so acclimatized to the phenomenon, it is difficult to articulate it *as* a phenomenon.[14] Resultantly, scholars have emphasized *speed*, which has received much more attention than slowness—although that is beginning to change.[15]

Human movement within the given apparatus (or geological feature) that provides the elevated view is likewise slow—often careful and steady, out of a sense of self-preservation. Viewers voluntarily grip the guardrail or the edge of the balloon basket, inching along. Although slow, the movement that spectators and passengers were once allowed in flying machines offered quite a bit of latitude compared to present-day flight. Even the original Ferris wheel—the most well known of the "observation rides," discussed in chapter 4—allowed its riders to circulate, unlike the seat-belted confinement of its descendants. The aerial view, when remediated, offers a relative freedom of movement: the virtual gaze is mobile rather than immobile, to use Anne Friedberg's well-known formulation.[16]

4. The Aerial View Is Intoxicating

Vertigo—or what is sometimes more carefully called "height vertigo," or in a clinical setting "airsickness," or in the nineteenth century "giddiness"—is one of the most widespread perceptual effects of the aerial view. The causes of this intoxicating feeling vary: high altitudes can cause lightheadedness, the act of ascension can send butterflies to the stomach, the perceived discord between mobility and stasis can provoke nausea. The connection between the aerial and dizziness was so immediately apparent in the balloon era that alcohol companies (Dubonnet, Cinzano) promptly began sponsoring balloons. One intoxicates the drinker; the other, the rider.[17]

Any few pages of a ballooning history will provide evidence of the intoxicating effect of the aerial view. This feature of the aerial in particular lends itself to jest, as in the poet Thomas Hood's "Ode to Mr. Graham, the Aeronaut," in which the author partakes of view and beverage at once, eventually asking for a Dollond telescope to bring the Earth closer to his eye:

Now for a glass of bright champagne
Above the clouds!—Come, let us drain
A bumper as we go!—
But hold!—For God's sake do not cant
The cork away—unless you want
To brain your friends below.

. . .

Ah me! my brain begins to swim!—
The world is growing rather dim;
The steeples and the trees—
My wife is getting very small!
I cannot see my babe at all!—
The Dollond, if you please![18]

Despite its potential for humor, such vertigo is occasionally treated seriously (Hitchcock's 1958 film named for the phenomenon being the most well-known example). In the playwright Henri Lavedan's short story, "Le vertige" (1896), a married woman boards a captive balloon ("un énorme et débonnaire point d'exclamation") where she chances to meet a persistent suitor. The combination of the social frisson and the view makes her succumb to "le vertige de isolement, de l'immensité, du loin de tout, presque un vertige morale enfin" ("the vertigo of isolation, of immensity, or remoteness from everything, almost a mental vertigo").[19] It is a worthy reminder that most aerial observations are made within a mental context of intoxication, and this intoxication inflects what is observed.

5. *The Aerial View Is Parallax*

Most aerial views were in history not perceived from a vertical position, like a map, but rather were ordinarily observed from an angle. The term *parallax*, here, is drawn from astronomy, where it characterizes the perceived difference in observation of celestial bodies that the various angles of vision provoke. (This is related to, but not to be confused with, "motion parallax," a related phenomenon discussed above.) A planet, for instance, appears different in size and shape dependent upon whether it is viewed from San Francisco or London. Ironing out the distortions of parallax via comparative data has been a major feature of astronomy (necessitating global collaboration and relying on an "aperspectival objectivity," discussed in chapter 1). The popular aerial views discussed here seldom have need for reliable measurement, so they need not reconcile data. All the same, *angle* is of vital importance in the aerial view; and relatedly, *scale*. The relative distance to the viewed object, and the perspective from which it is viewed, can mean the difference between an abstract geometry and a coherent space, between a Cubist tapestry and knowable city. This principle of the aerial view is so fundamental, so vital, and so neglected that a large part of the first chapter of this book is devoted to it, where the testimony of balloonists is also provided to this end.

AEROSCOPICS

These principles of the aerial view are also its problems. The aerial view is opaque, and so, hard to see clearly; it is plastic, and so, incoherently diverse; it is slow, and so, it punishes hasty analysis; it is intoxicating, and so, it denies a levelheaded understanding; it is parallax, and so, inconsistent and irreproducible. These features of the aerial recur throughout this book, as a series of apparatuses are discussed, apparatuses that reproduce the bird's-eye view and in so doing aim to remedy or remediate these problems: panoramas that beat the weather, models that slow down time, films that protect against intoxication, rides that toy with parallax vision. Collectively, I refer to these objects as *aeroscopics*, from a nineteenth-century term of art that is also the name of an observation ride treated in chapter 4. The aeroscopic, as I define it, provides a technologically mediated aerial view. The term *mediation* is here employed in a neutral sense, without the negative connotations that are often today attached to it in colloquial use, when discussing, for instance, the ubiquity of photography at museums and concerts, in which the art is nominally "mediated" by the camera and placed at an unfortunate remove from the viewer. Petran Kockelkoren's pithy distillation of Marshall McLuhan serves better: "The cultural process in which technology extends our ability to perceive, redistributes social relations, and thereby elicits new visual language and conferral of meanings."[20] The aeroscopic is, in short, a terrestrial spectacle that provides the bird's-eye outlook to a mass audience.

My first chapter examines what has been called the first mass medium: the circular panorama.[21] In film history, much has been made of this immense, immersive medium as the nineteenth-century's pre-cinematic object par excellence, trading in many of the same appeals that the movies would in decades to come. Much of this scholarship has, inevitably, marginalized the panorama as merely a forerunner to the later medium. Here, the original paintings are returned to via site visits and through neglected ephemera from the period. In particular, panorama paintings in the urban genre are considered, arguing that this first iteration of the form operates at a single, reliable altitude, one that is commensurate with—but reverses—the view from the astronomical observatory. I propose that the panorama painting was born atop the observatory, and sets the parameters for a "panoramic altitude," a scale of vision that aeroscopics share, and that carries with it distinct interpretive effects on the viewed subject. The vista that the urban panorama painting provided necessitates a curious hybrid vision: a push-pull between the particular and the expanse, the pedantic and the sublime, the close and the distant. This hybridity allowed for a unique form of play with scale in which observers could position themselves within competing possible systems of scalar order, from the human to the cosmological.

The second chapter recovers a medium that still exists, but that has changed its name. Today, we call them simply "model cities," but in the nineteenth century they were known as "panstereoramas." Immense models of Paris, London, and other metropolises toured within the same showman circuit as panorama canvases. The miniature model city—heretofore often a military artifact—was repurposed as a mass media approximation of the view from the balloon. This occurred before relief maps would become available to lay audiences, or indeed before tethered balloons provided genuine views for a paying public. Here surveyed, for the first time, is the panstereorama phenomenon: from Le Quoy's 1771 "model in relievo" of Paris, through the box-office successes of late-Georgian London, to the medium's ultimate adoption by the early world's fairs, whence they ceased to be named panstereoramas and became a commonly curated part of these new civic events. These spectacles, located at the juncture of the history of cartography and media history, recast the model city from a martial to a spectacular purpose and served quite explicitly as a proxy for a balloon view of the represented city. The panstereorama, like the balloon, slowed down civic life to a state that encouraged its contemplation, allowing for a careful accounting of a customarily fast-moving object: the city.

The third chapter begins by articulating a new concept: the "media pathology." An abiding response to new, twentieth-century media has been to focus on their accompanying physical maladies. Television brings the poor posture of "frogitis"; the smart phone breeds hunch-backed "text neck"; and cinema prompts, among many other disorders, "secretary's eye," a squint associated with excessive viewing. These pathologies—some bogus, some bona fide—powerfully inform the popular reception of the given medium, as well as (sometimes) their legal status and ergonomic design. Moreover, these media pathologies are almost invariably an extension of bodily media metaphors—the radio as ear, the camera as eye, the computer as brain—that can inform the laboratory and clinical practice of doctors and scientists.

One of the first media pathologies associated with the new medium of film was so-called "camera sickness," a vestibular malady that shared symptoms with other newly identified motion sicknesses. (*Motion sickness, car sickness,* and *space sickness* were all coined within a decade of 1900.) Dizziness, nausea, perspiration: many early cinema viewers simply dismissed the medium on account of these unintended effects, which were associated with the "sensory mismatch" that the immersive mobility of the cinema imposed on the stationary viewer. Cinema sickness was especially associated with aviation and balloon films. This chapter analyzes, with reference to early sociologies of the cinema, initial encounters with aerial films that resulted in symptoms of motion sickness, before pivoting to later scientific experiments that used cinema as a potential cure, through acclimatization, for actual motion sickness. The motion picture camera can be used as a device for habituating the viewer to height vertigo. The idea of the *pharmakon*—the ambivalent relationship between cure and poison—runs through aerial media.

My fourth chapter again aims to recover an overlooked medium; in this case, a genre of attraction that I dub an "observation ride," after the original name for the Ferris wheel (an "observation wheel"). Many devices fall into the category of observation ride, but they cluster at the turn of the nineteenth century, when the Ferris wheel (Chicago, 1893), the Aeriocycle (Buffalo, 1901), and the Flip-Flap (London, 1908), among others, were all introduced to eager publics. Such apparatuses—which often debuted at world's fairs but have had a varied afterlife in amusement parks—have fundamentally different values than the expected appeals of thrill rides, the erroneous genre of attraction into which they are often placed. Where a thrill ride such as a roller coaster offers velocity and shocks, blurring the rider's vision of the area, an observation ride offers a steady, languid trip; a frisson of unnatural movement (rotating, revolving, alternating, as the case may be); and a lightly intoxicated, not to say ludic, form of observation from above.

As a case study in the genre of observation rides, this chapter looks at the "Aeroscope," the device for which this book is named. This slow-moving, low-altitude, spiraling amusement ride offered visitors to San Francisco a bird's-eye view of the city during the Panama-Pacific International Exposition of 1915. Designed by the future engineer of the Golden Gate Bridge, Joseph Strauss, the Aeroscope was a curious machine, half-airplane, half-cinema. Its unique helical arc perpetually shifted the rider's perspective and distance from the subjects of the view, and further toyed with any appreciable scale markers. The Aeroscope, arguably a centering monument of the exhibition, promised cartographic information, but delivered instead an interpretive dizziness. It functions as an axial point from which to survey the debate over the place of aerial vision just prior to milestones in the use of aviation for war.

In the fifth and final chapter, the book pivots from the view from above, to the view from below. The objects that are my focus—panorama, model, ride, film—are spectacles of the bird's-eye view, but they are invariably connected to the worm's-eye view: the look up. The connection between the view from above and the view from below is sometimes literal: the balloon that the model city aims to simulate is sometimes tethered to the ground and gathers more spectators than it has riders. To be faithful to the experience of the period that is this work's focus is to notice not only that the view from above and the view from below are conceptually tied, and seldom uncoupled, but that the principal way that balloons, airships, and airplanes changed the direction or quality of a public's look was not by providing the view from above but rather by necessitating the view from below.

The history of flight is a history of entertainment. Lighter-than-air flying machines' overwhelming use was as spectacle for terrestrial viewers. The first appearance of heavier-than-air flying machines in the skies above major cities in 1909, when many caught their first glimpse of these strange new machines, was a major event in this aerial media history. Situating their arrival in the long history of heavenly spectacles, the panic and disorder that was anticipated on the streets is recovered, as is the sublime aerial "trainspotting" that accompanied these machines. Decades before contrails, the airplane turned the sky into a screen for their aerial animations.

FLIGHT PATH

These various objects and phenomena share many features. Aeroscopics provide their views, invariably, to a grouped audience—this is not the lone mountaineer enjoying the sublimity of distance, but rather the collective group appreciating the view from above as a spectacle. The view from the aeroscopic device is collectively imagined, and it shares, in this regard among others, an appeal with cartography, which has been described in similar terms.[22] One main endeavor in this work is to characterize the experience of such spectators, and to recover how they were positioned at the time. It can be difficult to imagine the curiosity of pre-flight viewers who had never, for instance, seen their city from above, and could not do so without an aeroscopic device. Accordingly, I resurrect several neglected categories of spectator—the observer, the sensation seeker, and the gazer.

Each type is determined by the given apparatus (respectively: panorama, observation ride, airplane), and their response is partially determined in kind. The observer is analytical; the sensation seeker, sanguine; the gazer, enraptured.

Aeroscopics, as apparatuses designed to simulate the aerial view, are produced to this day, and a number of contemporary aeroscopic devices are treated in the conclusion. Even so, as a genre of device they had their heyday, lasting from 1783, the date of the Montgolfiers' first balloon flight, to 1915, by which time new transportation technologies (the automobile, the airplane) began to have a large impact,[23] the status of world's fairs (a crucial site for the introduction of aeroscopics) began to decline,[24] and the First World War began to alter the predominant mood of the aerial.[25] There are ups and downs for aeroscopics within this period—panorama paintings boom in the early 1800s, and then boom again later in the century; model cities are popular throughout the nineteenth century, with a particular appeal in the 1820s; observation rides spring up at regular intervals with the ephemeron that is the world's fairs—but cumulatively, there is a steady trend of these apparatuses throughout the nineteenth century. This date range (1783–1915) corresponds, with slight modification, to what Eric Hobsbawm called the "long nineteenth century" (1789–1914, from the French Revolution to the First World War), a useful periodization for the book.

This span of time is long, and inevitably many of the objects that are recovered here have, like the literature of the balloonists, been neglected in media histories, despite once being abundant and popular, and despite their explanatory power today. Tom Gunning, in an essay that inspired my approach, claimed to be more of a burrower than a bird's-eye historian—more archivist than synthesizer.[26] Of course, Gunning is a master of both; but here, I hope to be the burrower *of* the bird's eye. His digging analogy is germane. In recovering these objects, the methodology of the media archaeologists has been encouraging: their insistence that we accord old media the stand-alone debt that they are owed, taking them in their own context and not as mere teleological forerunners;[27] their emphasis on unsuccessful or unremembered media as nevertheless important parts of the broader medial imaginary; their interest in media metaphors just as much as media hardware;[28] their reminders that media *topoi* can be cyclical, and accordingly we must be wary of firsts.[29] These good lessons have, to my view, positively altered the state of our media discussion today.[30] If this work succeeds, it is with their principles in mind.

This approach is one that is "anarchically undisciplined" (as Vivian Sobchack phrased it).[31] But it is also fitting, given that archaeology, in its ordinary sense, was one of the sciences that benefitted most from the aerial view, where it revealed countless heretofore unseen habitats and human cultures. This view, in its process of revealing, habitually (and historically) ignores boundaries of nation and state. It was tempting, methodologically, to follow the bird's-eye view as a structuring metaphor and maintain a borders-blind approach, but in the event, this book moves from England, to France, to Germany, to the United States, largely because these were the countries that played leading roles in the development of aviation technology, and thus had early interest in the popular remediation of it.

Readers may have noticed at this stage some terminological variation, as the terms for what we now call, inclusively, the *aerial view*, have changed: from the *bird's-eye view*, to the *balloon view*, to the *view from above*, and so on. *Bird's-eye view* will thus be the preferred and most historically consonant term for much of what is described in this book. Coined, it is said, by the author Horace Walpole in 1782, *bird's-eye view* is thus in use one year before the first balloon flight.[32] It remained the predominant term for an elevated perspective until after the postwar jet age, when *aerial view* came into fashion, where it more or less remains. This same trajectory of shedding the ornithological connotations of the view occurs in French, where the *vue à vol d'oiseau* (literally, "view as the bird flies") gives way to the *vue aérienne*, and German, where the *Vogelperspektive* or *Vogelschau* ("bird's perspective" or "bird's show") wanes and *Luftaufnahme* ("aerial shot") waxes. This trajectory of use is abided in what follows, while using *aerial* as the generalist and contemporary category.

The language of the aerial is very rich—a fact that speaks to the impact novel visions and sensations can have on expanding vocabulary—and varies dependent upon the reigning culture of the air. What was once the "celestial view" is today the "drone view." I have endeavored in the following to be attentive to the object that provides the given view, and the viewer who beholds it. Emphatically, the term *aeroscopic* (used as both noun and adjective, and etymologically situated in the fourth chapter) does not simply replace the catch-all *aerial view*, which unlike the aeroscopic view exists independent of apparatus. That is to say that one can have an aerial view from a mountaintop, but this would not be an aeroscopic one.

The panorama painting is a mass medium with one foot in the sciences: in geography, certainly, as well as (I argue) astronomy.[33] This scientific grounding is typical of all of the apparatuses considered here: observation rides have debts to engineering; model cities to aeronautics; and aerial films, via vertigo, to medicine. Accordingly, this work owes as much a debt to the histories of science, technology, and medicine as it does to media and cultural history. These disciplines are, moreover, converging, as the insights of media archaeology, characterized above, demand more knowledge of the history of technology;[34] as the study of "useful cinema" moves on to analysis of medical film;[35] as historians of medicine in turn examine the wider cultural life of their imagery;[36] and as historians of science consider whether there was a fin-de-siècle "cinematographic turn" in the sciences.[37]

The history of cartography—already and per se an interdisciplinary field, drawing from history, geography, literature, and art—also informs this work throughout, because aeroscopic devices related to and remediated contemporaneous genres of maps. The panorama incorporated the tools and imagery of star charts and nautical cartography.[38] Panstereoramas popularized and demilitarized the *plan-relief*.[39] Observation rides afforded the same angle as popular bird's-eye-view lithographs.[40] Each of these examples will be treated in more detail. Key here is the fact that aeroscopics were often *presented* as maps, albeit in spectacular form.[41] Maps that provide an inkling of giddiness, maps that seem to toy with the world pictured, maps with shifting scales. The aeroscopic skewed the epistemology of cartography. Aeroscopics, in the process of remediating flight, irrationalized routine processes of mapping. The compass of knowledge tilts from observation to intoxication. The meridian line becomes the rhumb. The game: spotting the spot.

1. The Panoramic Altitude

Percival Spencer—balloon photographer, balloon proselytizer—considered in 1907 the aesthetic particulars unique to specific altitudes of flight. His account followed the ascent of the balloon; here, I track its descent, reversing his journey, since my concern is ultimately with the lowest altitude. We begin one mile up (5,280 feet), where

> little detail can be distinguished, but nevertheless photographs result which seem to be of far greater use than those more artistic productions obtained at a lower altitude. For instance, one may obtain a whole coast line with all its bays, promontories, piers, harbours, &c., the towns which are situate [sic] along the shore, and the winding rivers which disappear up-country; or in the case of a fortified town the whole of the houses, the ramparts, moats and other safeguards around it, and the open country beyond. Such pictures seem to be of use to the military man and surveyor, whilst they may be described as not by any means the least interesting of a series of balloon photographs.[1]

Spencer, afloat above the citadel city of Gravelines, France (Figure 3), notes the fortifications that balloons can reveal, the same fortifications that the airplane would shortly superannuate. He apologizes for the abstraction of this scale ("little detail can be distinguished") and makes a case for its artistic appeal ("not by any means the least interesting"), allowances he will not make for lower altitudes. In essence, Spencer extenuates for the *utility* of the high-altitude balloon picture, contrary to the aesthetic inutility of the lower-altitude photograph.[2]

Releasing gas from the balloon, we lower to two thousand feet, where "railway trains may be observed moving along their rails over the country" and the "windings of rivers and other configurations of the country become more apparent."[3] Lower still, Spencer insists:

FIGURE 3.   One mile above Gravelines. This and figures 4–6
drawn from Percival Spencer, "Photography from Balloons,"
Ballooning and Aeronautics (1907), 84. Wolfsonian
Collection.

The most artistic photographs from balloons are those taken below
1,000 ft. because the objects of the earth are sufficiently large to be
distinguished. The sides of the houses and their windows may then be
discerned, traffic moving in the street, and human figures enter into the
picture. These views are generally most pleasing to the eye.[4]

The view below 1,000 feet is familiar to most. More familiar still, below
400 feet. One does not need to leave the Earth to obtain this view. This
altitude includes the view from observation rides such as the Ferris wheel
(the original, built for the Chicago World's Fair of 1893, was 264 feet), the
campanile (St. Mark's, in Venice, is 323 feet), the cathedral (St. Paul's, in
London, is 365 feet), and even the early skyscraper (the Flatiron Building,
in New York, is 285 feet). Readers will have their own private experiences
with this altitude and the vista that it affords. This altitude range has, as
with the higher instances, intrinsic hermeneutic effects on the viewed
subject: it allows for an overview of the city that is not detached from
its residents and their abodes. Berkeley architect and kite photographer
Cris Benton has called this altitude the "intimate aerial," and with good

FIGURE 4.   Two thousand feet above Greenwich Hospital.

FIGURE 5.   One thousand feet above the Thames.

FIGURE 6.   Well below one thousand feet. Originally
captioned "The friends we left behind us." I return to such
onlookers in chapter 5.

reason.[5] The process of abstraction that the aerial view, in rising, progres-
sively creates—the increasing alienation from the viewed subject that proceeds from a failure to comprehend it ("what am I looking at?")—is seldom
an issue below 400 feet.

The special properties of this altitude have been widely noted. H.G.
Wells, for instance, aimed to characterize the effects of low-altitude views
from a balloon. He begins from the summit of balloon flight:

> At first all the vast panorama below had been as silent as a painted picture.
> But as the day wore on and the gas diffused slowly from the balloon, it
> sank earthward again, details increased, men became more visible, and
> [one] began to hear the whistle and moan of trains and cars, sounds of
> cattle, bugles and kettle drums, and presently even men's voices.[6]

He later adds:

> The swaying view varied with these changes of altitude. Now they
> would be low and close, and he would distinguish in that steep, unusual
> perspective, windows, doors, street and sky signs, people and the
> minutest details, and watch the enigmatical behaviour of crowds and
> clusters upon the roofs and in the streets; then as they soared the details
> would shrink, the sides of streets draw together, the view widen, the
> people cease to be significant.[7]

Writing in the same year as Spencer's (1907) essay, Wells observes a
remarkably similar effect. For him, not only are people and houses surpris-

ingly interpretable, so, too, are sounds. In this "steep, unusual perspective," the sweeping prospect of the balloon view is paradoxically noted for its minutiae, its detail. There is a vacillation between the expansive view of the horizon and the focused view of the city, a hybridity of vision reproduced and remediated in the panorama painting, the main subject of this chapter.

As suggested in my introduction, distinctions regarding scale that were self-evident to the balloonists and writers of yesterday are often lost today. The "aerial view," as the term is used in the literature, collapses a range of viewing heights into a single perspective—the view from the cathedral is aerial, as is the view from the mountain, the view from the airplane, and so on up to the satellite when, finally, new terminology is available: the view from space that transforms the Earth into the "blue marble."[8] (Furthermore, this collective aerial view is ordinarily ascribed a single martial resonance, to be discussed in chapter 4.) There is a problem with this telescoping of distance. Take an example from film studies: a "camera view" would be an inadequate term to encompass all distances from lens to subject; thus, sub-divisions between close-up, medium shot, long shot, and so on up to the aerial are employed. These various distances have distinct perceptual effects. Recall, for instance, the abundant work on the close-up in recent years, which has restored it as a fundamental unit of film grammar—one tied to phenomenology and affect—well beyond its associations with promoting film stardom. As film scholar Mary Ann Doane asked of the close-up, "At what distance from the object or tightness of the frame does it begin? At what point does the . . . medium close-up become the pure close-up?"[9] These are valuable questions that we take as a given in film study, and that one might ask, in turn, not of proximity but of distance.

With this in mind, it is clear that to imagine all altitudes of the aerial view as a single complex is reductively to simplify numerous viewing per-spectives that instead have staged, even stepwise, differences. (It would like-wise be absurd to note these differences to a cartographer, for whom map scale—in essence, the height of the aerial perspective—is of fundamental and elementary significance.) In order to attend to these differences, it is indispensable to form a taxonomy of aerial scale, an altimetry for the aero-scopic. As a first step in this direction, I designate this narrow window of the troposphere—between two hundred and four hundred feet—and the oblique view onto the city that it provides, the "panoramic altitude."

The medium selected for analysis here, as the name of this altitude would suggest, is the panorama painting, which, being the mass medium that earliest traded in bird's-eye views, can be considered the first aero-scopic device. As a coda, I will turn to room-sized camera obscuras, which likewise functioned as a technology of panoramic altitude in the same long nineteenth century. I will introduce the panorama at length, but here it is worth noting that of the four main genres of panorama—urban, nautical, military, religious—I focus expressly on the urban, which is the first genre of the medium; it is also the least reliant on events (i.e., it usually captures a routine moment of city life rather than a historical battle or important event in the Bible), and the most reliant on elevation to deliver information: cities, unlike battles, always have a vertical dimension. Premised upon site visits to some of the oldest remaining panoramas, my analysis will draw here from a body of scholarship that seldom overlaps with media studies: the literature on observation from the history of science.

Observation is here taken in the general sense, as the key mode of looking in astronomy, botany, economics, physics, and many other social and hard sciences. It is also used in the specific sense, as it is tied to the *observatory*, those houses built for looking at the skies that boomed alongside the panorama rotunda and camera obscura room in the nineteenth century. Panorama, camera obscura, and observatory are linked, as I shall show, not only by adjacency—apparatuses first built on the hill, in the same period— but also by a shared interpretive outlook and a formal consanguinity. Architecturally, all are rotundas with apertures to the sky. For spectators, they encourage rotational viewing: to experience a panorama without turning around, or a camera obscura without circumnavigating the tabular screen, or an observatory without swiveling the telescope is to ignore a crucial feature of their construction. All are premised upon curvature. For the panorama, it is the curvature of the canvas; for the camera obscura, of the screening table; for the observatory, of the Earth.[10] The observatory is a "space of knowledge," designed and understood to produce through observation a certain kind of information; the panorama and camera obscura are also such spaces; and all are predicated upon a slow, comparative, contemplative type of looking.[11]

All demand a *hybrid vision* that, if it is to function, requires users to "double-check" what is seen in detail with what is seen in whole. In the observatory, it is to ask: is this star part of that constellation? In the panorama and camera obscura: where does a given building lie in relation to the city's plan? Where the observatory enables us to position ourselves within our galaxy, the panorama and camera obscura enable us to position ourselves within a city. In this way, the hybrid vision that each apparatus requires depends upon a conceptual scalar magnification: to project one's life into the city, or imagine one's size relative to the universe, is to become small against a new magnitude.

A PANORAMA OF THE PANORAMIC

"What," Roland Barthes asked fifty years ago, "in fact, is a panorama?"[12] The question remains surprisingly vexed. Standard histories agree, at least, that these 360-degree, circular paintings of immense scale blossomed in Europe at the end of the eighteenth century and were an extremely popular public spectacle for more than a century beyond, petering out after a minor renaissance at the fin de siècle.[13] Not unlike flaneurs, who have had too much conceptual baggage heaped upon their shoulders, the panorama painting is already an overburdened object in the literature on the visual culture of the nineteenth century. The panorama traded in specific effects, some of which have received more attention than others. Contemporary scholars have focused in large part on the panorama's capacities for simulation and constraint.[14]

Ralph Hyde, former head of London's Guildhall's Library and preeminent English historian of the panorama, tells a story of visiting the Panorama Mesdag in The Hague (1881).[15] Depicting a maritime scene viewed over sand dunes, the panorama includes an overcast sky and a beach cleared of people that suggests approaching rain. As with all circular panoramas in the original design, the Panorama Mesdag is lit naturally, from skylights above. Hyde, visiting on a cloudy day, and after an hour in the panorama, found himself reflexively reaching for his umbrella.[16] This is the "panorama effect"—a trompe l'oeil so persuasive, a simulation so successful, that even a panorama specialist can be involuntarily immersed. Accounts such as this are ubiquitous in period literature.

Historian Vanessa Schwartz gave a name to this widely noted, arguably structurally integral, effect of the panorama. Her account of its cause is insightful:

> The removal of all other visual points of reference outside the
> panorama made it difficult for spectators to judge size and distance. The
> circularity of the tableau created the illusion of depth. These elements
> comprise the "panorama effect." The panorama's visual trick, which
> relied on its erasure of the spectator's point of reference, also facilitated
> the sense that the panorama, a representation that effaced its status as
> representation, became a substitute reality.[17]

There are two components to the panorama effect. The first is the appeal to verisimilitude, an appeal that, in promotional literature for panoramas, would cite not only the accuracy of the image, but also its verifiable bona fides: a soldier at the battle depicted would vouch for the painting's factuality; artifacts from the source landscape (ranging from rocks to clothes to wagons) would be incorporated into the scenic frame; the handheld guide that accompanied all panoramas would place the locations depicted, adding further information. The panorama aimed for mimesis. In cultural historian Dolph Sternberger's elegant formulation, the panorama turned the spectator "from a passerby to an eyewitness."[18]

The second component of the panorama effect is its "substitute reality," which art historian Jonathan Crary has elaborated as a simulacral "reality effect" that offers an "imaginary unity and coherence."[19] Placing the invention in a proto-Debordian lineage, as Crary does, is a tempting move, given the panorama's position as the "first" mass medium and its nominal role as "one of the places in the nineteenth century where a modernization of perceptual experience occurs."[20] This simulacral property of the panorama has further been explored as a media metaphor for incarceration or constraint.

For this tendency, we can thank a footnote from Michel Foucault. In *Discipline and Punish*, he speculated briefly as to whether Jeremy Bentham's panopticon prison designs (1787) might have been impacted by the panorama painting, given that the viewer shares "the place of the sovereign gaze."[21] This historical observation has led to a considerable body of literature that takes this speculative conflation of the panoramic with the panoptic as a historical given.[22] The counterintuitive argument in such work is often not that the spectator is the "guard" in the panopticon, which could be plausible, given that the viewer is placed at the center (guard tower location) of the image; rather, the viewer is the prisoner incarcerated by the spectacle, and the world depicted in the painting is an entrapment. The panorama's celebrated framelessness is recast as inescapability, and the immersive surface of the painting stands emblematically for a global phenomenon. As Bruno Latour envisaged it: "In effect, the Big Picture is just that: a picture.... Panoramas, as etymology suggests, see everything. But they also see nothing since they simply show an image painted (or projected) on the tiny wall of a room fully closed to the outside."[23]

These critics could be discussing the movie theater, and it is quite possible that much of this consideration of the panorama projects later cinematic presumptions back onto a past viewing practice. Certainly, panorama paintings are one layer of the media history of cinema and new media; the parallels between the panorama and IMAX, for instance, or indeed between the panorama and virtual reality, are clear. One cannot fault this interest, and it has yielded some excellent scholarship.[24] However, we must not ignore the particularities of the medium in its time in favor of an understanding that reflects more neatly a recent medial moment. Panorama historian Stephan

Oettermann even places the panorama and panopticon in contemporaneous opposition, at opposing ends of a spectrum from confinement to freedom.[25]

We find above, then, attempts to understand the panorama by borrowing from related media and systems when a more useful structuring analogue sits next door to the panorama. Let us tear down the panopticon and erect instead an observatory.

OBSERVATIONS FROM THE PANORAMIC ALTITUDE

The characteristic elevation of the panorama painting has been twinned to that of ballooning, and the "discovery" of the horizon in the eighteenth century.[26] It also compares to the view from the cathedral steeple, a popular vantage from which to plan panoramas.[27] The range of concern here is thus between the low balloon and the high steeple. Thomas Hornor's *Panorama of London* from St. Paul's (1829), at 364 feet, is emblematic in this regard; as is Eduard Gaertner's triptych view of Berlin from the Friedrichswerder Church (1834), at 253 feet. There are, of course, many "sea-level" panoramas, usually executed in non-urban genres, such as the Panorama Mesdag in the Hague (1881); or the valley view of the Bourbaki Panorama in Lucerne (also 1881).[28] But in the urban genre, cathedral-height panoramas were the norm: a range of, again, 200 to 400 feet in height.

At this panoramic altitude, certain forms of information are made apparent, while others are made obscure: rooftop infrastructure is revealed, while facades disappear; depth is gained and open space rewarded, while narrow thoroughfares are occluded; the city is invariably emplaced within its surrounding rural context. All but the densest urban panoramas (of London, say) include the country beyond, for the simple reason that in most cities and towns of the nineteenth century, a high prospect would necessarily allow the viewer to see beyond the city limits.

The Swiss Thun Panorama (1809–14), the oldest surviving panorama, is exemplary in this regard (Figure 7). It takes as its perch an elevated building in the center of town. The view is first appreciated in its entirety—as much as two-thirds of the painting is given over to sky—and we situate the town within the surrounding landscape. Then, however, the Thun Panorama invites the viewer to notice the details of the painting. In the window of one house, a woman and children wave to the viewer, alerting them to the civic vignettes placed here and there, just as they are in a crowded hidden-picture *Wimmelbild* of Bosch or Breughel.[29] We note not just the citizens gathered in the town square, but also those drinking at the foot of an alley; we note the rooftop cats in battle; the labor of workers taking place on, as we know

FIGURE 7.   Marquard Fidelis Wocher's Thun Panorama, 1809–14, detail.

from the pictured clock tower, a typical day at 3:47p.m. Both landscape and landmark may be detected, both crowd and individual. There is a hybrid tension to the panoramic altitude, a tug of war for the viewer's attention: between citizen and city, detail and whole, even line work and brush stroke.[30] For all of its lexical afterlife as shorthand for the single "big-picture" view, the panorama is surprisingly dependent upon minute constituent properties. To upend a turn of phrase: with the panorama, we can't see the trees for the forest.

Pause here to appreciate the discursive irony in our colloquial use of the term *panorama*: the panorama, the original frameless medium is, likewise, semantically unbound: "The eye cannot range beyond the frame, because there is no frame."[31] This was somewhat true at the time, during the panorama boom that has been called variously the "o-rama craze" or "panoramania."[32] The panorama was so nomenclaturally generative, allowing for countless related media—the *diorama*, the *Maréorama*, the *Cinéorama*, the *panstereorama*, ad infinitum—that Balzac supposedly quipped that "certain painters' studios [now] joke of speaking in 'rama."[33] Today, the panorama has entered into the lexicon of promotional ubiquity. Any middling touristic prospect is a "panorama." There are more than one hundred streets in California named for the view: Panoramic Drives, Roads, Avenues. Historian of science Charlotte Bigg has provocatively suggested that the lexical drift of the panorama, its "material disintegration" to the point that we no longer remember, when we use the word, that we employ what was in effect a patented brand name, does not reflect the term's present inutility, but on the contrary the medium's complete incorporation into how landscapes are viewed: the panorama "has been forgotten [because it] has been naturalized."[34]

In the hybrid vision of the panorama painting, analysis of minute properties offers the viewer a sense of the city as a system in use, as a network. (The balloon accounts from Percival Spencer and H.G. Wells that began this chapter each note that the routes of traffic, human or otherwise, are visible at the panoramic altitude.) The panoramic altitude is low enough to see in windows, to appreciate manners and customs, to imagine oneself in the city square. Details were so crucial to the panorama painting that labor was sometimes divided among its creators down to the smallest unit of representation: one miniaturist working on the Panorama of Salzburg (1824) was individually responsible for painting buttons on vests. An old accounting for this focus on detail when faced with an elevated view comes from Samuel Johnson, writing of *King Lear*. Johnson proposed that this detail was merely a way to stave off vertigo and fear, just as, more prosaically, the common wisdom for beating car sickness is to focus on objects outside the front window alone.

> He that looks from a precipice finds himself assailed by one great and dreadful image of irresistible destruction. But this overwhelming idea is dissipated and enfeebled from the instant that the mind can restore itself to the observation of particulars and diffuse its attention to distinct objects. The enumeration of the choughs and crows, the samphire-man and the fishers, counteracts the great effect of the prospect, as it peoples the desert of intermediate vacuity, and stops the mind in the rapidity of its descent through emptiness and horror.[35]

In the panorama painting the focus on miniature detail is a tonic against a head-swimming magnitude. Operating at the panoramic altitude, this aeroscopic device offers signs of life, civic vignettes, and even narrative scenes that higher altitudes obliterate. The panorama painting offers a still-human scale of vision.

The panorama painting does not operate according to its reputation. In lieu of the standard accounts of simulation and constraint that have preoccupied some panorama scholars, I propose that the panorama painting is premised upon a hybrid vision promoted by a specific altitude, and that this hybridity is connected to *observation* and the astronomical observatory. It was at this scientific site that a parallel and symmetrical mode of looking established a framework for the appeal of the panorama painting.

OBSERVATORIES IN THE NINETEENTH CENTURY

The astronomical observatory has centuries of history, but scholars identify the nineteenth century as a time of immense change.[36] As the price of specialized instruments (such as telescopes) fell, a boom in observatories followed: observatories numbered fewer than thirty-six, worldwide, at the beginning of the century; by the end, there were more than two hundred.[37] The observatory became a widely celebrated site of scientific findings, and was open to the public much more than previously—more even than today. Nineteenth-century observatories "were expected to be the site of soirées and visits by dignitaries, state representatives, and the wider public: treating visitors to evening lectures, tours, or peeks through telescopes were important duties for professional astronomers."[38] By the 1870s, the writer (and stereoscope mogul) Oliver Wendell Holmes could write in *The Atlantic* with the assumption that every reader had visited an observatory: "I suppose everybody who reads this paper has visited one or more observatories, and of course knows all about them."[39] At the observatory, visitors would encounter novel instruments, sciences, and representations. Beyond the telescope and the clock, observatories quickly adopted the camera and the telegraph. Beyond meteorology, observatories were sites of physics, mathematics, geodesy, and cartography.[40] Beyond numerical tables, cosmologies, photographs, and almanacs, the observatory produced maps.[41] Maps—of the Earth, not only stellar maps—were one of the key products of the nineteenth-century observatory. The urban panorama painting emerges not just during, but also, as I will show, atop this flourishing of the observatory, in a period of public acclaim for a specific site of science. The panorama painting remediates not only the instruments and output of the observatory, but certain practices of observation.[42]

Historians of science now group many of the practices that were undertaken at observatories (including the above physics, mathematics, geodesy, and cartography) as *observatory sciences*, to be distinguished from field or lab sciences.[43] Not all sciences, of course, prioritize the type of analysis that observation requires, which was defined as "the attention of the mind turned toward the objects offered by nature."[44] The observatory sciences involve a patient mode of looking that depends upon both rare and scheduled events (e.g., the meteor shower, the eclipse). This form of analysis necessitates a comparative mode of viewing, in which the rarity is contextualized within the norm and the event compared to existing data. We imagine the archetypal astronomer, eye to the telescope, invariably with notebook in hand, simultaneously writing down observations. These notes, beginning in the nineteenth century, would be transformed into a range of output representations (including the above numerical tables, cosmologies, photographs, almanacs, and maps), which were in turn distributed either as specialist papers, popular accounts, or mementos for, respectively, the scientist, the public, and the visitor. The observatory was, as historian of science David Aubin termed it, a "laboratory of visuality."[45]

In part due to the popularity of astronomy in the period, as well as its new affordability and expansion, the observatory sciences were some of the first sciences to be globally networked: because of the visual discrepancies produced according to the location of a given observatory, these sites were in greater communication than were many other sources of scientific observation. The transits of Venus in 1874 and 1882 are often taken as emblematic of the globally collective enterprise of nineteenth-century observatories, as scientists the world over compared their mechanically derived data.[46] The monocular perspective of the telescope had to be cross-checked against a global range of monocular views (that also depended upon the above clock, camera, and telegraph). The astronomer, proverbially, "looks with his own eyes, but sees with the eyes of the collective."[47]

This collective data checking that aims to absolve individual scientists of the unknown errors of their perspective is what historian of science Lorraine Daston has called *aperspectival objectivity*, a form of scientific observation that was designed for "eliminating . . . human idiosyncrasies" in vision and judgment.[48] This is most notable in astronomy when observatories from across the globe share their findings in order to reduce errors of observation, or even institute new standards of timekeeping.[49] The idea was that if astronomers can eliminate the erratic or biased premises of their personal or geographic outlook—discrepancies caused by eye, elevation, angle, atmosphere—by comparing them with the findings of others, they might "escape from perspective" altogether.[50]

The panorama painting incorporates the logic of the observatory's aperspectival objectivity. The various angles of vision in a panorama provoke perceptual discrepancies between viewers. The panorama may be illusionistically isotropic, appearing equally distanced in all directions, but it is anisotropic by design. In cinematic terms: the immense aspect ratio and curvature of the screen warps the depth of field from viewing perch to viewing perch. A first principle: *the aerial view is parallax*. Both observatory and panorama accordingly depended upon "trained judgment," upon both the information captured by an instrument (the given lens, be it telescope or opera glass) and the interpretive rendering of the user (the astronomer, the panorama viewer).[51] This is not merely a case of adjacency (new, popular public spectacles in a century that was full of them) or chronology (although observatories of course precede panoramas, the rise of the observatory sciences occurs just as the panorama painting becomes a mass sensation).[52] Rather, the panorama painting was intrinsically tied—in patent, placement, technique, and mode of address—to the observatory. As we shall see, urban panorama paintings were often taken from heights adjacent to or on top of observatories and they addressed their viewers overwhelmingly as "observers." They were one spectacular public face of the observatory sciences.

The evidence that follows is informed by practical visits to panoramas. For this chapter, I visited not only the hillside site of Robert Barker's first, lost *Panorama of Edinburgh* (1789), but the extant nineteenth-century panoramas of (presented chronologically) Thun (Marquard Fidelis Wocher, 1809–14), which remains in Thun; Salzburg (Johann Michael Sattler, 1824) at that city's Panorama Museum; Scheveningen, the Panorama Mesdag (Hendrik Willem Mesdag, 1881), located at The Hague; the Bourbaki Panorama in Lucerne (Edouard Castres, 1881); the Civil War panoramas *Battle of*

Gettysburg (Paul Philippoteaux, 1883) and *Battle of Atlanta* (the American Panorama Company, 1886), both located at the sites they depict; and *The Crucifixion* (Jan Styka, 1896) in Los Angeles.[53] The following analysis will also rely on the many instructive panorama guides that have been preserved but that, because the connected painting has vanished, have been by and large neglected in the literature. (The images that follow are taken from these guides.) Also reconsidered in detail are two of the most well-known panorama paintings that only survive in reproduction: Barker's aforementioned *Panorama of Edinburgh*, which exists in rescued (lithographic) form at the University of Edinburgh; and Thomas Hornor's *Great Panorama of London* (1829), likewise preserved only as a lithograph. The urban panorama painting remains the focus throughout this study. To generalize, for the producers of spectacle in this book, it was felt that "the view of the country is not so interesting as that of the metropolis"—or so an English balloonist once phrased it, capturing the flyover ethic of the nineteenth century.[54]

SCAFFOLDS FOR SEEING

Few of the many panorama paintings produced in the nineteenth century have been preserved. According to the International Panorama Council's database, there is none on display in England or France, and only three in the United States. Of those that survive, some of the best-preserved panoramas are those that celebrate military milestones (in Atlanta, Lucerne, Moscow, and many other locations) or that feature biblical subjects (usually maintained by churches, as in Sainte-Anne-de-Beaupré, Quebec; Einsiedeln, Switzerland; and Burbank, California). Because there is no obvious institutional reason for cities to preserve urban panoramas, fewer remain. Accordingly, one must return to surviving ephemera rather than merely the surviving paintings, in order to obtain a clear picture of the concerns of the urban panorama painting and the panorama painter. Following Lorraine Daston's aphorism that "choosing how to observe in some cases dictates what is observed," the following analysis of panorama ephemera clusters around two central themes.[55] The first is the way that panorama creators selected their sites according to height and vista (the panoramic altitude), and second is how they relied on the concept of the panorama as a kind of instrument built for observation.

Urban panoramas made the most sense, according to their makers, in rationalized cities with on-site geographic or built elevations, and broad boulevards. New York City, for instance, was a poor choice for a panorama location in the 1800s. Although we think of the elevated skyscraper views of New York as intrinsic to the place today, for much of the nineteenth

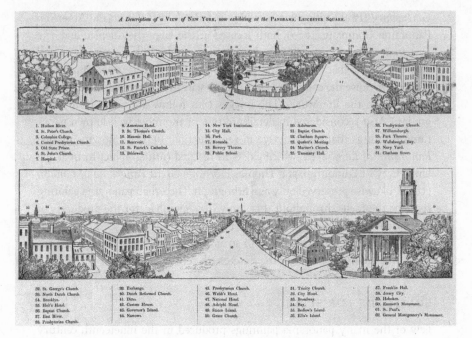

FIGURE 8. "A Description of a View of New York, now exhibiting at the Panorama, Leicester Square," 1834. Library of Congress.

century the city made for unsatisfactory panoramas: dense, with no natural elevations and few tall structures (St. Patrick's Cathedral was not built until 1878; skyscrapers began rising there in the 1890s). When, in 1834, a panorama of New York was exhibited by Robert Burford at his panorama rotunda in Leicester Square, it was "taken opposite the city hall, about the middle of the Broadway"; the view was so superficial—a few open boulevards framed by facades—that the proprietor apologized in the accompanying guide: "Being built on nearly level ground, it does not present any very marked or romantic features"[56] (Figure 8).

Venice was worse: "Totally without that great convenience and ornament—a wide street."[57] Again, when a panorama of Venice was made—this time by Burford and Barker, in 1819—it was regretted by its makers that "notwithstanding the frequency of canals in every part of the city, amounting to four hundred, not one can be seen from the Place of St. Mark, owing to the height of the houses and their being so close together."[58] Nevertheless, they took their view from St. Mark's, but elevated a scaffolding of their own design in order to reach a greater open height, "so placed as to have an elevated view of the whole square."[59]

Panorama planners have an ideal spot that they are looking for, a vantage from a certain height. When it is not available, they create it. In this way, a standardized panoramic altitude may be maintained (Figures 9, Vienna; 10, Madrid; 11, Florence; and 12, Mexico City).

Creating a new panoramic vantage was sometimes part of the advertising for a panorama. Take Thomas Hornor's well-known view of London from St. Paul's Cathedral. It was developed, rendered, and executed over seven years and finally displayed on an acre of canvas.[60] The idea was to reproduce a true "aërial perspective" of London.[61] St. Paul's is, of course, already an immense structure—but Hornor, a former cartographer, wished to go higher still, and to have a secure purchase from which to sketch the city. He was allowed to build scaffolding over the dome and cross of the cathedral. This he called, tellingly, his "observatory." The panorama was to be no mere landscape painting to eyeball and scale according to thumb; it was an "invention," an "apparatus for extracting," as Barker's patent claimed, "a proper disposition of the whole."[62]

Hornor brought a number of instruments into his observatory to render the view. He used a form of camera lucida to improve his mapping; a rotating frame to hold the paper on which he would sketch the panorama, so that he could capture those parts of London unobscured by weather as they appeared; and, crucially, he used a telescope.[63] The telescope was almost always mentioned in period accounts, indicating that the reader was to think of the structure as a kind of astronomical observatory. Hornor himself described in his prospectus the "mathematical accuracy" with which he made his sketches.[64] His observatory generated considerable public interest, functioning as a billboard for the panorama to come, as it was visible from all over London. Here was a panoramic astronomer who, high in his observatory, had tilted his telescope back toward the city.

By most accounts, Hornor's panorama was a success. One anonymous visitor noted how the view produced knowledge of both the details and the expanse of this immense city:

> So plain are the principal streets in the view, that thousands of visitors will be able to identify their own dwellings. . . . Thousands of spectators will therefore become rivetted [sic] by some particular objects, for every Londoner can name a score of sites which are endeared to him by some grateful recollections and associations of his life; whilst our country friends will be lost in admiration at the immense knot of dwellings, till they contrive to pick their road back to their inn or temporary abode in this queen of cities.[65]

Hornor's observatory (Figure 13), positioned at the panoramic altitude, produced a hybrid mode of looking that will seem characteristic by this stage:

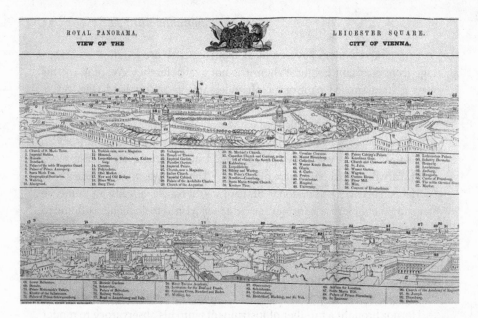

FIGURE 9.   "View of the City of Vienna," 1847. Getty Library.

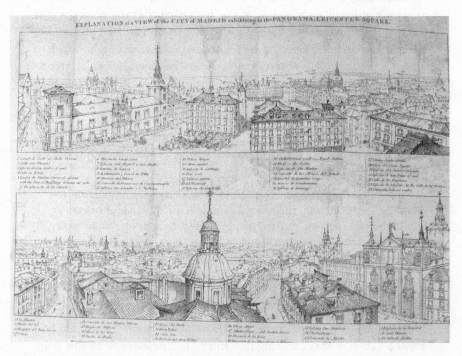

FIGURE 10.   "Explanation of a View of the City of Madrid," 1825. Getty Library.

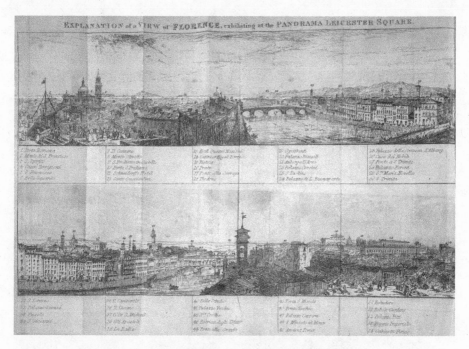

FIGURE 11. "Explanation of a View of Florence, exhibiting at the Panorama, Leicester Square," 1832. Getty Library.

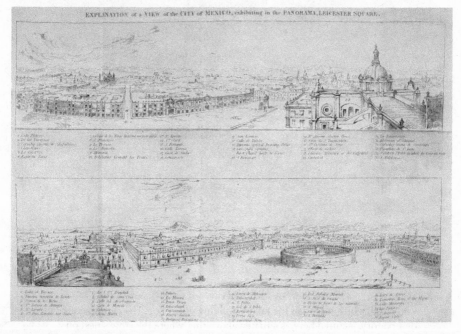

FIGURE 12. "Explanation of a View of the City of Mexico, exhibiting at the Panorama, Leicester Square," 1826. Getty Library.

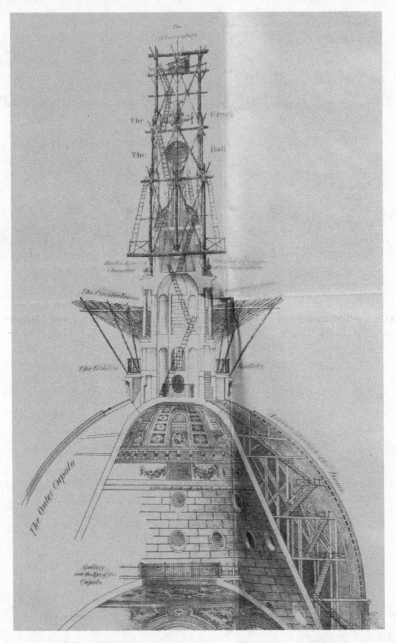

FIGURE 13. Thomas Hornor's scaffold covered the cross of St. Paul's Cathedral, which was then the tallest building in London. His manufactured observatory, pictured here, is situated above this, where the crow's nest on a ship might be. "Prospectus. View of London" (London: Hornor, 1823), foldout.

from the "particular" to the "immense." The magnitude of the panorama, and the new scale it seemed to produce, was also much commented upon:

> The great size of the picture, added to the number of objects contained in it, gives it indeed the appearance of a model on a gigantic scale, rather than that of a painted panorama; and the first impression that strikes the general spectator is, how little he was acquainted with the great outline of the city, in which, perhaps, he habitually resides.[66]

The reference to a model is intriguing and speaks to a problem of the bird's-eye view—its perceived artifice, both simulated and not—taken up in chapter 2 as well as in the conclusion.

The nineteenth century was important for the invention, production, and dispersal of countless instruments, both scientific and recreational.[67] The number of instruments used to produce Hornor's panorama was great, and a selling point, but it was not atypical in panorama creation. Just as there is an instrument behind and beyond every map, there is an instrument behind and beyond every panorama. Cartographers rely on data produced by (among countless other devices) sextant, compass, and observatory; this data, embedded in a map, may be extracted by the map reader with the help of a stereoscope or a magnifying glass. Panoramas used many of the same devices for planning and magnification. Scientists advised panorama painters to use optical devices like Hornor's (not uncommon) camera lucida and telescope.[68] This suggestion was made based on an understanding that the size of the panorama had already been standardized by "optical science" to mark, and set at a limit, the "distance at which ordinary panoramic painting becomes illusive."[69] This included classical objects of surveying and location: Henry Aston Barker's Panorama of Spitsbergen (1819), for instance, taken by "celestial navigation," used some form of sextant in order to give a more accurate rendering.[70] Others, like Hornor, relied on sui generis inventions: Joseph Stöger created the obscure "cubigraph" to correctly render perspective in his panorama.[71] Hendrik Willem Mesdag designed and employed a circular glass attachment with preliminary etchings of the larger panorama, to be worn around his head while he painted (Figure 14). As for new technologies, photography was incorporated into panorama planning by the mid-1800s.[72] Once a panorama was on display, opera glasses and telescopes were commonplace so as to better appreciate the details (see Figure 15). To this day, the Panorama of Salzburg has a telescope permanently installed. These instruments were put to use in an observatory-style system of examination and representation, a practice that dates to the earliest panorama; they also

FIGURE 14.　Mesdag's glass cylinder apparatus, The Hague. Author's photograph, 2013.

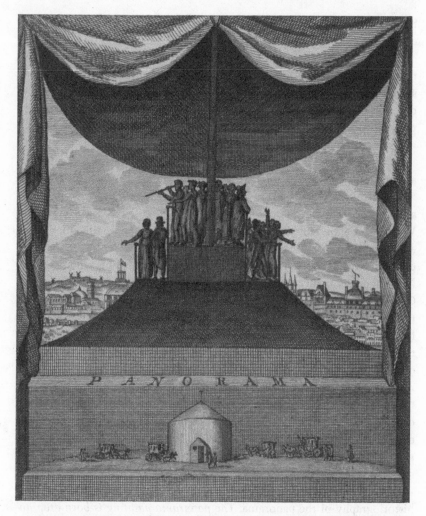

FIGURE 15. A panorama of Paris as shown in Amsterdam. Note the viewer using a telescope. Atlas Dreesmann Collection, Amsterdam City Archives. Panorama historian Gabriele Koller, whose work alerted me to this image, dates it to 1803–04.

enabled the revelations of scalar magnification that were crucial in both observatory and panorama.

In each site, experiments with scale were taking place, experiments with both the scale of the viewer and the object of scrutiny. The panorama painting was executed on an unprecedentedly large canvas, one that dwarfed the viewer; it further aimed to reproduce the particular scalar effects of a low altitude; and finally offered viewing apparatuses in order to capture detailed images. Viewers are made giant (high above the city), yet small (within the expanse of the city), and their view is likewise giant (the sublime expanse of the panorama), yet small (seen through the telescope). Viewers could measure themselves against the system of the city, and within several possible scales. This process mirrors that of the observatory, which made the observer small, first, within its immense dome, and small again, through the lens of the telescope, looking out at the infinite; but it also provided maps that offered a scalar magnification of the individual.

Barker's *Panorama of Edinburgh*, mentioned above, is widely understood as the first panorama painting. As a later Edinburgh panoramist noted, "There are many spots from which Edinburgh may be seen from great advantage."[73] Edinburgh does not have the flat, dense problems of Venice. Why then Calton Hill? Why not, say, Arthur's Seat? To begin with, Barker stipulated in his patent that "the painter or drawer must fix his station, and delineate correctly and connectedly every object which presents itself to his view as he turns round."[74] An apparatus was needed, so, in Stephan Oettermann's account, "Barker envisioned a stand with a rectangular frame that would revolve above a fixed point. After one sketch was finished, the frame could be turned until the new stretch of landscape exactly adjacent to the first appeared."[75] Much of today's literature considers the panorama as only an invention for *display*, when in fact, and as addressed, it invariably required new instruments for *production* as well. Crucially, there stood at the time of Barker's first panorama (1789) an existing observation technology: the observatory on Calton Hill. The optician Thomas Short had kept an observatory on the hill since the 1770s (it has subsequently moved and is now a Royal Observatory; a different, City Observatory remains on the site). Barker drafted the first panorama from the roof of this observatory.

This is a fundamental, medium-defining fact that is neglected in the historiography of the panorama. *The panorama painting is born atop an observatory.* In my introduction, I speculated regarding the impact that various perches can have on the experience and quality of an aerial view; I ask now, what does it mean to take one's view at the top of a structure built for stargazing, but turn one's head from the stars? It means, first and most conspicuously, that the trappings of astronomical observation are in the frame. In Barker's first panorama of Edinburgh, the chimney of the observatory dominates the picture on the right; beyond, in the observatory gardens are a number of orreries—astronomical models of the heavens and their movements (Figure 16). It is as great a hint as we shall ever receive, as to how the first viewers of the panorama painting were meant to view the city below. If the observer in the observatory aims to see past the weather,

FIGURE 16.   Detail, Robert Barker, *Panorama of Edinburgh* from Calton Hill, 1789 showing the observatory garden with orreries. Barker completed two panoramas of Edinburgh. This is the first, less-viewed example preserved at the University of Edinburgh.

to pick out the thoroughfares of the stars, the spectator in the panorama painting clears the city of fog and rain and vacates much of the populace, but leaves enough of each—weather, thoroughfares, citizenry—to connect them in relation to architectural monuments of the city: constellations, major and minor. This is in evidence again and again in the city panoramas.

The encouraged act of seeing was, indisputably, observation—not *spectating*, not *viewing*: *observing*. Barker uses the term "observer" six times in his panorama patent of fewer than five hundred words. This nomenclature, with its implied strategy of "watching, noticing, or subjecting to scientific observation," was by and large maintained in the period literature on the panorama.[76] So, too, was the infrastructure of the observatory. Hornor's makeshift "observatory" over London has been discussed. The *View of St. Petersburg* (1818), shown at Barker's rotunda in Leicester Square, was taken from an observatory in the city.[77] At Burford's panorama rotunda in 1836, the Panorama of Lima did the same.[78] When an observatory is not the viewing apparatus, it may be included as a subject, as in the Panorama of Boothia (Burford, 1834).

My account of the shared features of the urban panorama painting and the observatory by no means erases the differences between them. The observatory, for instance, has a single peephole in the telescope, and accordingly accommodates only a single viewer at a time, whereas the panorama painting, a *mass* medium, offers an arena for multiple viewers. Meanwhile, the panorama offers a snapshot of a given moment, whereas the observatory provides what we might now, ahistorically, call a "live stream." However, these differences are subtle. If compared to other, fast-moving nineteenth-century media—the moving panorama, the zoetrope, the motion picture—both panorama and observatory encourage that slow, analytic mode of examination known as *observation*. So, too, does the room-sized camera obscura, which we might understand as a synthesis of the observatory and the panorama.

OBSERVATORY OBSCURA

The camera obscura has, like the observatory, two histories, one in art, the other in science.[79] My concern here is not with the small-scale, portable darkened chamber version of the camera obscura that assisted in the production of proto-photographic verisimilitude in seventeenth-century painting, with Vermeer's use as the prime example.[80] Rather, my focus is on the large, darkened-room format of camera obscura, which I shall call "camera obscura rooms" despite the redundancy (*camera*, etymologically, relates to *chambers* or *rooms*). With an outlet for daylight and a system of lenses and mirrors embedded in the domed roof, these rooms projected an image of the surrounding world onto a surface, typically a slightly curved viewing table set at a horizontal axis (Figure 17). Both the small and large systems of camera obscura were based on the same "pinhole camera" principle of light passing through a small aperture into a darkened space, where an image of what is outside materializes, albeit inverted. These different camera obscuras also share a history of use in astronomy: the original purpose of the camera obscura was to safely view eclipses and sunspots, a practice dating back to antiquity and predating the telescope. However, the role of the camera obscura in astronomical observation ends, according to most historians, by the eighteenth century.

But then the room-sized format of the device is added, at considerable expense, to some of the leading observatories of the world during the nineteenth century. They were, as one historian of the camera obscura has suggested, "sideshows" with an observatory affiliation if not a useful observatory function.[81] (Some readers may have visited the one at the Greenwich Observatory, as many historically did.)[82] Simultaneously, independent camera obscura rooms were opened in tourist towns and dense

FIGURE 17.   Observers in a seaside camera obscura. From *Coney Island and What Is to Be Seen There* (New York: C.J. Macdonald, 1879), 36.

cities, sometimes called "splendid camera obscuras."[83] They were added to repurposed towers or mills or found in purpose-built structures; they might also be located in temporary tents at a fair or amusement park. Even in these circumstances, they maintained something of the pedigree of the observatory sciences. In the words of one camera obscura visitor in the 1880s: "The astronomical dignity of the place is not great, but still it is an agreeable and civilized institution."[84]

Camera obscura rooms were aeroscopic media, typically placed at the panoramic altitude. The camera obscura in Bristol (1828) sits 338 feet above the River Avon, which it overlooks. The camera obscura in Edinburgh (1835) looks down some 304 feet to the base of the Royal Mile.[85] The camera obscura in Dumfries (1836), high on a hill, is at least 386 feet over the River Nith.[86] These examples all survive today, and there are a number of others that remain open, with a particular concentration in the United Kingdom. Beyond the aforementioned camera obscuras, for this brief section I am also indebted to visits to and tours of those in Douglas (1892) and San Francisco (1946).[87]

These rooms, although placed at a similar altitude, nevertheless varied in their internal mechanisms and intended audiences. The lenses would have been built by a variety of glass manufacturers to unique specifications. (That is to say, there was not a camera obscura company that provided a standardized room kit, as such; each one was tailored to the given location.) Most camera obscuras allowed for a periscopic rotation of the view, but how they achieved this also varied. Some were meant for locals, some for tourists. Compare the differences between two surviving camera obscuras.

In Dumfries, Scotland, local residents paid a monthly subscription fee to access the room, which was housed at the top of a former windmill. There, they had access to an elaborate device that employed a system of pulleys. The camera's lenses could rotate around the city and even change focus, drawing attention to proximate gardens or distant farms. To operate the device required a certain amount of expertise. Witnessing someone manipulate the focus of the Dumfries camera obscura today, just as it was done in 1836, is not dissimilar to watching someone skillfully operate the ropes of a ship's rigging. As with the panorama, the camera obscura is both instrument and display.

Others were popular tourist attractions that required no expertise. Douglas, on the Isle of Man, was in the nineteenth century a booming seaside resort. Its remaining camera obscura (there were at one time three operating in the town simultaneously) has a remarkable design. A hidden central aperture room with twelve lenses, accessible by ladder, that face different directions, correspondingly projects into twelve separate open screening booths below. It is named the "Great Union Camera Obscura," and patented as such (Figure 18) because it offered a unified, panoramic vision of all that surrounds it, split up into small, digestible scenes. The viewer walks around the interior circumference of the space and takes in each scene, one by one, accessing the whole view and its component parts.

These two domed structures, in Dumfries and Douglas, each situated on a hill, each overlooking the town, the water, and surrounding paths, may be said to be typical (if exceptionally well preserved) examples of the nineteenth-century camera obscura phenomenon. A visit today gives a strong sense of how they were once employed. As with their designs, the precise purpose and appeal of camera obscura rooms historically varied. It was a medium in search of its métier. Was it to be popular science, a furtive look, or plein-air appreciation?

These are the three advertised appeals to the camera obscura room. First, the science and technology itself. This is the "operational aesthetic," in which how the device functions—the optical phenomenon involved in seeing the outside world projected onto an interior screen—is part of the draw.[88] Camera obscuras then and now include some discussion of the science involved, and period guides for creating your own camera obscura room emphasized this feature, just as optical toys such as zoetropes and kaleidoscopes offered "object lessons" in optics—and just as observatories

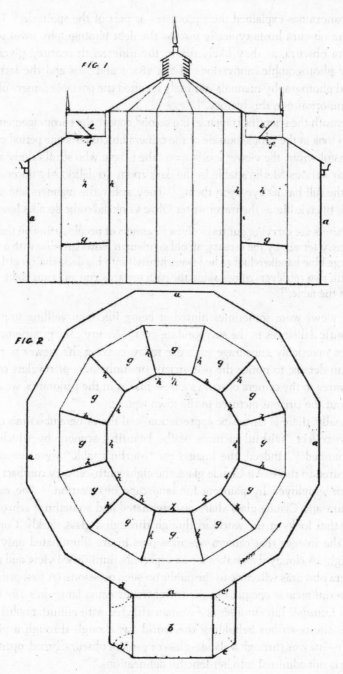

FIGURE 18.   Designs for John Richard Fielding's Great Union
Camera Obscura, from the patent, 1892.

and panoramas explained their processes as part of the spectacle.[89] Today, camera obscura hosts typically discuss the debt photography owes to the camera obscura, as they likely did in the nineteenth century, given the many photographic innovations of the 1820s and '30s and the fact that period photography manuals routinely credited the portable camera obscura's importance in this history.[90]

Beneath the scientific trappings is a second appeal: the encouragement of a stolen look at the people outside of the camera obscura. As one period visitor in Bristol wrote, the viewer looks upon "the people who stroll calmly across the mysterious Merlin's table in the dark room, so deliciously unconscious that the hill has its eye upon them."[91] They notice the manners and minor details of civic life, as the travel writer Olive Cook did some decades later:

> Waiters are carrying out trays of tea to groups of people sitting on the grassy terrace by the estuary, an old gentleman blows his nose with a large blue handkerchief as he lowers himself into his deck-chair, a girl with two retrievers comes along the path towards you and runs right off the table.[92]

Such views were sometimes hinted at being illicit, surveilling improper romantic dalliances in the surrounding area.[93] In any case, proprietors and guides invariably encourage such use today, coaxing the viewer to notice human details; to notice the pedestrians or sunbathers or revelers caught unawares in the camera obscura's gaze—just as in the panorama, we are to pick out the citizens pictured in the town square.

Finally, there is landscape appreciation, and the camera obscura's capacity to reflect "faithful pictures of the beautiful scenery by which it is surrounded."[94] Indeed, the images on "Merlin's table" were sometimes compared to those of a Claude glass, the eighteenth-century compact black mirror employed by painters for landscape observation.[95] The camera obscura and Claude glass share an attenuated and sometimes achromatic view that looks at the world as though through a glass, darkly. Consider that the images that camera obscuras pipe in are illuminated only with sunlight. A cloudy day makes for an especially diminished view, and many camera obscuras will close to the public on such occasions. (A first principle: *the aerial view is opaque*.) In the travel writer Anna Jameson's *The Diary of an Ennuyée* (an *ennuyée* is a woman afflicted with ennui), published in 1836, she describes beholding the world "as though through a picture frame—nay, as through a claude-glass or camera obscura; broad, open daylight is not admitted into her fanciful delineations."[96]

The camera obscura synthesizes, at the panoramic altitude, these qualities of optical science, unnoticed examination, and landscape appreciation, much as did the panorama painting. Viewers even discussed camera obscura rooms in panoramic terms, sometimes directly: "Visitors looking at the table obtain a panoramic view of all that passes across the field of view outside the building."[97] And sometimes the description is indirect, using the same keywords and themes:

> On the summit is placed a very large and excellent Camera Obscura, [which has a] most magical effect, the whole of the scenery being brought in succession upon the table, with figures, animals, and carriages in motion. . . . The varied effects of light and shade upon the landscape afford a high gratification to the observer.[98]

This account, describing the camera obscura in Bristol, is reminiscent of the balloon voyage that began this chapter; it has all the expansive (*whole*) and detailed (*figures*) properties of the hybrid vision that the panoramic altitude encourages. And note the final term: *observer*.

THE POST-PANORAMIC OBSERVATORY

The observatory—its instruments, its architecture, its address, its aims—is felt everywhere in the urban panorama painting and camera obscura. This combination of apparatuses lingers on in displays such as the planetarium, which increased the panoramic debt to the observatory sciences. Planetariums have important historical precedents, including the many popular astronomical magic lanterns shows, the aforementioned orreries, and the astronomical lecturer Adam Walker's "Eidouranion."[99] But planetariums are not in play during the long nineteenth century in the sense that we understand them today, as a relatively fixed genre of popular science with overhead display. Rather, they arrive just beyond: visual studies scholar Alison Griffiths proposed that the first modern planetarium begins with the Zeiss display in the 1920s; and they really only have public success as a midcentury attraction.[100] Nevertheless, and to the point, planetariums do display many features of the panoramic—circularity, rotation, hybrid vision—as Griffiths makes plain. Panoramic astronomy lives on.

Likewise, observatories, if they may be said to have a technological memory, seem to remember their connection to panoramas. The panorama was born in the observatory, and so it has been kept, terminologically, by the structure of the observatory. Observatories still trade in panoramas. Today, the promotional materials for almost any English or French observatory will include the term; the Besançon, Bordeaux, Greenwich, Griffith, Lick, and Yerkes observatories—a random, typical sampling—promise "panoramas" of the heavens or the city. Media scholar Lisa Parks, in her book *Cultures in Orbit,* refers to the images that a space telescope gains as "satellite panoramas."[101]

But "big science" demonstrations such as the Hubble telescope to the contrary, the observatory was also a site of popular science, and this history is still present.[102] Although astronomers debated the relative public value of the observatory, its connections to spectacle were there from the nineteenth century on. The American astronomer Richard Anthony Proctor argued beginning in the 1860s for the observatory to be a public face of the sciences and rejected calls for his discipline's professionalization.[103] (For film historians, a useful analogy between the muddled popular–scientific face of the observatory would be Eadweard Muybridge, whose chronophotographic work was likewise, and famously, both science and art.) This would later change, of course, as observatories became sites largely for specialists. By 1909, the popularizer of astronomy Garrett P. Serviss complained that the professional astronomer "is like a selfish spectator at a panorama who holds possession of the only peephole."[104]

Observatories afforded the panoramic altitude in the nineteenth century. (High-altitude mountaintop observatories such as the Lick, in California, begin to arrive at the end of the century.) They allowed viewers to practice their trained judgment on the city, that "celebration (not denigration) of the human (rather than mechanical) ability to seize patterns."[105] The altitude allowed for close consideration of the details of the city, simultaneously slowing its movements down and arresting its growth long enough to constellate it. To perform this imaginative feat, observers reduce their scale in the place lived: the viewer's surrogate in the simulated space of the apparatus—the citizens in the market square of the panorama, the locals that pass by on the camera obscura's table—are likewise made small. This miniaturization, this *scalar magnification,* is a necessary feature of the constellating, hybrid vision described here. Although astronomers seldom use the word "constellate," this is what was done: mapping the stars and their movement, and size, noting unusual phenomena. The representational theater of the observatory delivered "cosmological narratives" that thematized "the place of man in the universe,"[106] giving a sense of the infinitesimal scale of humankind. The panorama and camera obscura in turn zoomed in from the celestial to the bird's-eye view, showing the place of the citizen in the city. Atop the observatory, looking down rather than up. Turning from the heavens and taking in the Earth.

2. The Panstereorama

Three-dimensional models of the Earth's surface and human settlements have a history dating back millennia and exist to this day. From a sculpted plan of Maltese buildings in the late Neolithic; to a model of the Alps in the eighteenth century; to a 3D-printed miniature of Chicago today, the purpose, scale, materials, and names of these maps differ.[1] The large-scale map of Malta, chiseled out of limestone, has a now unknowable purpose and name; Franz Ludwig Pfyffer's immense small-scale "Relief der Urschweiz," made of sand, wax, and wood, aimed to depict a tenth of Switzerland; the Chicago Model, which includes every structure currently in the city, cast in plastic, does not use the term *relief* and is geared to the architectural aficionado. These three-dimensional models, in their diversity, sometimes strain the limit of what is considered cartography.[2] They share, however, a plan view as rendered in three dimensions, as though seen from a great height, and they use models in relief to achieve this effect.

Although such three-dimensional models are, like other urban mediations, "rooted in deep time," this chapter focuses on a particular, largely nineteenth-century genre of urban model called the "panstereorama."[3] Made of cork, pasteboard, grasses, and silk, panstereoramas presented existing cities in miniature for public amusement.[4] Panstereoramas aimed to present the entirety of a given municipality, each extant structure rendered at a scale between 1:72 to 1:600.[5] This scale is, by way of comparison, much smaller than that of a doll's house, which, although unstandardized, have always been many degrees larger than the panstereorama. Nevertheless, although made up of individual miniature structures, panstereoramas were cumulatively immense mosaics spread over large tables. A model of 118 square feet was typical, and viewers could circle the perimeter of the city in order to view it from every angle.

49

The panstereorama phenomenon occurs in the wake of the Montgolfier Brothers' first balloon flight (1783), and the "balloonomania" that swept Europe and the United States in the years that followed. Many people had never viewed their city from above, and there was a thirst for such representations, one that balloonists (who, for a variety of reasons, did not customarily make maps) did not quench.[6] This chapter argues that the panstereorama was a major cartographic output of ballooning, and one that cast the map on the center stage, displayed as a popular amusement. What unites these urban models is that they offered a simulation of the view from a balloon to a public that did not otherwise have safe or reliable access to this perspective.

Panstereoramas were inflected by the balloon view. Like a ride in a balloon, they offered travel, albeit virtual: a trip to a new city, or a trip above one's own city. They offered a sense of the city in its fragile entirety: the term that balloonists and panstereorama promoters alike employed was *the whole*.[7] Finally, they offered a view of the city slowed down to a stop, stripped of its citizens, and without the clutter and noise of the nineteenth-century metropolis; this, too, corresponds with the accounts of balloonists, who wrote routinely of the peace that flight afforded.[8] In sum, although a terrestrial amusement, the discourse on the city and cartography that the panstereoramas offered was elevated in altitude, and distinctly related to period notions of flight.

The contours and scale of the panstereorama phenomenon have been neglected, as has their important role in communicating civic information as cartographic spectacles. After discussing two affiliated media forms that help to explain the panstereorama—panorama paintings and *plans-reliefs*—this chapter presents studies of two urban regional practices of city modeling (London and Paris), and examines two panstereoramas in detail (representing Paris and New York). The fortunes and features of this medium changed after the beginning of the world's fairs (1851), when such models became a routinely exhibited feature, and the afterlife of the panstereorama is considered at the close of this chapter.

PANORAMAS AND PANSTEREORAMAS

The term *panorama* is conspicuous in the word *panstereorama*, and this section explores the relation of panorama painting to model cities. *Panstereorama* is a portmanteau word that takes the *pan* (all) and *orama* (view) of *panorama* and, as a period encyclopedia noted, adds to it "*stereos, solide*, qui indique que la *vue totale* ou *générale* se compose d'objets non plus simplement apparens, mais *solides* ou de relief" ("*stereo*, solid, which indicates that the *total* or *general view* is composed not simply of the semblance of objects, but *solid* or in relief").[9] Its use of the "-orama" affix makes plain that the panstereorama was part of the "o-rama craze" that entered with Robert Barker's painted circular panorama (patented in 1787) and, arguably, exited with the moving panorama at the fin de siècle.[10] Panorama paintings, as discussed in chapter 1, typically offered immersive views of cities, harbors, battles, or biblical scenes, rendered at an immense scale in purpose-built rotundas. A typical urban panorama might show the town square, the many streets that lead to it, as well as the rural landscape beyond. Successful panoramas, of which there were many, could remain on display for years, or travel across Europe and the Atlantic to new audiences.

Amid the many singular o-ramic media devices that blossomed during these years—including the previously mentioned *diorama, maréorama,* and *cinéorama,* one could add the *cosmorama,* the *georama,* and the *myriorama,* among many others.[11] Most of these traded in either simulated travel experiences or popular science, and the panstereorama was often perceived to be a pinnacle of the form. This recollection, from London's *Saturday Review* of 1913, provides a popular late genealogy of the word:

> Among the delights which were grouped under this magic name was a thing first called in the days of its innocence a Panorama; which afterwards gave itself the more sophisticated name of Diorama, and finally, as art and science were enslaved to its elaboration, blossomed into the thrilling title of Panstereorama. I have never again recovered the sense of intoxication with which my annual visit to this entertainment was accompanied.[12]

Walter Benjamin, in his *Arcades Project*, noted a similar lineage that likewise culminated in the panstereorama.[13] Certainly, these models presented something novel, even within the o-rama craze: where most panoramic media devices used canvases, directed lighting, cutouts, and various tromp l'oeil effects to produce a sense of scale, depth, and immersion, the panstereorama relied on three-dimensional objects, albeit miniaturized, to produce an impression of relief and distance.

Panoramas and panstereoramas shared audiences, networks, and appeals. Each was a relatively affordable amusement that offered popularly intelligible maps of a city. As industrialization brought more and more people into the cities, and the cities grew, and workers migrated between them, a parallel network of itinerant cities in miniature emerged. These cities traveled along the same routes as panorama paintings: Rome went to Paris; Paris to London; London to New York. In each case, the untraveled could take a substitute "trip" to a foreign city, whereas the cosmopolitan could retrace the steps of their last visit. The panorama painting, as discussed, often reproduced elevated perspectives, ordinarily from city structures or topographical features that would afford the finest vantage point. It was, by and large, limited in this regard—it went as high as the cathedral spire, seldom the balloon. The panstereorama, by contrast, in offering the "all-solid-view" of large conurbations, had to go higher still, to the height of a balloon, in order to fit in the entirety of the city. Although the panstereorama is thus no longer at the panoramic altitude, it is this feature above all, this amplification of a bird's-eye view, that makes the panstereorama *panoramic*.

The relationship between panorama paintings and cartography is conspicuous, and the impact of the panorama can be seen in bird's-eye-view lithographs and the expanded horizontal frame of panoramic maps. As for maps in relief, as many have noted, they require the least expertise of any form of cartography to understand, as they do not rely on the same coded representation as two-dimensional maps. They are thus an obvious format for a publicly displayed cartographic spectacle. Both panorama and panstereorama likewise share a cartographic clarity of vision that pictures a city under ideal circumstances of visibility.[14] (This may explain the special popularity of both media in London.) Panstereoramas were cartographic in many other regards. To take the most conspicuous instance, unlike architectural maquettes, which often envision a public inhabiting the proposed structures and thus include miniature denizens within the display, the panstereorama was devoid of represented inhabitants.[15]

The panstereorama did not propose new constructs or envision cities to come, but rather, like the panorama, reflected preexisting cities. The art historian Malcolm Baker has articulated the basic categories of use to which models (broadly conceived) in the eighteenth century were put, categories that still applied in the nineteenth century, as indeed today. These categories of use may be summarized as *anticipatory, reconstructive, reflective,* or *detailing*. Panstereoramas, unlike later urban models, were never anticipatory (e.g., "the city of the future") or reconstructive (e.g., "London before the Great Fire"); rather, in the main they existed at the axis of the reflective (e.g., "London as she is") and the detailing (e.g., "key monuments of Paris").[16]

The panstereorama, as Baker's categories suggest, connects to an extant popular practice of modeling that existed in the eighteenth and nineteenth centuries. These were models not only for scientific or pedagogic demonstration, connecting to, for instance, embryology or archaeology, but also models for mass spectacle.[17] The Crystal Palace Dinosaurs, on view since 1854, are perhaps the great public example from this period of modeling.[18] Panstereoramas, which emerged from this practice, and doubtless employed many of the same craftsmen, may be viewed in part as a preexisting culture of the miniature rising to meet, and compete with, the immense size of the panorama painting. If, as the historian of science Simon Schaffer argued, "models make the sublime into the artificial, measurable, and thus manageable," then the panstereorama, through relentless miniature accretion, places the minute newly into the panoramic category of the sublime.[19]

PLANS EN RELIEF

The most abundant literature on the subject of model cities relates to the French collections of *plans-reliefs* once stored at the Louvre, and now held by the Musée des Plans-reliefs at the Hôtel National des Invalides in Paris, and the Palais des Beaux-Arts in Lille (as well as, in smaller numbers, several regional museums).[20] These models of French territorial possessions (from Antibes to Verdun), of citadels, forts, and walled cities, commissioned by rulers from Louis XIV to Napoleon III, were a type of military technology, but not in the ordinary sense. As "objets de prestige," they were too large and fragile to be useful in the battlefield, so they stayed in Paris as a kind of Wünderkammer of the empire.[21] They were often shown to visiting dignitaries.

Historians who have worked on the models tend to place the entire prehistory of model cities into the context of the *plan-relief*, citing an early modern (1521) model of Rhodes as the first such object.[22] But this model of Rhodes was not just used for military purposes: it was also employed for city improvement; later, it was given as a gift. A useful distinction, proposed here for the first time, is to consider the *plan-relief* a military technology, and the panstereorama the popular variant. For this reason, the Rhodes model cannot be considered a true *plan-relief*, and the descriptor must be limited to *military* objects made between the seventeenth and nineteenth centuries.[23] Nor should a public city model advertised as a panstereorama in France be called a *plan-relief*, although some have done so—erroneously, according to the distinction presented here.

There are of course many and important infrastructural relations between the *plan-relief* and the panstereorama (and even fusions of the two, as in the "panstereomachia" discussed below), not least among them the fact that statecraft *plans-reliefs* were, after the death of Louis XIV in 1715, placed on display in the Louvre; thus, they ceased to be framed exclusively as objects of martial-cartographic value, and became objects of aesthetic contemplation. Art historian Quatremère de Quincy, for instance, writing in 1825 notes that "Il faut placer sous cette dénomination

FIGURE 19. *Plan-relief* of Tournai, 1701 (detail). No panstereoramas remain extant; the historian of the model city depends upon the adjacent medium of the *plan-relief* to provide a semblance of the craft and experience of the panstereorama. Palais des Beaux-Arts, Lille. Photograph by Pierre André Leclercq, CC BY-SA.

[panstereorama] la collection de représentations semblables, en relief, à l'hôtel royal des Invalides, où l'on voit la plupart des forteresses et des ports de mer de la France" ("one must place under this term [panstereorama] the collection of similar representations in relief at the Hôtel Royal des Invalides, where we see the majority of France's fortresses and harbors.")[24] In short, he argues for recategorizing the *plan-relief* as a panstereorama to suit the new, o-ramic media taxonomy.

Plans-reliefs remain important media a priori for panstereoramas. In Choffin's panstereorama of London in 1825 (detailed below) advertisements noted that the engineer had designed such maps for Napoleon Bonaparte. Likewise, *plans-reliefs* remain vital for our consideration of panstereoramas in the eighteenth and nineteenth centuries, since, perhaps owing to the fragility of the model city, and the mobility of the popular variant, none has been preserved.[25] The collections of *plans-reliefs* held in France today have thus become the clearest window into the craft and presentation of panstereoramas that survives (Figure 19).[26] Readers wishing to gain an impression of a panstereorama would do well to visit the collections in Paris or Lille, rather than a contemporary model made in this century.

"A PERFECT MINIATURE": LE QUOY'S MODEL IN RELIEVO OF PARIS

Le Quoy's model of Paris, which showed in London and (at least, but probably beyond) York in the late 1760s and 1770s, cannot be classed a *plan en relief*, given that it does not emerge from the same military infrastructure. Rather, this was a privately funded endeavor intended for public exhibition, advertised as a sui generis object: "the only thing of the kind in the world," viewed for a shilling.[27] The construction of the large-scale model was an immense procedure and investment. As described in the narrative guide, or "little summary Extract" that accompanied Le Quoy's exhibit, the "infinite Pains and Labour attending such an Undertaking" were considerable:

> Our Artist, from the kind Countenance shewn him by the Nobility and Gentry, [was permitted] to visit the internal Parts of their Hotels and Gardens, to render his Model compleat, useful and entertaining. . . . After Twenty-two Years close and diligent Application [this model] truly represents the City and Suburbs of *Paris*, as well in Regard to its Ground-plot, as the Elevation and Extent of each particular Edifice, and its Subdivisions, upon a Scale of seventy-two Feet to an Inch [1:864].[28]

The twenty-two-year length of construction time is improbable, given the routine exaggeration found in civic spectacles of the age, and the financial backing that this relatively untested display would have required. But the list of depicted features of Paris, which some in the audience could verify for themselves, suggests that whatever the exact building timeline for Le Quoy's model, the level of detail would have necessitated an extensive assembly. "The public Buildings of the City, and even the private Houses of the Citizens, are so exactly copied, that not only every Ornament in Architecture, but the Doors and Windows of the common Houses are distinctly seen."[29] A sense of the innumerable miniature details built into the immense model may be located in the announcement of its sale in 1777 ("worthy a place in the finest Museum in the World"), where it was reported that the size of the model was eighty-two square feet.[30] "The Number of Houses is reckoned to be 3,019, and upwards, the greatest Part of which are seven Stories high, besides many small Shops."[31]

The guides to the exhibit narrate several itineraries through the network of Paris, approaching from different directions and noting key buildings and features of the city. In a section on "curious observations on the city of

Paris," further details are listed for the visitor to look out for—a scavenger hunt of embedded particulars. Paris is reported to have, among dozens of other entries:

26 Hospitals.

An Opera House.

One ditto for Oratorios.

12 Prisons or Gaols.

6200 Lanterns to light the City.[32]

This index, vouching for the model's status as a bona fide surrogate for Paris, provides a sense of verisimilitude that the visitor will nominally appreciate as supporting the sense of virtual travel that the model provides. Le Quoy's model "will convey to those, who have never been in that metropolis, a stronger idea of it than can be acquired by a transient inspection of the place itself; and those ladies and gentlemen who have been there, may distinguish the very houses they resided in."[33]

Absent from the streets of the model are representations of its residents, which other miniature media—including doll's houses and board games—might lead a viewer to reasonably expect, in the eighteenth century as today. Nevertheless, Le Quoy's original public model testified to the comprehensiveness of the city, to its "wholeness," a promotional refrain that occurs on countless occasions in the literature. "The Whole is exactly like the Object itself, and may be said to be in every Respect, natural."[34] In offering the "whole," the panstereorama provides a system map of the city, one in which itineraries may be plotted or not, free of human and other traffic. This process makes the city into an individual entity, rather than an inhabited space; it makes the city, as we shall see, into something that must be cared for and preserved.

PANSTÉRÉORAMAS IN PARIS

At the beginning of the nineteenth century, after Barker's panorama in Leicester Square had engaged the media imagination of Europe, the term *panstereorama* came to be employed. The precise location of the first panstereorama is unknown, as is its architect, but it is certain that by 1802 the Pavillon de Hanovre in Paris (which remains, rebuilt in a park in Sceaux) hosted so-named panstereorama displays. Once again, the most substantive source of information is found in the guide that accompanied the *Panstéréorama Ville de Londres* (1802), "enrichie d'un plan esquissé" (Figure 20).[35] It may seem unusual for one form of popularized cartography (the panstereorama) to come with another (the *plan esquissé*, or sketched map), but it speaks to the novelty of the balloon view that the model provided. Although interpretation of models in relief is not difficult, orientation can be, and this small accompanying map acts as a key to the larger map, allowing bearings to be located via two modes.

The Panstereorama of the City of London's accompanying guide suggests a generic familiarity, given that it rehearses many of the same claims as Le Quoy's. It proceeds directly to the annotated list of important London landmarks and an index of its features that almost seem to build on Le Quoy's, including:

25 Hôpitaux (hospitals).

5 Théâtres royaux (royal theatres).

8,005 Cabarets (cabarets).

21 Prisons ou maisons de correction (prisons or houses of correction).

There is an assumption, evidently, that the viewer who buys a ticket for the panstereorama is familiar with the premise of the medium; there are fewer instructions in the particulars of the form. Further, the *plan esquissé* and the list highly resemble the format of the travel book at that time, speaking to the appeals of virtual travel that the panstereorama offered.[36]

There were at least two panstereoramas in Paris in the early 1800s: that in the Pavillon de Hanovre discussed above and another in the Jardin des Montagne Russes et du Panstereorama (Figure 21).[37] The precise location of this second attraction is unknown, as is its operator, and in the instances that follow, it is not always apparent which panstereorama writers were visiting. It is worth noting that the panstereorama was here paired with the fairground attraction of the *montagne russe* (an early form of roller coaster, and still the preferred term for such rides in several languages today) situating the medium at this historical juncture in the pleasure garden and fairground milieus within which panorama paintings often operated, and which were abundant in France at the time.[38] Indeed, in 1814, the *Theatrical Inquisitor* lists the *panstéréorama* alphabetically between some media cousins, the *ombres chinoises* and the phantasmagoria, noting only that "at this place of amusement cities are represented, painted in relief, with a precision and effect that command universal attention."[39]

In keeping with the popular etymology of *panstereorama* noted above—emergent from *panorama*—these model cities were likewise seen as structurally improving upon the root, panoramic attraction. Several guidebooks to Paris mention this: *How to Enjoy Paris* (1818) notes that the panoramas

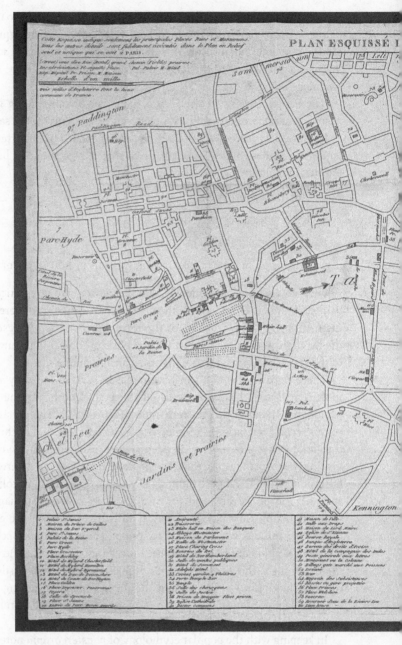

FIGURE 20.   This engraving was inserted into the slim booklet produced to help visitors orient themselves as they viewed Le Quoy's Panstéréorama Ville de Londres displayed at Sceaux, Paris, in 1802. It resembles the maps published in tourist guidebooks in the period. British Library.

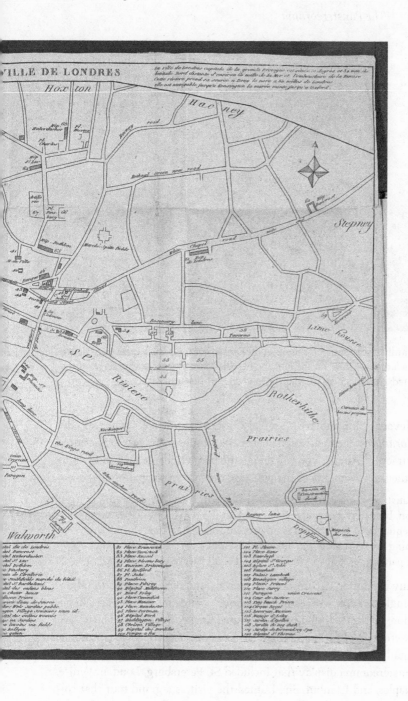

FIGURE 21. Jardin des Montagne Russes et du Panstereorama. The panstereorama would be stored in the large structure on the left; the Montagne russes are on the right, in the distance. Undated; circa 1814–1830. Marmatton Monet Museum, Paris.

on Boulevard Montmartre "scarcely merit attention," whereas the *Panstéréorama* is deemed worth seeing, its "Cities in relief . . . presented with accuracy."[40] August von Kotzebue, the playwright, echoed this evaluation of the improvements of the panstereorama over the panorama:

> The Panstereorama exhibits, in two apartments, Paris, Lyons, and London, beautifully executed in relievo. In the two former cities even the inequality of the ground is preserved; and, at any rate, this charming art represents the objects chosen in a very striking manner. Other panoramas, but too well known, I shall pass over in silence.[41]

In many exhibition circumstances, the panstereorama offered several cities in a single location. Von Kotzebue (above) visited models of Paris, Lyon, and London; *Le Vie Parisienne*, the illustrated weekly, advised readers to "see the Panstereorama. . . . You'll travel to London, Vienna, Constantinople, etc."[42] Finally, Stéphanie Félicité, the comtesse de Genlis, reported visiting a single panstereorama display that included St. Petersburg, London, Venice, Rome, Naples, and Istanbul. She framed the visit as a grand tour that collapsed space and time, using a formulation that speaks once again to the appeals of virtual travel that the models provided: "Après avoir bien voyagé pendant une heure en Russie, en Angleterre, en Italie, on descendit dans le jardin" (After having traveled, within one hour, in Russia, England, and Italy, we descended to the garden).[43]

PANSTEREORAMAS IN LONDON

The circulation of miniature cities in Europe at this time becomes difficult to encompass, so many are on tour; the focus of this section, however, is London, where there were many. The audience required to support such traffic in model cities must have been large, and it included at least one famous visitor. Wordsworth, who was writing *The Prelude*, looked in on one of these models and came away impressed by its technical ingenuity.

> More mechanic artist represent
> By scale exact, in model, wood or clay,
> From blended colours also borrowing help,
> Some miniature of famous spots or things,—
> St. Peter's Church; or, more aspiring aim,
> In microscopic vision, Rome herself.[44]

The model of Rome to which he refers does not survive elsewhere in the historical record. But other displays that Wordsworth may have visited do. In 1826, for instance, Antoine de Flossi built a model of St. Petersburg some two hundred square feet in size, with "55 craftsmen invited from Italy and France."[45] Later in the 1820s, Messrs. Williams debuted their new model of the City of London, which increased Le Quoy's 3,019 represented houses to a purported 78,000. The Thames was rendered in glass. Visitors who lived in the city could have their house pointed out to them by the proprietors. And as was now commonplace, the bird's-eye effect of the model city was noted: "One of the most ingenious and perhaps extraordinary works of art, now exhibiting in the Metropolis, is this magnificent Model—it can only be compared, with that of a person hovering over a city, on a fine bright day, seated in the car of a balloon."[46] Certain panstereoramas in this period offered a second story from which to view the models, so as to offer an even higher altitude of "flight."

The institutional affiliations between the creators of the *plans-reliefs* and the panstereoramas have to this point been nebulous, although it is a safe assumption that there was a certain degree of migration between models of state and models of spectacle, given the expertise required. The few reports of the Panstereorama of Paris, which showed in London in 1826, confirm this connection, for its engineer, Mr. Choffin, was noted in the advertisements to be the "Author of several models on the principal towns in Europe, that have just been bought by Napoleon Bonaparte."[47] In the interim between Le Quoy and Choffin (between 1760 and 1826) the repute of the panstereorama had only grown, given that now advertisers were able to note that "This model has been honoured by several Branches of the [British] Royal Family, who were highly gratified by its correctness and beauty."[48] Again, all such boasts must be met with skepticism—the promotional materials of various popular media at the time were rife with proclamations of blue-blooded clientele—but the fact that panstereorama promoters would be so bold as to make such a claim suggests a change in status, and indicates the abiding level of interest in this type of exhibition.

Certain components had altered in Choffin's model and had lined up more exactly with the understood practices of ballooning. "The respective palaces and other public buildings, are seen with the utmost distinctness; and, by the occasional aid of magnifiers of large power, a more accurate idea of the great city of Paris is impressed upon the mind."[49] These magnifiers were most likely telescopes of some variety, designed to observe the detail of the forty-two-square-foot model. By this stage in the history of flight, it was understood that aeronauts traveled with such optical devices; so too, then, would the panstereorama.

The balloonist's luxury of taking in the entire city in one view was once again noted ("the eye not only takes in at a glance—say all the city from Chelsea to Wapping"), as was, corresponding to the addition of telescopes, the detailed particulars the model makers embedded in the city. As one reviewer vividly explained:

> Every spectator, looking at the town of his own inhabitancy, finds something in the *minutia* to attract him. . . . A young lady, the instant she enters, looks for "Covent-garden Theatre"; her old aunt for "Wesley's Tabernacle." . . . 'Prentices would see "Pocknell's lobster shop in the Strand"; antiquaries (without spectacles) the "British Museum"; the gambler's eye would vacillate between the "Hells" in St. James's and the "Tread-mill"; and the hackney-coachman would know "Essex-street," and every other street in town.[50]

Paradoxically, although no one is depicted in the model, there is a place for everyone in the panstereorama.

By 1826, the term *panstereorama* was evidently familiar enough to warrant, or explain, an ancillary attraction, the *panstereomachia*. Charles Bullock, the proprietor of the display, which showed at Regent St.'s Spacious Room, presented the medium as though it was an established type in the epigraph that begins the accompanying guide: "Derived from *pan* (all) *stereo* (solid) and *machia* (battle, or combat). The representation of a Battle, entirely composed of solid figures in their relative proportions."[51] The battle, in this instance, is that of Poitiers (1356), between France and England; to an extent, the panstereomachia may be viewed as a patriotic national retort to the French *plan-relief*.[52] Bullock's guide seldom discusses the model itself, preferring to narrate the battle and its many details.[53] Notices in the popular press are more explanatory:

> This celebrated Military Engagement is represented by upwards of 1500 figures, modelled in solid materials, and finished with strict regard to historical truth, and with accurate attention to the heraldry, chivalry, and costume of the period to which it relates.[54]

This fusion of the military and popular model would continue to be a desired combination. For instance, James Wyld, the proprietor of the famous cartographic spectacle, the Great Globe, produced a model of the Siege of Sebastopol that went on display in 1855.[55] By this stage, balloons had been used for observation purposes in war, which helps to account for the new focus.

BELDEN'S MODEL OF NEW YORK

It is likely that versions of the panstereorama were presented in North America prior to Ezekiel Porter Belden's model of New York (1846)—for instance, there is evidence that he completed a model of New Haven in advance of this larger venture. Certainly, American audiences expressed familiarity with the form when greeting Belden's model, but it is nonetheless one of the earliest records of a panstereorama in the United States. Fortunately, Belden's promotional publications ensure that there remains an abundance of primary materials with which to reconstruct an idea of the model. Indeed, Belden published a 125-page history of the city—*New York: Past, Present, and Future*—to accompany the model. This in turn has a standalone appendix, *New York as It Is*, which collects many construction facts and press responses to the model itself. Belden's model displays what may be seen as the typical features of the panstereorama—some 137 square feet in size (accounts differ); with every notable and non-notable building produced in relief, in this instance, carved in wood; and small features such as lampposts likewise crafted in miniature. It rendered all of Manhattan, and a portion of Brooklyn in the vicinity of Brooklyn Heights.

Diverging from the norm, however, is Belden's willingness to share recognition for the construction of the model (despite taking mayoral responsibility for "the whole" model city); previous examples invariably attributed the given model to an individual maker. Belden provides a list of credits for those involved in producing this spectacle:

Architectural Work and General Superintendence—By Mr. W.P. Whitey.

Platform of the Model—By Messrs. A.E. Moulthrop, E. Bishop, and Assistants.

Surveying and Map Department—By Messrs. J. Murphy, R. Morrison, and Assistants.

Modelling of Buildings—By Messrs. P.A. Edinger, R. Moley, E. Brown [et al.].

Trees—By Messrs. C.H. Judson, J.B. Hinton, A.P. Butler, and C.H. Lewis.

Elevations, Depressions, and Wharves—By Mr. H. Stow.

Steamboats—By Messrs. E.B. Cunningham and S.R. Cunningham.

Shipping—By Messrs. C. Davis, A.W. Hogg, T. Hogg, Jr., and S. Hogg.

Painting of the Public Buildings, Steamboats, Shipping, &c. —By Messrs. E.W. Jackson, J.Y. Brush, H. Rover [et al.].

Painting of the Private Buildings—By Messrs. J.W. Rover, A. Eiffe, A. Miller [et al.].

Scenic Effects—By Messrs. C. McDonald, E. Richmond, B. Clark [et al.].

Inspection of the Modelling—By J.H. Plumb, F.B. Booth, and J.J. Palmer.

Framework of the Canopy—By Messrs. P. Tiers, J. Crisp, H.L. Farnham [et al.].

The Painting of the Canopy—By Messrs. J. Evers, E.P. Barnes, E.C. Coates, and J.H. Kimberly.

Canvas for the Paintings—By Messrs. T. Kelly, S.N. Dodge, and E. Dechaux.

Carved Ornamental Work—By Messrs. J.H.B. Jackson, J.D. Darlington, T. Millard [et al.].

Gilding—By Messrs. J. McPeake., H. Cunningham, and H. Scardenfield.

Ornamental Painting—By Messrs. T.T. Hogg, J.C. Whitmore, S.A. Dodge [et al.].

Iron Frame Work—By Messrs. Cornell & Jackson.

Drapery—By Messrs. Solomon & Hart.

Lights and Glasses—By Messrs. Benjamin Pike & Son.

Book-Keeper and Treasurer—H. C. Hall.

The Whole—By H. Porter Belden.[56]

The distribution of labor for the model was extensive. Belden further had all parties above agree to a proviso to the effect that, "if this Model should be destroyed by fire, or other accident, while we are living, we will hold ourselves in readiness at a moment's warning to rally to the standard of Mr. Belden for its re-construction."[57] Given that the model opened one year after the New York City fire of 1845, there was poignancy to this agreement.

Belden's model was complex and used multiple techniques in order to give a sense of the entirety of the metropolis (Figure 22.) In addition to a background canvas, which would have blocked off what lay east of Brooklyn, the model also included a type of canopy, ringing the top of the model with detailed paintings of key New York buildings. Further, its lighting scheme was advanced, with directional lamps on the posts supporting the apparatus. This late panstereorama mirrors some of the elaborate cartographic spectacles that were on display in England in this period, such as the aforementioned Great Globe of 1851, which likewise aimed to present an entire system, in this case the Earth in toto, and did so by forging a complex intermedial device with viewing ramps, maps in relief, unique lighting apparatuses, and more. The panstereorama, in its ornate 1840s iteration, was "a piece of mechanism entirely different from a Map or Painting," as indeed it needed to be to present the city comprehensively.[58]

Belden's model encapsulates the central features of the panstereorama. It was received as a purposeful simulation of a balloon view, one that offered a network map of the city. Contemporaneous journalists noted this. The *American Whig Review*, a short-lived arts publication, expressed familiarity along these lines:

> Among the many happy productions of the modern art of perspective drawing, we have always been particularly interested in the aeroscopic, or *bird's eye* views of great cities. . . . But no such pictorial view, however skillfully executed, can equal in faithfulness and reality of impression the exhibition of a city in carved blocks of wood. . . . We do not know that we have ever been more struck with any curious work of art than with the "Model of New-York city."[59]

Another period journalist noted that it captured the city in "a single *coup d'oeil*"—a rare elevated view of New York City at a time when there were no skyscrapers to provide one.[60] *Coup d'oeil* here is a clear synonym for the more frequently adopted *whole*, but it speaks to the complete, sudden, holistic

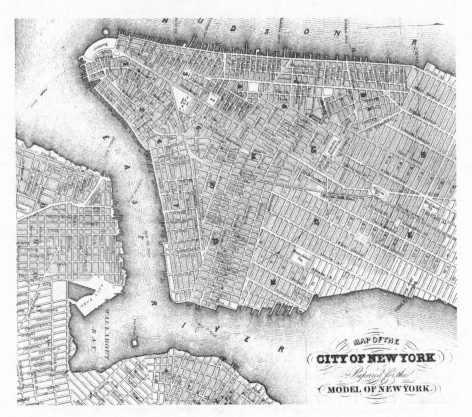

FIGURE 22.   Eziekiel Porter Belden, "Map of The City of New York: Prepared for The Model of New York," 1849. As with the map of London in Figure 19, Belden's map was produced to accompany the model guide *New York: Past, Present, and Future* (New York: Prall, 1849) and was inserted before the second page. It shows the southern end of Manhattan and part of Brooklyn. The axis of the map has north on the right side.

view of a complicated system (in this case, a city), which Lorraine Daston has investigated as a mode of vision that thrived in the nineteenth century.[61]

Belden's model included detailed features of New York, from awning, to tree, to window: "even in the minutiae, all was correct."[62] The great silence of this model, like the others, was the citizenry. The throngs of New York were not included. The absence was not noticed in any of the existing accounts, although viewers might have plausibly expected such a representation. One author wished to add some dynamism to the model by having actual fire in the lamps.[63] In any case, Belden's hyperreal model was one of the last typical of the strategies of the panstereorama; after 1851, the intention of such city models changed.

FIGURE 23. Lithograph of Eziekiel Porter Belden's panstereorama of New York. The lamps attached to the supports provided illumination. The reproduction represents the island of Manhattan as seen from the west, with Brooklyn Heights to the right, but visitors could walk all around to inspect the buildings, streets, and other details of the urban landscape. From Eziekiel Porter Belden, *New-York—As It Is* (New York: Prall, 1849), 2.

BEYOND 1851: WORLD'S FAIRS, ALFRESCO PANORAMAS, AND CINEMA

The model city has, to this point, largely been concerned with reproducing the balloon view, with providing a virtual trip, and with aiming to display the "whole" system of the city. In the latter half of the nineteenth century, however, the context and intention of these models changed. This may mirror the popularization and ubiquity of balloon views, which were increasingly offered to the public at fairs and celebrations. Panstereoramas, as proxies for a balloon view, were no longer required to serve this purpose. Indeed, the term *panstereorama* experienced a semantic drift, ultimately encompassing a broad a range of practices.[64] Nevertheless, the popular model city lived on, at world's fairs, in alfresco panoramas, and in early film.

At London's Great Exhibition of 1851, which set many of the standards of later world's fairs, an altogether different logic of miniaturization and scale was found, one that did not marshal the effects of miniaturization toward aerial use. Instead, the famed "world in miniature" presentation style of the fair insisted upon a topsy-turvy organization that not only magnified the size of small technical objects, but also miniaturized larger places and structures. At the Great Exhibition alone, there were models of a number of cathedrals, as well as "plans of towns in relievo," and the Great Globe.[65] The idea behind these modeling strategies was to fit the technical wonders of the world in a single place. Such scale-based exhibits continued as a mainstay of world's fairs, from the historic model of Jerusalem at Vienna's *Weltausstellung* (1873), to Henry Dreyfuss's futuristic "Democracity" in New York (1939), to the most recent world's fair, held in Milan in 2015, which included a model of historic Chicago.[66] Such models were invariably either reconstructive (Jerusalem, Chicago) or anticipatory (Democracity), not reflective of extant metropolises as were the panstereoramas.[67]

Simultaneous with the rise of the world's fairs and the decline of the panstereorama, what Ralph Hyde called the alfresco panorama emerges. This related medium takes some of the craftsmanship of the panstereorama and, again, applies it to different aims. The alfresco panorama was a genre of display popular in English pleasure gardens, such as Vauxhall, and included, typically, a relief model combined with painting, sound effects, and "concluding pyrotechnics"—pyrotechnics that would often result in the model's nightly destruction: Vesuvius erupts, London burns, Lisbon quakes.[68] Evidently, the alfresco panorama has much in common with the later panstereoramic complexes, such as Belden's model of New York, inasmuch as they combined multiple representative strategies. But in their focus on the destruction of the city, these models have a clear continuity with early cinema, which also modelled the city pyrotechnically.[69]

It is likely that the modeling culture of the eighteenth and nineteenth centuries fed directly into the craft of early cinema. The panstereorama, given its half-century profusion and later iterations, was within popular memory and existing stagecraft. Correspondingly, the trick film tradition employed miniature, model cities from the earliest days of film. While the French fantasist Georges Méliès's technique was to employ laterally shot cut-outs in films such as *Eruption on Mont Pelée* (1902), the American Mutoscope & Biograph Company built solid models of San Francisco for its 1906 film of the city in flames (Figure 24).[70] English director Walter Booth created large solid models of London for *The Aerial Anarchists* (1911), which is regrettably lost, as well as in *The Airship Destroyer* (1909), which combines a backdrop with solid models for his prediction of aerial warfare on Britain. As the film industry grew, production guidebooks routinely gave detailed accounts of model city construction, borrowing much of the language of the panstereorama guide, noting the lengthy build times, the artistry, and the detail of the models.[71] Once again, there is a focus

FIGURE 24.   A promotional still for *San Francisco* (1906), advertised as "The Only Complete Moving Picture Production Showing the Fire in Progress." This image shows "the conflagration at its height." The model was built in their New York City studio, and the film was "tinted red to represent the glare of the fire."

on the destruction of the model city—by volcano, airship, or simple dynamite—rather than the contemplation of "the whole."[72]

• • •

This destructive aim is meaningfully different from how panstereoramas were received and understood in their heyday. There is a contrary ethic of care and preservation for panstereoramic models—remember the builders' promise to reconstruct Belden's model of New York—and it is one that I have observed firsthand. Although public response has been understandably difficult to reconstruct, since it is impossible to visit a panstereorama (as such) with an audience, analogous experiences may reveal something of historic reactions to such models.

In Lille, for instance, where some fifteen *plan-reliefs* are on display in the basement of the Palais des Beaux-Arts, there is among them a model of the city itself (made in 1740–43). When visiting the collection for research, I overheard residents of the city speculating about the orientation of the model, using surviving city landmarks and digital maps to get their bearings. Having done so, they noted the immense changes that had been made to the city (and that had been thrust upon it through war) in the interim

FIGURE 25.   A model city designed by Martin J. Doner, from an unidentified film, c. 1920s. The caption that originally ran below the image notes: "More than two thousand miniature buildings, with their design architecturally perfect, were placed in this scene," a line that could have come straight from Le Quoy's guide of 1768. The caption further informs the reader that they "will be able to visualize the proportions upon which this miniature city was constructed . . . from the two men who are placing the dynamite under the viaduct." Once again, the destruction of the city. Image from Lee Royal, *The Romance of Motion Picture Production* (Los Angeles: Royal, 1920), 47.

centuries, aiming to reconcile what remains with what is lost, picturing the city today in their mind's eye as they looked at the city yesterday.

Another example: in San Francisco in 2019, they placed on display a model of the city originally built by the Works Progress Administration in the late 1930s. Broken into pieces and spread throughout San Francisco Public Library branches, it included every structure of the city circa 1939.[73] Every home and street, every field and dune, every pier and monument, all cast in miniature and spread out over fifteen hundred square feet, capturing the city as it appeared at the time of its manufacture. Speaking to visitors who attended the model exhibit, there was a pronounced sense of tenderness toward the model—this facsimile of the whole seemed vulnerable, a physical synecdoche for the city. The public hoped to preserve it. The reaction is not unlike historical descriptions of the "blue marble" effect: that moment when we first saw the Earth from space, a vision that helped to catalyze global environmental efforts.[74]

Perhaps a "ship in a bottle" is the better, more historically appropriate image. The resilient seafaring vessel now delicate, too fragile to touch, looked at from above. Most models, being scaled down rather than scaled up, provide a simulation of the aerial view regardless of the modeling objective, through incidental miniaturization of the object, which is made small in order to offer something large in a single, viewable entirety—again, like a ship in a bottle. This incidental product of model craft is integral to the panstereorama, which marshals this effect as an attribute: miniaturization for the sake of clarity is simultaneously deployed as miniaturization as a scale effect of viewing from above. Thus, the aerial effect of the panstereorama that was lost in the model city beyond the mid-nineteenth century is a feature that is intrinsic, but unintentional, to modeling.

Friedrich Kittler once observed that "technologic media miniaturize the city, while magnifying [its] entropy." By "technologic media" Kittler meant digitization, but he might as well have been speaking to the panstereorama.[75] A first principle: *the aerial view is slow.* The model city, in its popular, nineteenth-century variation, offered a quality of civic and indeed infrastructural information that was otherwise unavailable to the average citizen. It allowed visitors to note major change, infrastructural or entropic, and to attempt to grasp the totality of the city. In the model city era, the (per Wordsworth) "microscopic vision" of the panstereorama allowed for macroscopic understanding.

It is in the balloon era, and not beyond, that this mobilization of the aerial effect of modeling makes sense. Features of balloon trips that were widely reported—the escape from the crowd and the total view of the city that it offered—were provided by the panstereorama. The producers of these models, borrowing from the appeals of panorama paintings and *plans-reliefs*, made alterations to better communicate aerial aesthetics, even going as far as to include optical apparatuses typical of the balloon basket.

The success of the medium in translating these appeals can, finally, be evidenced in the writings of balloonists. The English aeronaut James Glaisher, describing a first trip in a balloon ride over Paris in 1871, noted that "the whole town of Paris is reduced, after a little while, to the size of one of those maps in relief which we see at the Museum of the Invalides."[76] In the history of ballooning literature, the chosen terminology for describing what the Earth looked like from above was first a "map," and then a "panorama." After the panstereorama, balloonists also used the terms *model, miniature,* and *relief,* marking the impact of the panstereorama, and attesting to a reciprocity between model and balloon.[77]

3. Vertigo Effects

The "vertigo effect," as a filmic shorthand for perceptual imbalance—be it dizziness, epiphany, psychosis—has its eponymous origin in Hitchcock's *Vertigo* (1959).[1] A technique designed to register the fear of heights protagonist Scottie (James Stewart) suffers, as he hangs from the ledge of a building, looking down, the camera simultaneously zooms in and backs out, combining lens and camera movement to provide the unusual effect of objects remaining in their (relative) fixed positions on screen, while the viewer's perspective on them subtly changes. The repetition of this strategy in countless films has secured it a place and meaning, but it is not the only vertigo effect in film history. The dissolve long served as code for fainting and reverie. In the silent era, the custom was to repeatedly rotate the camera 360° clockwise while maintaining a close-up on the vertiginous face of a character.[2] Our vision swirls parallel to the onscreen sufferer's.

This chapter concerns the intersection of vertigo and cinema, but rather than the onscreen depiction of vertigo, it investigates the cultivation of vertigo in audiences *by* cinema. Film was an aeroscopic medium from its inception, simulating flights for a decidedly grounded audience, but the type of aerial viewing experience that it provided was altogether different from the relatively static, observational, studied approaches of the panorama and panstereorama. Film offered a physiological dimension to aeroscopics; namely, dizziness. What kind vertiginous responses can film produce? This chapter answers the question. Although I will not return to Hitchcock, I ask that you hold in mind the image of Jimmy Stewart dangling precipitously from a San Francisco skyscraper as a symbol for what follows and, indeed, imagine yourself in this position, and thus consider your own susceptibility to vertigo effects.

HOW TO DIAGNOSE A MEDIA PATHOLOGY

As children, many of us were once cautioned against sitting too close to a television screen, and we may have in turn, as adults, issued this same caution to our own progeny. This concern was based originally, and briefly, upon legitimate worry concerning radiation; it survived as a half-life of parental worry surrounding damage to children's eyesight. It remains a cliché.[3] It is an example of a media pathology.

An abiding, historical response to new media has been to focus on their accompanying physical maladies. It is a cyclic, if accelerating concern, perhaps earliest associated with music and musical instruments. This is for good reason. "We cannot," as Wordsworth noted, "bid the ear be still."[4] Unlike the eye, the ear has no naturally available lid to close. The idea of music as a cause of disease, as historian of medicine James Kennaway frames it, is centuries old. The most vivid example of this is likely the glass armonica of the eighteenth century, a retooled and refined adaptation of that impromptu instrument, the wine glass partly filled with water, which is played by rotating a damp finger around the lip of the glass. The story of the glass armonica includes a surprising cast of characters, including Benjamin Franklin and Franz Mesmer; ultimately, the sounds that emanated from the instrument became associated with madness and ill health.[5] To hear its unearthly noise accompanying a magic lantern phantasmagoria today remains unsettling.[6]

Media pathologies proliferate in the twentieth century. In its first decade, hysterical responses to music—"amusia," "hypermusia," "paramusia"—are first recorded.[7] "Radioitis," a mode of listening to the new technology that borders on obsessive and would include "the person who literally falls asleep wearing headphones," arrives by 1930.[8] Television brought a symmetrical media pathology in the form of impaired growth and leg deformity caused by excessive viewing, the so-named "frogitis."[9] Video games, meanwhile, have an immense toxicology. They encouraged the carpal tunnel–like syndromes known as "Nintendo thumb"[10] and "Tetwrist," named for Tetris, the addictive game designed by Alexey Pajitnov.[11] Novelist Martin Amis, an eager anthropologist of video games in their early days, identified four more: "Asteroid Elbow, PacMan Finger, Galaxian Spine, and Centipede Disc."[12] Such ergonomic anxieties continue to the present day. A book could be written about the panoply of virtual reality pathologies. And in this book, the example of the smart phone-bred "text neck" is discussed in chapter 5.

Media pathologies are sometimes moral arguments cloaked in the language of medicine. Any media pathology that ends with the suffix -*mania*, as in "kaleidoscomania" or "cartolinamania" (postcard mania) is likely an admonishment masquerading as a diagnosis, a form of social hypochondria tied to novelty.[13] The same is true of -*itis* (seen twice already in this chapter), a tongue-in-cheek use of the clinical suffix, applied to "a state of mind or tendency fancifully regarded as a disease."[14] These diagnoses chide the enthusiast, the fan, the cinephile, even the bibliophile was not immune, suffering from "febris bibliophilis chronica."[15] At other times, the sufferer has a real ailment but may be misdiagnosing the cause, using *technophobia* as a pretext.[16] Electromagnetic hypersensitivity, memorably depicted in the television series *Better Call Saul* (2015–), is one such case. And occasionally—as in what follows, drawing from medical, popular, and philosophical sources—media pathologies describe legitimate ailments or physiological effects of such new technologies. Whether or not they exist, media pathologies powerfully inform the popular reception of the given medium, as well as (in some cases) their legal status, design, and pedagogic or medical use.

The media theorist Friedrich Kittler argued that disability lies behind media invention: Edison was half deaf when he invented the phonograph; the typewriter was first made for people with vision troubles.[17] Correspondingly, media, as Marshall McLuhan argued, extend our senses: the wheel as extension of the foot, the book as extension of the eye, electric circuitry as extension of the nervous system.[18] This is a useful way of understanding these technologies, which earn a status as corporeal media metaphors. When successful, these metaphoric extensions creep, reciprocally, into our understanding of how our own sense organs operate. Jonathan Crary, for instance, made the case for the camera obscura as historic analogy for the eye, and the ear was widely analogized to the radio.[19] Today, it's the computer as brain, a "cognitive prothesis": the body a cyborgian, Saul Steinberg amalgam of media devices.[20]

The media metaphor informs the laboratory and clinical practice of doctors and scientists since at least the nineteenth century of Hermann von Helmholtz.[21] Take, for example, the case of German physiologist Wilhelm Kühne. Inspired by an understanding of photography, he began his optical experiments with the idea that "the retina behaves not merely like a photographic plate, but like an entire photographic workshop."[22] With this premise, that "retinal purple" has *au fond* the same mechanism for developing an image as wet-plate photography, what kind of tests does one run? For Kühne, it was to take gruesome "optograms," or photographs taken with the eyes of living organisms, by developing the image preserved on the retinas of first, a decapitated rabbit, and later, a guillotined man.[23] Kühne's successful experiments informed folktales that continue to this day, that the eye of a dead person contains within it, undeveloped, an image of the last thing that person saw.[24]

Corporeal media metaphors inform our own sense of hearing, vision, and memory. Once the metaphor takes hold, media pathologies follow in kind: radio static is often used to describe tinnitus; analogies of data retrieval, storage, and glitch are used to describe memory loss; and below, I will explore the analogies between cinema and optical and vestibular health.[25]

This chapter will analyze, with reference to classical film theory and spectator response, initial encounters with aerial films that resulted in motion sickness, before pivoting to later medical experiments that used cinema as a potential cure for motion sickness itself. Aerial simulation films provided the first approximations of airsickness for millions of people who could not otherwise reach the heights and technologies required to experience it, comprising an early cinematic "body genre."[26] The motion picture camera has been used as a device for habituating the viewer to motion sicknesses, implicitly and explicitly, throughout the history of the medium.

CINEMA SICKNESS

The cinema was the greatest vector for media pathologies in the twentieth century. Most of the ailments were, from the first, associated with eyesight.[27] Entries from a prospective media-diagnostic manual follow.

Picturitis (1908): Ocular discomfort and headache due to rapidity of scenes; likened to the effect of looking out of the window of a fast-moving train or car.[28]

Cinematophthalmia (1909): Conjunctivitis, lachrymation, and photophobia caused by motion picture viewing.[29]

Moving picture eye (1913): Widespread ocular fatigue, once studied by the Cleveland school board.[30]

Kinema headache (1920): Eye fatigue and pain caused by poor cinema design, namely, low illumination and uncomfortable viewing angles.[31]

Movie strain (1933): Serious eye fatigue that necessitates a visit to the optometrist.[32]

A New Jersey doctor in 1912 summed up the effects of cinema as "intense ocular and cerebral weariness, a sort of dazed, 'good-for-nothing' feeling, lack of energy, or appetite, etc., to which almost as frequently may be added 'upset stomach,' even vomiting, [and] sleeplessness." Similar to other reports published in medical journals at this time, the author was quite suspicious of the cinema, reporting: "I have had so many patients who have been made sick at these places of amusement that I now ask routine questions to elicit this etiologic factor."[33]

Suggested therapeutics and prophylactics for these media pathologies were creative, varying from an eye-wash "containing cocaine and adrenaline," the wearing of colored spectacles to limit excess exposure to the illumination of arc lamps, or "azurine goggles," to be worn in the movie theater.[34] Later, in the 1920s, there was a medical preference for color film over black and white, arriving with the reasoning that "absence of natural color in a photograph renders identification of the objects more difficult."[35]

Ocular media pathologies appeared on movie sets, as well. And they boomed again publicly with the 3D resurgence of the 1950s.[36] The key symptom was eyestrain, with sympathetic ophthalmologists brought to the pages of industry bulletins to reassure producers and exhibitors that the fault was with the viewer, not the stereoscopic technologies.

> *Klieg eyes* (1926): Temporary blindness and conjunctivitis caused by exposure to arc lamps (such as the popular brand named for the Kliegl brothers) on a movie set.[37]

> *3-D headache* (1953, and subsequently perennial): Eyestrain caused by the "unnatural optical gymnastics" of the viewer wearing stereoscopic lenses in the cinema.[38]

Another branch of pathology associated with cinema was vestibular. While the above citations have been drawn from medical journals, classical film theorists were just as innovative in diagnosing media pathologies. The poet Vachel Lindsay named three synonymous variants on a single page of his *The Art of the Moving Picture*.

> *Motion picture nausea* (1915)

> *Moving picture sea sickness* (1915)

> *Photoplay delirium tremens* (1915)

For Lindsay, these were the result of an excess of viewing motion pictures; what might now be called, anachronistically but nevertheless aptly, "binge watching." These are examples of what have cumulatively been dubbed *cinema sickness*, a vestibular malady that shared symptoms with other motion sicknesses.[39]

As Alison Griffiths identified in *Shivers Down Your Spine: Cinema, Museums, and the Immersive View*, immersive motion sickness traces back at least to painted panoramas, which were static to cinema's kinetic.[40] The sense of transportation to the new space was so verisimilar, the "panorama effect" so strong, as to prompt the queasy response that one might have traveling in the flesh. This desire to dip a toe into seasick waters is a fundamental appeal of the cinema as such; film scholars have variously called this allure its "proprioceptive aesthetics," or noticed its role in a broader "somatic visual culture."[41] From the beginnings of cinema, it was recognized by doctors and critics alike that "to many sensitive organizations the flicker of the cinematographic film alone is sufficient to cause vertigo and nausea."[42] Worse still were films that added movement to the brew.

FLYING TRAINS AND PHANTOM RIDES

Film historians have long found fascinating an unusual early-cinematic apparatus that aimed to move the audience along with the image.[43] Hale's Tours, a financially successful if short-lived (1904–1906) film ride that showed across the United States and Great Britain, was premised upon point-of-view shots from the head of locomotives traveling down the track; these shots were projected in a theater space designed to resemble a railway car. In addition to this décor simulation, Hale's Tours added electric fans to simulate the rushing of wind and shook the viewing space from below with mechanical girders.

Hale's Tours also had a proprietary aerial variant, but their mainstay was to provide a simulation of railway travel, and one immersive enough to cause motion sickness in some viewers. This has been given as one reason for the company's rapid decline from (at its height) five hundred franchise locations in the United States to none.[44] Many viewers were not return customers. As a representative, if perhaps apocryphal, example, Mary Pickford reported visiting a Hale's Tour as a teenager. It was her first experience with film, and the shaking floor and tunneling point-of-view shot produced nausea, which led her to assume that all films would produce this type of motion sickness. She left partway through the screening and did not return.[45]

Hale's Tours blurred the line between moving image and attraction in a way that Sergei Eisenstein, famously hiding firecrackers beneath the seats of the theater, might have liked.[46] But such extreme measures were unnecessary for producing cinema sickness. Aerial "rides" were enough.[47] The "phantom ride," a genre of early cinema to which Hale's Tours is related, provides the best example of such attempts.[48] Phantom rides, which had hundreds of examples in the early history of film, were ordinarily shots taken from the front of trains as they hurtled down the tracks. A popular and international genre, their titles often reflected the passage of railway track or geography over which the camera passed: *The Haverstraw Tunnel*

(1897), *Phantom Train Ride to Conway Castle* (1898), *Frazer Canon* (1902), *Canadian Car Ride* (1908). All were premised upon what Charles Musser has called the "spectator as passenger" convention, discussed in chapter 4.[49] But the phantom ride was not unique to the railway.[50] Any moving vehicle could take the viewer on its simulation, and so they did: on funiculars, gondolas, automobiles, and balloons.

Many an industrious filmmaker in the era of early cinema provided films that captured a ride in a balloon. Although some are lost, such films can be found in the catalogs of countless fly-by-night producers (so to speak), as well as luminaries including Edison and Porter (*Bird's-Eye View of San Francisco, Cal., from a Balloon*, 1902), Méliès (*L'ascension d'un ballon*, 1897), and the Lumières (*Panorama pris d'un ballon captif*, 1898).[51] This film from the Lumières is a representative example of a balloon phantom ride. Shot from a captive or tethered balloon (the balloon tied to the ground, never free floating), the passenger/viewer rises vertically over the city, obtaining not the oblique perspective that we are acclimatized to today by airplane windows, but an overhead, vertical view, looking directly down over the side of the balloon. Balloons, of course, offered a much freer viewing prospect than later flying machines, given that they are open-air devices. This view from the balloon is, like all vertical views, somewhat disorienting, making the space seem abstract and unfamiliar.[52]

The most well-known aerial simulation to film historians is Raoul Grimon-Sanson's Cinéorama (Figure 26), born late in the o-ramic moment but early in the cinematic one, around 1900. The goal was to produce an immersive, 360-degree surround-screen simulation of a ride in a balloon over Paris, and to "move" the audience through immersion rather than mechanics. Using a circular array of projectors, with patrons seated in an ersatz basket of a balloon, Grimon-Sanson's goal was that the "spectateurs éprouvaient le même vertige que celui que donne une ascension vraie" (spectators would experience the same vertigo as a real ascension would provide).[53] It was ultimately abandoned on account of the excess heat produced by its ten projectors.[54]

Certain aerial phantom rides flipped the concept on its head, as in the film *Flying Train. Flying Train* was shot in Wuppertal in 1901, the same year that the *Schwebebahn* (suspension train, in which the cars hang from tracks above) there, one of the first, was opened. At first glance, this is just another railway phantom ride, except that it has essentially been flipped upside down; the tracks are above, the expanse down below. Hanging from the tracks, the train wavers and shakes; there is the sense that it might fall at any moment, that it is being held aloft precipitously (Figure 27).

FIGURE 26. Cutaway drawing of the Cinéorama at the World's Fair of 1900, showing its interior and the crowds in attendance. *Paris Exposition, 1900* (Paris: Hachette, 1900), 426.

FIGURE 27. *The Flying Train,* Mutoscope and Biograph Company, 1901. The Wuppertal suspension train was a futuristic icon of modern transit in these years. Here we see its elevated tracks; in the distance, above the horse and carriage, hangs one of its train cars.

There is much in the historical record in terms of audience responses to such films. The author Elizabeth Stocking, for instance, gives a strong sense of the crowd who might have seen a film like this, and how they responded at the time in 1912.

> It seemed as if the audience were sailing above the world in an aeroplane. Below sped fields, woods and cities, seen as the bird views them in his joyous flight through the air. They could look down upon the bustling city, the peaceful country, lakes and rivers shining far below. They might have been disembodied spirits or angels gazing from afar at the earth's life and turmoil.
>
> The front seats were occupied by a row of small boys, their restlessness and mischief quelled for the time, their gaze intent upon the wonderful spectacle. There were little girls, quiet and absorbed; young men and maidens, their interest in each other superseded for the moment by the scene before them; there were whole families, the grandfather and the youngest child equally engrossed.
>
> They had each paid five cents to watch these speeding pictures taken from a flying machine as it swept through the air.[55]

It is a well-observed piece. Stocking captures the joy and freedom of flight, but also the powerful remove from earthly matters—both the peaceful absorption of the audience and their immersion in these not "moving pictures" but "speeding pictures." In her gesture to the acceleration of the image, one can almost imagine a separate timeline of film history in which we watch not movies but *speedies*. The images that she described were presented as the futuristic forefront of cinema in the article titled "Motion Picture Possibilities," a pinnacle of technology, worlds away from the Nickelodeon. The audience she characterized was facing this new dizzying technology among many others: "scraps of film," to borrow from the land artist Robert Smithson, "powerful enough to hurl one into a lucid vertigo."[56]

THE RISE OF MOTION SICKNESS

Motion sickness is historically contingent. The malaise-inducing cluster of symptoms that includes nausea, fatigue, perspiration, vomiting, and vertigo is a signal ailment of modernity. Until the late 1800s, seasickness was the only motion-based sickness cited in literature or indeed in medical journals. Then, coincident with new transportation technologies, an outbreak of motion-based sicknesses was diagnosed.

Following the first recorded usages of these coinages in the *Oxford English Dictionary* gives an indication of the spread of the illness. *Airsickness* is diagnosed in the balloon era, in 1862, well before the airplane, and there are some

FIGURE 28. A "Seajoy" morphine-laced bandage used for treating motion sicknesses; the drug would seep in through the skin. London, England, 1928–30. Science Museum.

twenty years where the only such sicknesses are derived from *air* and *sea*—a natural pairing. *Motion sickness*, the general category, is named in 1881, and followed soon after by *rail sickness* in 1892. *Carsickness* arrives in 1908. *Space sickness* is predicted as early as 1912. And half a century later, in 1962, *simulation sickness*, perhaps the most useful term for describing the cluster of media pathologies that lead to motion sickness, is added to this list, and it is connected to *virtual reality sickness*, which is actively combated today.

In the first decades of the twentieth century, cures for this outbreak of motion sicknesses were needed. Press reports about potential remedies were widespread, with treatments ranging from the surgical removal of polyps, to operations on the inner ear, to sedatives (Figure 28).[57]

Airsickness received particular attention. For one thing, it had novelty appeal: the newest pathology associated with the newest form of transit. As a Boston doctor wrote in 1911, only two years after most people had even seen an airplane (more on which in chapter 5):

> With each new form of locomotion . . . arises some form of minor
> injury which, from some mechanical peculiarity, it is particularly liable
> to produce. . . . Aviation, the latest step in human progression, has
> brought too its peculiar types of risk [including] the interesting medical
> condition of airsickness, a phenomenon of cardiovascular physiology.[58]

Airsickness was widespread among aviators. The same article reported that "there is no aviator who has not spoken of dizziness."[59] As commercial and military flight needs increased in the United States, so too did the drive to find a cure for airsickness and vertigo. Pilots who did not suffer from these

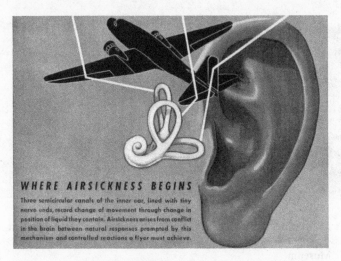

WHERE AIRSICKNESS BEGINS

Three semicircular canals of the inner ear, lined with tiny nerve ends, record change of movement through change in position of liquid they contain. Airsickness arises from conflict in the brain between natural responses prompted by this mechanism and controlled reactions a flyer must achieve.

FIGURE 29.   Decades later and after another world war, doctors were still studying the problem of airsickness. Andre Berniere, "Why You Get Airsick," *Flying Magazine* 36, no. 2 (February 1945), 39.

afflictions—who would not be dizzy or nauseous in flight—were needed. The *New York Times* advised in 1918 that "persistent headaches, vertigo, and easily induced fatigue are serious defects" in the selection of a pilot.[60] These issues remained throughout the twentieth century and formed a major part of what is now aviation medicine.

Evidently, a reliable account of the cause of motion sickness was required. There was a general consensus, one which abides, that motion sickness is produced by "sensory conflict or sensory mismatch"(Figure 29).[61] In simple terms: the eye, the inner ear, and the body are all giving different, incompatible cues about motion to the brain. In a modern airplane, for instance, the inner ear insists upon perceived movement; the body and eye report otherwise. Why this mismatch should in turn cause illness, however, remains much less settled. There are two reigning theories. The first, the punishment hypothesis, contends that the body reacts negatively to sensory conflict as a "punishment system" that advises against moving in what is perceived to be an inefficient manner; the body is signaling, *do not fly; walk*. Second, the poison hypothesis, argues that the body provokes the symptoms of motion sickness—which lead in extreme cases to vomiting— because, prior to modern technology, the only conceivable cause of such conflicting internal signals would have been a mistakenly ingested toxin. In an effort to expel the (in the case of modern transport, nonexistent) poison

FIGURE 30. Aerial intoxication on the occasion of the first
Los Angeles aviation meet. *Los Angeles Sunday Times,*
16 January 1910.

or parasite that would cause this dissociative mind-body experience, the
body produces the physical manifestations required to eject it.

The body's response to excessive amounts of alcohol is another illustration of this mechanism; taken in excess, the body rejects alcohol as a poison.
In the popular imagination, flight and alcohol were intimately related.[62]
Balloonists had long been known to bring aloft a brace of champagne for
their midair picnic. The similarity between the effects of motion sickness, in
particular airsickness, and the effects of an excess of alcohol, were widely
assumed in the years following the advent of flight; so, too, was the thrill of
flight compared with the elation of alcoholic intoxication (Figure 30). In the
airplane age, the parallels were marketable. The sponsors of some of
the earliest aviation meets included alcohol manufacturers. Dubonnet, the
French aperitif producers, who had a famous balloonist in the family, and
Cinzano, the Italian vermouth manufacturers, were both aviation patrons
in Europe, and their advertising reflected this investment (Figure 31). A
first principle: *the aerial view is intoxicating.*

A film such as Edwin S. Porter's *Dream of a Rarebit Fiend* (1906), staple
of the film studies curriculum, contains a precise equation made between
the intoxication of flight and the intoxication of alcohol. A nominal

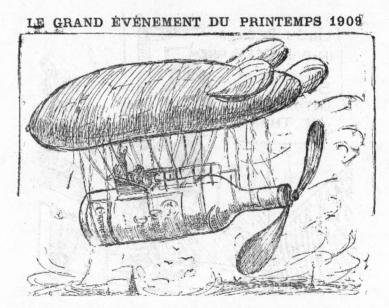

FIGURE 31. "This will be the launch of the airship 'Dubonnet,' whose platform represents exactly the bottle of this excellent tonic." *Le Temps*, 18 February 1909, 4.

adaptation of the cartoonist and animator Winsor McCay's newspaper strip of the same title, in the film, the gourmand "rarebit fiend" drinks to excess, tipsily journeys the whirling streets, and retires to his bed, which quickly transforms into a flying machine.[63] He ultimately lands on a weather vane, spinning vertiginously; an image that often occurs in Winsor McCay's oeuvre. In the equation between the intoxication of flight and the intoxication of alcohol there is the visual representation of motion sickness on screen. Both flight and alcohol can cause this effect on the body. So, too, can cinema.

A CASE OF "KINOTOSIS" FOR THE CLASSICAL FILM THEORISTS

Those philosophers, psychologists, and critics who wrote what we now call "classical film theory" placed great emphasis on the physiological power of cinema.[64] Emblematic in this regard is the work of Electra Sparks, whom I have written about elsewhere.[65] Sparks argued that our minds and bodies are "photosensitive" to moving pictures. "We know," she wrote in 1912, "that the eye learns more rapidly than the ear; and that it is the scenes impressed upon this brain-camera that make indelible impression."[66] The indelibility of the brain and the body was her concern. Sparks went so far as to program a series of films—including scenics and fairy tales—designed for pregnant women in New York, believing that exposure to beautiful imagery could physically strengthen them.

If a scenic film could be a cinematic tonic, what then about an aerial phantom ride—was it a cinematic toxin? Many classical film theorists, writing a little later than Sparks, noted the physiological response that such simulated flight films could have on the viewer. Take for instance the Weimar author Arno Arndt, describing an aerial film like *Flying Train*: "It whips back and forth, turns, and leans into the curves in such a way that it is frightening just to sit before the screen."[67] By 1932, psychologist Rudolf Arnheim could characterize the effects of cinema on the body as well established:

> It is well known that a feeling of giddiness . . . of vertigo, intoxication,
> falling, rising . . . is produced by watching a film that has been taken
> with a camera traveling very rapidly. This giddiness is caused by the
> eyes participating in a different world from that indicated by the
> kinaesthetic reactions of the body, which is at rest.[68]

Paul Virilio once argued that "child society . . . looks for sensations of vertigo and disorder as sources of pleasure."[69] This is the miniature version of Roger Caillois's proposal, discussed at length in the next chapter, that this desire for vertigo was not unique to children; it was merely easier for them to access it. Rather, vertigo play aims to "momentarily destroy the stability of perception and inflict a kind of voluptuous panic upon an otherwise lucid mind. In all cases, it is a question of surrendering to a kind of spasm, seizure, or shock which destroys reality with sovereign brusqueness."[70]

The keyword *shock* conjures up a world of scholarly debate. The human response to fast-moving modern entertainments of the twentieth century, and the possibility that these technologies held to habituate us to the shocks of modernity, was of course a major part of Walter Benjamin's writing on cinema. They led, ultimately, to what have been called the modernity thesis debates.[71] The modernity thesis takes a "neurological conception of modernity,"[72] arguing that the cinema historically served an ameliorative function against the urban shocks wrought by new technologies, against a nominal "annihilation of space and time" (belabored though that phrase may be).[73] By providing these shocks in a diluted, safe form, it was argued, the cinema mitigates them in the wider world.

On the other side are those who argued that these effects were overstated (our perceptual apparatus not so plastic as that), ahistorical (are we still being inoculated?), and in general airily detached from physiology and cinemagoing practice. This is only a summary account of a lively feud.[74] This chapter, on the vertigo effects of film, can be taken as a further case study, bringing concrete historic examples to what have sometimes been speculative discussions considering the role of cinema in its early years. I show that these debates were not confined to recent film history but were rather a matter of practical experiment for doctors, researchers, and psychologists throughout the twentieth century.

In that regard, what follows is in line with film historian Ben Singer's examination of the modernity thesis, and his focus on the scientific literature demonstrating that the shocks of modernity can in fact be measured, and later were (via, e.g., the stress levels of city dwellers who live near airports).[75] Film scholar Linda Williams's important article on "body genres" is also germane here. Focusing on horror, melodrama, and pornography as film genres in which a mimicking process takes place between the portrayed body onscreen and the viewer's body, and a physiological response is shared (horror produces shudders, melodrama tears, and pornography arousal), Williams allows for "other film genres which both portray and affect the sensational body."[76]

Certain aeroscopic films baldly promised such a sensate response—they promised, in a word, cinema sickness. Take *Fond of Sensation?*, a British Pathé newsreel item from 1925, which increases the *sensational* component considerably. The question mark in the title of the film quizzes the audience: *Are you fond of sensation?* Implied: *Are you certain?* A camera is placed on the exterior of an airplane, and the viewer is treated (or subjected) to loop-the-loops, spins, and volplanes. The title card promises that viewers may "enjoy air thrills from the safety of your seat," and I can attest, having screened the film to many audiences, that it still has the power to instill vertigo almost a century later. We might, in keeping with the poison hypothesis of motion sickness, class a film such as this as part of a "poisoned-body genre." The spectator's seated body rebels at the disjunction between their visual, vestibular, and corporeal experience: cinema sickness is in the offing. Many in the audience look away from the screen.

One film is unique for having debuted with both the promise of cinema sickness as well as its cure. *Flight of the Lost Balloon*, a colonialist B-movie from 1961, offered motion sickness pills to viewers as a theatrical promotion (Figure 32). In the event, the film offered neither vertigo nor its cure—rather, a landlocked melodrama—and there is no record of anyone taking the pills. Nevertheless, their strategy reflects an ongoing understanding of film as an agent of a particular kind of motion sickness. Indeed, as we have seen, motion *pictures* have always caused motion *sickness*. They even share the same root word, etymologically. A clinical term for motion sickness is *kinetosis*; like

FIGURE 32. A promotion for *Flight of the Lost Balloon*;
pictured to the left of the balloon is the sachet of motion-
sickness pills that viewers would ostensibly receive at the
theater.

cinema, it derives from the Greek for "movement," and is still heard in the
word for cinema in German, Russian, and many other languages: *kino*.

Cinema sickness? Call it *kino-tosis*.

FILM AS CURE

Historically, the only cure for seasickness had been habituation. You suffer
until your body adjusts, or habituates. Seasoned sailors did not suffer from

seasickness. They had their sea legs. In the many attempts to treat the new motion sicknesses outlined above, heavier-than-air flight posed a particular challenge since, in its earliest days especially, it was a comparatively brief activity; one might go to sea for days or weeks at a time, but flying was measured in minutes and hours. Habituation did not seem to be an option in the air.

Therapeutics are, as the historian of medicine Guenter Risse has observed, a "social ritual very much shaped by the prevailing cultural milieu" (1991).[77] Thus a twentieth-century American solution to airsickness was to use the prevailing medium of the culture (namely, cinema), and to acclimatize people on the ground using filmic simulations. In other words: might not airsickness be treated by habituation to cinema sickness? The reasoning has a pharmakon logic to it: that which might cause the problem can also solve it. The cinema could mitigate the symptoms of motion sickness via exposure and resistance, a ground-level inoculation against the real thing, a useful cinema doubling as exposure therapy.

There were many medico-cinematic devices constructed to test the causes and remedies of vertigo and airsickness throughout the twentieth century. Built by academics, inventors, pilot training schools, and sometimes the military, these devices reached many of the same conclusions in their design. They were typically premised upon bodily rotation, movement as perceived by the vestibule of the ear, and immersive mechanics. There is some crossover with the history of flight simulators in what follows, but the focus will be on devices that included a media apparatus such as a screen or canvas.[78]

Physicist Ernst Mach's "cyclostat," was used to study the relationship between the physical and psychical in small vertebrates (Figure 33). The Aerostructor (Figure 34) showed loops of film and isolated the viewer in an attempt to create the feeling of flight and its attendant vertigo. Others used a variety of simulation methods and contraptions to visually deceive the potential pilot. Some employed panoramic paintings in lieu of film, but to the same desired end (Figure 35). Movement was as much part of the training as was the image. There were various strategies for its inclusion; some were simple laboratory chairs (Figure 36). Others were apparatuses that used pneumatic or human power to provide a semblance of the movement of a flying machine—roll, pitch, and yaw—to induce vertigo in the viewer (Figure 37).

The most sustained documented attempts to use film as a habituation device for motion sickness were completed in the early 1970s, when David Parker, professor of psychology at what is now California State University, Northridge, published two articles in the *Journal of General Psychology*: "A Psychophysiological Test for Motion Sickness Susceptibility," and its sequel, on the "Effects of Repeated Administration of the Psychophysiological

FIGURE 33. One of the earliest vertigo machines is physicist Ernst Mach's "cyclostat," designed to produce rotary vertigo in small vertebrates. The animal (he used birds and fish) is placed in the glass cylinder marked *g* and spun rapidly. Mach, *The Analysis of Sensations and the Relation of the Physical to the Psychical*, trans. C. M. Williams (Chicago: Open Court, 1914 [1886]), 150.

Test for Motion Sickness Susceptibility."[79] In his first test, one hundred students from the college were shown a "five minute film depicting a ride down rough, twisting mountain roads in a speeding, open sports car. Filming was done from a tripod mounted beside the driver's head. Right and left turns were in no discernable order, and as many straight stretches as possible were edited out. Speeds were maximal for the automobile and road conditions at the times."[80] The student viewers, meanwhile, were each "seated in a dentist's chair which was provided with a head rest to restrict movement," and the film was shown on a screen six feet away, aiming to approximate the view of the driver.[81]

Subjects in the test were fitted with a variety of electrodes connected to a Polygraph machine, and their sweat glands were monitored. An observer also made sure that none of the viewers closed their eyes. (The similarity of this apparatus to the exposure therapy indoctrination device depicted in Stanley Kubrick's *Clockwork Orange*, of the same year of publication, 1971, is striking.) Those who felt some sense of motion sickness were then

FIGURE 34.   Aerostructor, c.1930s. This device is also part of a concerted effort in the period to use cinema to teach aviation skills. The many aviation magazines from this period are enlightening as to the breadth of the instructive impulse. The British *Flight* magazine repeatedly emphasized the filmic component of flight, reporting on those who had taken cameras into the air. Moreover, it regularly advertised for educational film programs whence the viewer could "Learn to Fly in Pictures." *Flight*, February 21, 1914, 195.

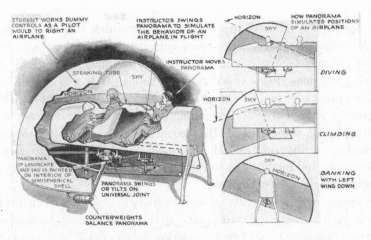

FIGURE 35.   A painted, "rocking panorama" flight instruction apparatus. *Popular Science*, March 1932, 63.

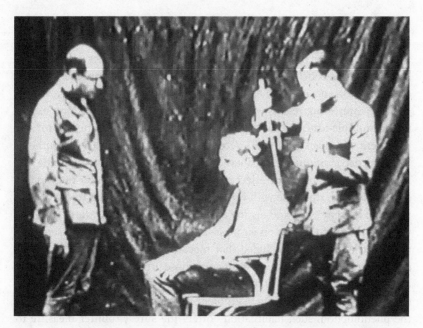

FIGURE 36. A laboratory chair designed for testing vertigo, shown in the film *Fit to Fly* (1919). See W. H. Wilmer, "Introductory Remarks, Exhibition of Film, '*Fit to Fly*,'" *Transactions of the American Ophthalmological Society Annual Meeting* 17 (Philadelphia: American Ophthalmological Society, 1919), 271–72.

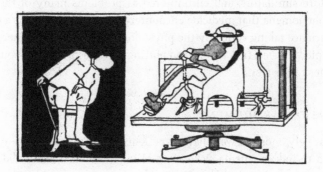

FIGURE 37. A more advanced laboratory chair designed for testing vertigo. "Science Explains Many Tragic Mysteries of the Air," *Washington Times*, January 5, 1919, 10.

randomly selected to be taken aboard a research ship for several hours in order to test for seasickness. The results showed that those prone to motion sickness from the film were correspondingly made seasick on the boat, leading them to conclude that "camera sickness" is an accurate predictor for other forms of motion sickness.

More interesting results were revealed when Parker repeated this experiment multiple times in the hope of eventually using the same test for the treatment of airsickness.[82] His second article began with the hypothesis "that the deconditioning or adaptation effect of repeated viewing of the test film has some prophylactic effect in motion sickness."[83] Parker ran the test described above, this time with varying degrees of immersion in the "phantom ride therapy" prior to testing for seasickness. Reliably, those who had watched more of the motion sickness–inducing films had less motion sickness on the boat. He concluded that repeated viewing, or habituation, so drastically reduced the motion sickness of those previously vulnerable to the ailment that midway into the experiment their responses were no longer classed as "susceptible."[84] As psychologist John Golding later summarized the phenomenon, such habituation "offers the surest counter measure to motion sickness. Habituation is superior to anti-motion sickness drugs, and it is free of side effects."[85]

There was nothing about the establishment of this scenario that does not essentially resemble a phantom ride, nothing that could not have been achieved in the silent era, nothing that a film such as *Flying Train* did not implicitly accomplish. Film in the silent era provided, sub rosa, simulators before simulators, and encountered as problems many of the same bodily phenomena that medicine encountered as evidence. This is a case of period science taking seriously the physiological properties of cinema that preoccupied classical film theory and putting their observations about these properties to the test.

MAL DE DÉBARQUEMENT

Cumulatively, most viewers have experienced as much exposure to films that aim to induce cinema sickness as David Parker's students did in the 1970s. Any experience with a 4D film that brings motion into the mix is likely trading on similar appeals. Have we likewise been habituated to motion sickness in wider life?

Those who have gone to sea for some time on a passenger ship or for their profession sometimes return to shore with what is called *mal de débarquement*, or "disembarkment sickness." Their bodies continue to sway with unseen waves, a lingering aftereffect of the acclimatization that they undertook to the motion of the waters. It is not rare; I saw it growing up in the Maritimes. The same can also occur with air travel. Indeed, in the early years of flight, after a dizzying descent, a typical pilot was said upon deplaning to understand "but vaguely what is said to him and sometimes is taken with vertigo and tumbles into the arms of his friends."[86]

Transportation pathologies such as *mal de débarquement* (or "railway spine" or the "aeroplane gaze") are closely related to media pathologies; indeed, as proposed in chapter 5, they are sometimes one and the same. Have we not all suffered from *mal de débarquement*? Many readers may have experienced a similar strangeness. Recall that dreamlike feeling that occurs when you enter a movie theater in the afternoon for a film, and after, emerge outside at night. It seems suddenly, artificially dark, and one feels unsure of one's footing, a little punch-drunk. Roland Barthes wrote memorably of that particular sensation: "Back out on the more or less empty brightly lit sidewalk (it is invariably at night, and during the week, that he *goes*), and heading uncertainly for some café or other, he walks in silence (he doesn't like discussing the film he's just seen), a little dazed, wrapped up in himself, feeling the cold—he's *sleepy*, that's what he's thinking, his body has become something *sopitive*, soft, limp, and he feels a little disjointed."[87] Barthes feels both disjointed but, as he says later in the essay, as though he has taken part in a "healing." A cinematic *mal de débarquement*.

The assumption here is to treat "media technology as medical technology," as the historian of medicine Jeremy Greene has encouraged.[88] If we accept the findings of the California State study, then many films function as an incidental public inoculation against vertigo, a prophylactic that limits future susceptibility to these ailments. Just as a frequent viewer of other body genres becomes inured to the shudders of horror, and no longer jumps at its startle effects, the vertigo effects of these aeroscopic films acclimatize the viewer to future problems with motion sickness.

It goes without saying that film did not "cure" motion sickness; we still have it with us today. However, it may have offered some a boost against other types of vestibular confusion. In defeating the fundamental vertiginousness of moving images—something we all must defeat in order to watch them—we see how these other motion sicknesses can be overcome, through habituation. In the mythology of seafaring, as mentioned above, the only cure for seasickness was to endure the discomfort and wait for the body to habituate, to adopt what were called "sea legs." Since "air legs" were not an option for most early film viewers, then cinema—to place it in the Benjaminian terms of the modernity thesis, as film scholar Miriam

Hansen once did—"could at the very least neutralize, on a mass basis, the traumatic effects of the bungled reception of technology."[89]

At the outset, I traced some of this "bungled reception" in the form of the media pathology, and outlined a few of its features (social hypochondria, misdiagnosis, physiological response), including its relation to the corporeal media metaphor. We still use corporeal media metaphors, of course; we routinely analogize the mind to the computer (something that may appear highly contingent to future historians). But in the twentieth century, the abiding media metaphor for the mind was the cinema. As early as 1916, classical film theorists were using cinematic terms to describe its functions. Hugo Munsterberg characterized our memory as a *flashback*, and our imagination as a *flashforward*. Electra Sparks referred to our "brain camera" that watches the movies. If the mind is a kind of film, how to cure physiological disequilibrium? The answer: with more film. This is the counterintuitive final feature of the media pathology: it carries with it its own cure, which is only a greater dosage of the medium. Motion pictures cure motion sickness.

4. Observation Rides

World's fairs were known for debuting new technology to the public. Some of these technologies lasted—many people encountered their first dishwasher, telephone, and X-ray at a world's fair—but others did not. One world's fair technology that has largely been forgotten is what I call the "observation ride." After the Eiffel Tower (Paris, 1889), after the Ferris wheel (Chicago, 1893), each fair wanted an immense engineering monument that could provide a slow, bird's-eye view, be it in elevator or gondola, to the visiting public. In quick succession arrived the Giant See-Saw (Nashville, 1897), the Aeriocycle (Buffalo, 1901), the Flip-Flap (London, 1908), and the Aeroscope (San Francisco, 1915). Drawing from a tradition of "technical monumentalism," of tower lights and observation towers, while simultaneously borrowing from the thrill ride and the cinema, the observation ride was a unique genre of aeroscopic device.[1]

The Aeroscope is emblematic of the appeals of observation rides and will be the focus of this chapter. Produced originally for San Francisco's Panama-Pacific International Exposition (PPIE) of 1915, and designed by Chicago bridge engineer Joseph Strauss, the Aeroscope was situated at the gateway to the exposition's concessionary area, the "Zone." This steel observation tower on hinges operated with hydraulic and pneumatic power and rose to a panoramic altitude of 265 feet (one foot higher than the Ferris wheel, as was often commented upon), or 330 feet above sea level (Figure 38). In its double-decker viewing theater, 120 people at a time could take the ride, which turned in a helical pattern to offer a view through a plate-glass window of the exposition grounds, San Francisco, and the (then bridgeless) Golden Gate to the Pacific. Auspiciously, Strauss would later go on to be the chief engineer of the Golden Gate Bridge.

The ambitions and cultural expectations for the Aeroscope were great, as the archival sources that surround the device reveal. The Aeroscope was

NIGHT VIEW
of AEROSCOPE
PAN.-PAC. INT. EXPOSITION
SAN FRANCISCO, 1915.

E 76

FIGURE 38. "Night View of Aeroscope," postcard, 1915. Wolfsonian Collection.

heralded in engineering magazines for years in advance, and became a trial-run monument for San Francisco, a prospective Eiffel Tower for the city. Its failure to serve this purpose is another motivating question of this chapter. I propose that the Aeroscope, monument *manqué* of the PPIE, provided an ambivalent type of managed dizziness, one that was, compared to the vertigo machines described in the last chapter, controlled, even subdued. Slipping between the observational appeals of the panorama painting, the vertiginous frisson of the amusement ride, and the travelogues of the cinema, the Aeroscope was medially indiscriminate. It depended upon cartographic ratio play, upon a shifting scale that worked expressly with the unique and topsy-turvy design of the exposition. By design, it moved strangely, and slowly, spiraling up into the sky above San Francisco to offer an experience of inter-pretive imbalance: not a thrill ride, but an enthrall ride.

The Aeroscope debuted on the American cusp of war. Fears of aerial bom-bardment were already on the horizon—in 1908, H.G. Wells had published *The War in the Air* and Albert Robida *La guerre infernale*, each presenting nightmare scenarios of aviation and warfare. The PPIE received a proposal for a display that captured these anxieties. "The Air Demons; or, The Holy War" would have built on such dark aerial prognostications, modeling a miniature New York City that, in combination with dioramic light technolo-gies, would be destroyed nightly by a fleet of air ships. "Rapidly the destruc-tion goes on,—Crash after crash,—Horror upon horror, the points of attack selected with diabolical ingenuity."[2] This account is in line with much of today's historiography on the aerial view; it confirms our assumptions about the aerial anxieties of the age. Yet the exposition committee rejected this proposal. It was the Aeroscope that would define the aerial view at the PPIE, and the view it offered was both highly idiosyncratic and a barometer—or better, an altimeter—of the aerial view circa 1915.

Given its peculiarities, the Aeroscope poses problems regarding how to describe those who rode it, problems common to the study of consumers of world's fair attractions. The available terms all have their drawbacks. Indeed, *consumer* implies a market logic that does not always apply. *Audience* sub-tly prioritizes listening. *Spectator*, as Jonathan Crary has argued, implies passivity.[3] *Observer* has been carefully employed in chapter 1 for another specific circumstance. *Visitors* might be apt, and appropriately noncommit-tal, but it suggests a passing lack of engagement. When movement is added to the attraction, portmanteaus develop. Charles Musser has, with reference to Hale's Tours, referred to a convention of "spectator as passenger," reflect-ing the "vehicular amplification" in media that Erkki Huhtamo has else-where described.[4] The spectator-passenger is a useful historical actor, but perhaps too unique for broad roles. Returned to here, then, is the encompassing character of the *sensation seeker*, as employed in literature of the 1910s and earlier. The relatively dispassionate value of this type is to be distinguished from the reckless thrill seeker, since the two are often treated synonymously in psychological literature today. The sensation seeker is that broad class of person who attends amusements without devotion to a particular object—who, neither cinemaniac nor balloonatic (to cite two contemporaneous types of devoted fans), does not suffer from an excess of allegiance to a single object, but rather is curious about a range of sensations and experiences.[5] They might, in a single day at the fair, perform the function of the audience, the observer, the passenger, and so on. The sensation seeker, in short, visits the fair undecided, precise activities up in the air.

SENSATION SEEKERS

Consider three sets of sensation seekers who found the Aeroscope. A series of news items documented the unusual happenings at the pinnacle of the Aeroscope.[6] One was the visit by the blind and deaf author Helen Keller. The *San Francisco Chronicle* reported that she "was delighted at the experience, enjoying the sensation of the car rising . . . and seeing the many varied sights beneath her through the eyes of Mrs. Macy," her teacher.[7] Although this is evidently not the traditional "viewing" experience of the Aeroscope, one can imagine other sensationalists who, on account of vertigo, keep their eyes closed, and yet still appreciate the occasion. Indeed, Keller's account speaks to fundamental components of the ride: its gentle somatic appeals, and the variety of views on offer, which would shift throughout its course.

Some merely saw the device and wondered. In 1915, film comedians Fatty Arbuckle and Mabel Normand made a lightly fictionalized documentary for Keystone Studios, *Mabel and Fatty Visiting the World's Fair at San Francisco*. Touring the PPIE, the film documents many exhibits at the fair, both nautical (the US Navy battleship *Oregon* and the miniature yacht harbor) and altitudinal (the "tallest flagpole in the world" and the Tower of Jewels).[8] The penultimate shot in the film is of a "night view of the entire fairground." An intertitle card suggests to the viewer: "Notice the captive aeroplane above the maze of lights." This "captive aeroplane," so misnamed after a preexisting English fairground ride, is, of course, the Aeroscope.[9] Amid the electrically lit structures of the fair, their contours "sketched" by illumination,[10] the crane-like device, framed off-center, twice ascends at an angle, and when reaching its highest point, takes a panorama of the fair that almost slips beyond the frame, before descending. The entire circumrotation on screen takes about ten seconds; in fact, a ride on the Aeroscope took ten minutes for passengers in real time.

The represented speed of the Aeroscope is a puzzle. The only other filmic citation of the device, this time from a newsreel, has the same ten-second rate. This speed discrepancy is not attributable to particularities of frame rate or projection speed. The pace of increase is too great. It is plausible, then, that in its renaming (as "captive aeroplane") and acceleration, Keystone aimed to fit the Aeroscope into the amusement park genre of the thrill ride; the Aeroscope was, after all, positioned next to a roller coaster. Although this categorization does not fit the gentle pace of this observation ride, it may be indicative of how the Aeroscope was interpreted by passing sensation seekers.

John Henry Goldfrap, author, under the pseudonym Howard Payson, of a popular series of Boy Scout adventure novels, had already directed his characters in separate books to, among other locations, the Arizona desert, the Panama Canal, Mexico, Belgium, and France before bringing them to San Francisco in 1915 for *The Boy Scouts at the Panama Pacific Exposition*.[11] It is evident from the novel that Goldfrap visited the fair, and indeed rode the Aeroscope, for it occupies a central, detail-filled fifteen-page set piece over two chapters ("A Strange Meeting in the Air" and "Four Scouts in the Whirl"). These chapters provide the clearest and most substantial record remaining of the Aeroscope; and the sensations his scouts experience point the way to the greater concerns of this chapter.[12]

The Boy Scouts Rob, Andy, and Hiram (later joined by Tubby)—as though travelers on the grand tour of Europe, visiting a city for the first time and seeking out the cathedral's vista—are encouraged to ride the Aeroscope upon initial arrival at the fair, "because you get a comprehensive idea of the lay of the land that serves you better than any map you can buy."[13] Hiram voices some anxiety regarding the safety of the machine: "I hope now they don't have any accident to the machinery while we're taking our look."[14] But appeals to investigate its engineering are met with dismissal by Andy, who complains that Hiram is "like the geologists, with your nose pointed toward the ground all the while; I'm built more after the style of the astronomers who keep looking up and see the glories of the firmament that beat the fossils all hollow."[15] This divide between the operational and spectatorial appeals of the Aeroscope form a basic binary that functions as a through line in the consideration of the device and of observation rides more widely.

Goldfrap's articulation of the view from the Aeroscope is the most in-depth record that we have.

> The view was, indeed, becoming grand . . . and both boys were soon
> copying Andy, who was staring first one way and then another, as sea

and shore began to be spread out before him like a Mercators [*sic*] chart. Although the huge arm of the giant had by no means reached the upper limit of its sweep, the great buildings lying below had the appearance of squatty "ant-heaps," as Andy termed them; and the crowds that swarmed many of the walks of the Exposition looked so minute that it was hard to believe they were human beings.[16]

Once again, the cartographic appeal of the ride is foregrounded. Likewise, the familiar trope of the insectoid human, miniaturized to the size of an ant, makes an appearance. The process of miniaturization is key, and will be returned to, for the Aeroscope posed unique trompe-l'oeil scale issues that are alluded to here. The Aeroscope also, as the following, final description makes plain, occupied an unusual position between terrestrial and aerial attraction, between panorama as media metaphor and panorama as medium.

"It's well worth coming a long way just to get such a panoramic view of the City, Bay and Fair." "Panoramic whew!" whistled Andy; "but I guess that covers the ground as well as any word you could scare up, Rob; for it is a panorama a whole lot better'n any I ever saw painted on canvas, like the Battle of Gettysburg and such." They remained at their several posts drinking in the wonderful features of the magnificent view until finally the machinery was set in motion again, and they found themselves being gradually lowered toward the ground. The buildings lost their squatty appearance, the moving throngs of human beings ceased resembling crawling flies, and finally the four boys issued from the cage satisfied that they had experienced a sensation worth while.[17]

"Panoramic whew!" This exclamation encapsulates the appeals of the observation ride: part panoramic, part dizzy astonishment. Given the charms of the panorama painting, which (in its urban genre) are premised upon the registering of specific locations, the Aeroscope is correspondingly cartographic. It differs, however, in its shifting scale: buildings are "squatty" and then not; humans are as small as flies, and then not. For ten minutes, scale is "gradually" unfixed. The themes introduced by the ride of *The Boy Scouts at the Panama Pacific Exposition*—vertigo, miniaturization, mapping, slowness—are uniquely arranged within the device.

The quality of the sensation that Helen Keller, Fatty and Mabel, and the Boy Scouts experienced divides along corporeal and ocular lines; lines that are not indelible. Compared to the first two objects under study in this work—the panorama painting and the model city—this observation ride is in keeping with Thomas Elsaesser's claim that "the main organ of perception is no longer the centered eye of Renaissance perspective with everything aligning along the visual cone, but a different kind of scanning of the optical as well as sensory field, leading to an involvement of the body."[18]

The Aeroscope is neither exclusively a vertiginous ride nor purely a carto-graphic device, but something in between. A possible reconciliation of these countervailing tendencies is located in other firsthand accounts of the Aeroscopic experience, which note that the spiral arc of the Aeroscope was its signal feature, a proprioceptive quality as important for the body as the eye (just as the up-and-down perpendicularity of the Eiffel Tower elevator and the rotation of the Ferris wheel were key to their appeal). The Aeroscope did not offer a clarifying perspective, as the Boy Scouts claimed, but a hermeneutic challenge.

AERO-, -SCOPE / AERIAL VISION

I have borrowed this ride's name, the Aeroscope, as a title for this book, and as a category name for the aerial simulations discussed throughout. The word encapsulates the notion of a technologically mediated aerial view. The union of the prefix *aero-* and the suffix *-scope* seems historically inevitable. Beyond the many aeronautic and scopic derivatives that remain with us today (from aerospace to microscope), both of these affixes had broad lexi-cal lives in the arts. Genres of painting such as the Futurists' *aeropittura* or Henry Dumoutet's *aérochromographe* were marginal compared to the wide application of aerophotography. The use of *-scope*, meanwhile, had been steadily on the increase, and the nineteenth century afforded such media as the phenakistoscope, stereoscope, and indeed bioscope.

Aero-, which refers in this usage to practices affiliated with aviation and flight, and *-scope*, which refers to ocular scientific observation instruments, combine in the form Aeroscope to make an incidental declaration about the practice of aerial vision in the period. What were the connotations of the Aeroscope's view? A standard account might argue that the outlook that the Aeroscope provided was—given the imperialist logic of the fair, which celebrated the American completion of the Panama Canal—primarily one of mastery. A "prosthetic of empire," envisioning American domination: here is the landscape, tamed; foreign countries come to genuflect in their exhibition embassies; the masses below imperiled by the underlying threat of bombardment.[19]

This manner of reading the aerial view is seen most clearly in the work of Paul Virilio, who argued in his polemical *War and Cinema: The Logistics of Perception* that aerial vision is, by its very nature, threatening: a hawkish viewpoint that facilitated guiltless destruction by its ethical distance from those on the ground.[20] It's the original sin of flight technology, echoing Walter Benjamin's famous line: "There is no document of civilization which is not at the same time a document of barbarism."[21] This position has had widespread currency, and has produced some sophisticated work; understandably, given our current era of the drone's-eye view.[22]

Nevertheless, it can be teleological to project this argument on the very long history of the aerial view, and to imagine that our own experience with the aerial is the historic norm. The military component of flight only really begins to become plausible during World War I, after more than a century of failure, as discussed in detail in my final chapter.[23] Moreover, the idea that there is a reliable aesthetic equation to be made, that the aerial invariably equals ethical distance, is as simplistic as reading every shot in a film that angles upward as being about the hierarchical power of the pictured subject—a formula that even introductory film textbooks warn against.[24] A number of scholars have come to question this "dystopian discourse of aerovision," arguing for a more ambivalent, and less technologically determinant, reading of this view. In lieu of a totalizing account of aerial vision, recent work has located other models for understanding this vision based on, for instance, local knowledge of the landscape, the scientifically educative capacity of this new type of looking, and the conceptual implications of altitudinal difference.[25] As Le Corbusier observed in his celebration of the airplane, the bird's-eye view is held by "dove or hawk."[26] A first principle: *the aerial view is plastic.*

The Aeroscope arguably arrives at the interchange of perceptions of the aerial view, just prior to the United States' entry into the war. Certain properties of the Aeroscope—its helical movement, pacing, and upending of scale—were noted often enough as to suggest that the aerial vision that the Aeroscope provided was not one of domination, mastery, or control, but rather disorientation, observation, and playfulness. Furthermore, within the context of world's fairs, amusement parks, and the various media that functioned adjacent to the Aeroscope, from cinema to panorama, the Aeroscope offered a particular mode of spectatorship, one that has been neglected. Offering a vertigo that was decidedly not abrasive, the Aeroscope gave instead a vertigo of contemplation: here is a map with a key from *Alice in Wonderland*, a map that changes as you examine it, prompting a hermeneutic dizziness.

AERONAUTICA AND ORIENTATION

Where previous world's fairs and expositions had introduced ballooning to a broad public, or perhaps had a demonstration of an airplane, the PPIE was to be the first aeronautic exposition. This ambition of the organizers was

FIGURE 39. Art Smith's "nightwriting" display at the PPIE. University of California at Santa Cruz Special Collections.

central from the earliest stages of planning. A *San Francisco Chronicle* cartoon of 1911, "A Peep into the Aerial Future," promised towering docking stations for aircraft that left for "all points." Farcical, the cartoon nevertheless anticipated the revolutionary capacity of flight-based travel, speculating in the lower margin that "transportation to the exposition may be in the above manner, by 1915."

An air show was held at the PPIE, still a nascent genre of event in 1915.[27] One tourist guide to the fair anticipated that "there is going to be twenty machines or more in the air all at once."[28] There was an airplane race and a number of aviation displays. A nighttime skywriting display by pilot Art Smith was demonstrated (Figure 39). Various scale models that gave a simulation of an aerial perspective were attractions, including, most famously, a colossal model of the Panama Canal.[29] A statue of the angel of aviation was often reproduced on postcards, and the Aeroscope presided over all these lower aeronautics. Indeed, the analogy between Aeroscope and

FIGURE 40.   Panoramic photograph with silhouettes of anticipated fair structures, displaying the linearity of planning involved. Library of Congress, 1914.

airplane was not accidental. Cosmetic propellers were added to the Aeroscope's frame to give the impression of airfoil thrust.[30] Some passengers considered a ride on the Aeroscope, with its diagonal ascent, to be a simulation of an airplane ride.[31]

Although the emphasis on aviation at the PPIE was unprecedented, the logic of aeriality had been embedded in world's fairs for some time, as Anders Ekström has persuasively shown, instancing the Scandinavian Art and Industry Exhibition of 1897. Arguing that "a bird's eye view was built into the planning and architecture of the site," a cursory look at contemporaneous and subsequent major expositions (Chicago 1893, Paris 1900, Buffalo 1901) reveals that they built upon similar principles of embedded belvederes, observation towers, and elevated access.[32] Indeed, balloon rides were often available to a broad public at the Paris International Exposition of 1867 and beyond. At the PPIE, these overlooks were meant to allow for a clear view down its various roads (Figure 40).

The literature and maps accompanying the PPIE further served to embed the bird's-eye view into the logic of the fair. The most literal example of this is the promotional booklet, *Gullible's Travels to the Panama Pacific International Exposition*. In this fictionalized travelogue, a San Francisco seagull flies to the PPIE and takes "a 'bird's eye' view of the many wonders."[33] "Gullible" mistakes the various embassies for countries, the Japanese village for all of Japan, and the exposition as the entirety of the world. It is essentially a rube narrative in which the thing displayed is mistaken for the thing itself: an *Uncle Josh at the Moving Picture Show* (1902) written for a world's fair. ("Tourists," as a later critic framed it, "are willing gulls."[34]) Implicit in *Gullible's Travels*, and instructive of the goals of the exposition, is

the notion that the fair does contain the "world in miniature," and that if a visitor could obtain a comprehensive, bird's-eye view of the PPIE, one would have a global perspective.[35]

Even with the countless aerial views of the fair found in promotional and documentary photographs, maps, and paintings, the fair was confusing. A particularly revealing passage, in which Gullible flies over the concessionary amusement Zone, described the bewildering arrangement of perspectival looks at play on the ground level: "Many had their heads reclined either to the right or left, some had their eyes turned inward, others directly up to the heavens."[36] In *Mabel and Fatty Visiting the World's Fair*, the Aeroscope was described as presiding over a "maze of lights." To navigate this labyrinthine space, a period newspaper cartoon that depicts a visitor staring at a map of the PPIE advised, "Memorize your map, make your notes, wind up your compass," and only then, "start."

The exposition was not an easily navigable space; it required an expertise, an axis: the Aeroscope ostensibly served as this clarifying axis. In *What We Saw at Madame World's Fair*, a contemporaneous travelogue of the PPIE, the rationalizing component is made plain: "Then we zigzagged across again and did things on the other side of the [amusement] Zone, like going up in the funny thing which gives you a ride in the air, so you can see all the Fair at once."[37]

CLOUS AND VIEWS

The historian Alexander Geppert has usefully reintroduced the concept of the *clou* ("nail") into the study of world's fairs. Geppert defines the clou as the "pre-eminent exhibit," the most important structure, of the fair: Paris's Eiffel Tower, Chicago's Ferris wheel, even Knoxville's Sunsphere. The clou provided "the entire site with a central, clarifying perspective." Many were thus "observation posts or lookout towers from which one could survey the whole exposition."[38] The clou functioned not simply as the central structure around which the fair was planned, but moreover as the ideal vantage point from which to take in the totality of the fair. The Eiffel Tower, again, is probably the archetypal example of axis and vantage point combined. It provides a centralizing logic to the grounds, as well as a method for appreciating this design.[39] Clous were, unlike the Eiffel Tower (which was originally to be disassembled at the end of the fair) sometimes planned for permanence, and have occasionally achieved monument status, coming to stand synecdochically for the city they represent, as in the case of Seattle's Sky Needle, originally built for the Century 21 Exposition of 1962.

Was the Aeroscope the clou of the PPIE? The Tower of Jewels is the more obvious candidate. The latter was more often pictured on promotional items, a rainbow of colors representing the searchlights of the "scintillator" behind it. But it was the Aeroscope that was explicitly positioned in the architectural and engineering lineage of the Eiffel Tower and the Ferris wheel. Popular scientific magazines, which had welcomed the Ferris wheel as a marvel of engineering—"As the Brooklyn Bridge and the Eiffel Tower have been as milestones to mark the progress made in engineering in the past, so will the Ferris wheel be added to mark another advancing step"— anticipated that the Aeroscope would surpass these wonders.[40]

The Aeroscope was to be the clou of clous. *Popular Electricity*, evidently working with limited access to Strauss's designs, and two years before the Aeroscope's debut, imagined it as a kind of hinged Eiffel Tower (Figure 41). It was depicted towering over a Ferris wheel and a Great Globe, its spotlight capturing an airplane in its sights (a strategy for making scale evident that was frequently employed in postcards of the Eiffel Tower.)[41] Upon the Aeroscope's launch, *Scientific American* gave it the cover along with a feature article (Figure 42). The *Edison Monthly* declared it a success, noting that "the huge Aeroscope ... was built to outdo the Ferris wheel of the Chicago World's Fair, and judging from its popularity among visitors it accomplished its purpose."[42] The *New York Tribune* indulged in hyperbole for its lengthy profile of the machine:

> Later came fire and gas balloons, aeroplanes and stationary devices, such as the Ferris Wheel and the Eiffel Tower, all designed to lift man, for a moment, above his cares and follies. Every world's fair has had

FIGURE 41. "The Aeroscope," *Popular Electricity* 6. no. 1 (May 1913): 65.

something of the sort, but all have to yield the palm to the great aeroscope at the Panama-Pacific International Exposition. . . . The movement, rising, is slow and majestic, as is becoming in a machine that sets gravitation at naught and competes with the celestial bodies. And here comes its first great departure from other devices. Your Eiffel Tower is merely an edifice; the Ferris Wheel a gigantic whirligig. But as the aeroscope rises and describes a slow gesture in midair it might very well be the air of the presiding genius invoking a blessing upon the fair.[43]

The *Tribune*'s "presiding genius" is, of course, Joseph Strauss. Why not, then, if it is Gustave Eiffel's tower and George Ferris's wheel, Joseph

FIGURE 42.   The Aeroscope on the cover of *Scientific American* 112 (10 April 1915): 15.

Strauss's 'scope? The promotional literature and press response framed the Aeroscope, like its forerunners, as a potential civic monument. Instead, the Aeroscope became a monument *manqué*, in effect a trial run for Strauss, who would in the 1930s engineer San Francisco's enduring monument, the Golden Gate Bridge.

It may be that the Aeroscope, part of the genre of the observation ride, was, as a device, too indiscriminate and diversely isomorphic—too much like a cinema, an airplane, a tower, a balloon, a thrill ride, a bridge—to function as an abiding monument. Period commentators grasped for analogies, comparing it to "some huge prehistoric monster," a "bascule bridge turned into an amusement device," an "Enormous Inverted Pendulum," "one of those new-fangled wireless masts on the latest war vessels, which has been thrown over a cyclone upon its side," "a giant see-saw," and so on.[44] Of course, all new media technologies are met with antecedent analogues. The sensation seeker compares the novelty to a repertoire of known preexisting technologies, which in turn become the prehistory of the new device. But the Aeroscope was met with markedly disparate and grasping comparisons and haphazard positioning—more, even, than the Ferris wheel.[45] And these may have contributed to its ultimate decline.

The Aeroscope's capacity for mixed understanding is revealing. The ride was reliably described, even in non-promotional literature, as "unique." What was most often remarked upon as novel is evidenced in a final example, from *Popular Electricity Magazine*: "Thus the old fashioned well sweep idea will be found in a new vocation doling out joy. In spite of the unique twist passengers will experience in this joy ride they are not expected to be 'all turned around' when they land again."[46] Indeed, in a culture of ambulant "mobilized gaze," as Anne Friedberg framed it, the Aeroscope's particular type of movement, its twist, was distinct.[47]

THE UNIQUE TWIST

What was the quality of movement that the Aeroscope provided? Period authors old enough to remember previous American expositions sometimes compared the Aeroscope to a captive balloon, but many visitors to the fair would not have this frame of reference.[48] Furthermore, unlike the captive balloon, the Aeroscope did not ascend vertically, but rather, as the guide to the exposition noted, its "car described a huge helix as it rose in the air."[49] (Without access to a film record of the Aeroscope in motion, the phantom lines indicating movement that are included in Strauss's blueprints for the machine give the best sense of its path through the air. See Figure 43.) This coil-like movement was likewise different in kind from the circular visual logic of the panorama painting, to which the Boy Scouts compared the Aeroscope. If anything, the Aeroscope more resembles the spiral stairway of the panorama rotunda, the path to the panoramic view, than the panorama itself.[50] The act of ascension is pivotal. The most vivid account of this spiral rotation comes from *Popular Mechanics*, which noted that as the "whole contrivance revolves, the sensation of the passengers [is] described much like that of 'ascending an enormous spiral stairway' that

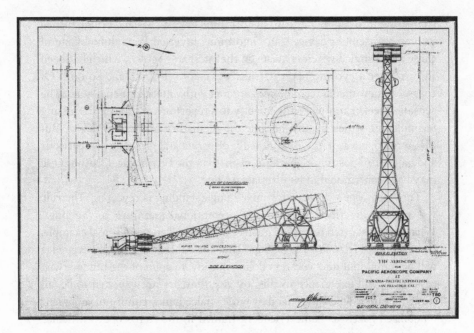

FIGURE 43.   Strauss's blueprints for the Aeroscope. Note that when the car is on the ground, the "Mayas village concession" rests beneath it, giving a sense of the scale of the device and the extent to which it was a neighbor to the other amusements on the Zone. "Aeroscope, for the Pacific Aeroscope Co., Panama-Pacific Exposition, San Francisco, California," 1914. Joseph Strauss Bridge Plans, M163, Department of Special Collections, Stanford University Libraries, California.

has a constantly narrowing diameter as the top is approached."[51] This leisurely helical arc is key to the Aeroscope's model of aerial vision, which despite intentions was less clarifying than puzzling.[52]

"Spirality," wrote the art critic Theodore Cooke in 1914, "is a generalization of far-reaching importance."[53] The spiral is, in this period, the visual emblem of vertigo. Recall the emergent cliché of spiral hypnosis, which is meant to dizzy the receiver into a receptive state of mind; or, to use a more popular example, the iconographic dizzy symbol of the early newspaper comics, the so-called "spurl" that floats above a character's head to indicate dizziness or confusion.[54] The connection between spirals and dizziness has ancient roots. In his taxonomy of play, French sociologist Roger Caillois equates the term *vertigo* with the Greek *ilinx*, which originated from the term for a whirlpool. The whirlpool, the vertigo spurl, the Aeroscope's helix—there is a visual consanguinity to these forms. Caillois considered vertigo a form of play, albeit an enigmatic one. Some varieties of dance, whirling dervishes, and hypnosis: all are examples of vertigo play, all activities that might fall under the visual sign of the helix.[55] "Vertigo games attempt to momentarily destroy the stability of perception. . . . In order to give this kind of sensation the kind of intensity and brutality capable of shocking adults, powerful machines have had to be invented. The Industrial Revolution had to take place before vertigo could really become a kind of game."[56] Caillois refers to thrill rides, such as roller coasters, but it is argued here that this application of the concept of the vertigo game can be used to think about the Aeroscope as a subtler, less "brutalizing" form of vertigo machine. Film, a fast-moving medium, felt compelled to speed up the maneuvers of the Aeroscope precisely because an observation ride is a "slow" medium, operating at an unhurried pace that allows for a careful mode of observation—not unlike a panstereorama. It is no wonder that the Aeroscope could not serve as the central monument of the exhibit: compared to the centering and centripetal arrangement of the canonical clous—the verticality of the Eiffel Tower, the revolutions of the Ferris wheel—the Aeroscope is by design decentered and centrifugal. Not an exclamation point, but a question mark.

The vertiginous component of the Aeroscope is one important facet of the ludic quality of aerial vision that it offered. The other is scale. The PPIE, as part of its aerial logic, radically toyed with scale. In addition to the scale model of the Panama Canal, it contained as discrete exhibits the "world's largest" typewriter, flagpole, and relief map of the United States, as well as a number of colossal displays in immediate proximity to the Aeroscope. It will be useful at this stage to examine in detail the pictorial evidence of the view from the Aeroscope. No filmic account of this view remains, so the Aeroscope exists chiefly in the photographic record, in both the many postcards produced with it as the focus, and in the photographs shot from the Aeroscope's car. The following figures track the trajectory of the Aeroscope's arc.

Interestingly, the Aeroscope souvenir booklet does not include any views of San Francisco, which was apparently considered incidental to the exposition and geographic prospects that the ride afforded. However, one private photo has been preserved, facing south (Figure 44). The slightly canted angle gives what is probably an accurate impression of what a ride on the Aeroscope would have resembled—the other photographs, taken for promotional purposes, and considering exposure time, would likely have been taken from a static Aeroscope.

Facing the Golden Gate and capturing the Tower of Jewels in the upper left, Figure 45 is the most reproduced image from the Aeroscope.[57] The large structure dominating the middle right, below the rotunda, is an outdoor, scale model of the Grand Canyon, providing an aerial view of that

FIGURE 44.   Anonymous photograph from Aeroscope.
Glenn Koch postcard collection.

FIGURE 45.   Aeroscope
souvenir postcard.
Accompanying text reads
"Birdseye View of
Exposition Grounds and
Golden Gate as seen from
Aeroscope." Glenn Koch
postcard collection.

geographic landmark long before touristic flyovers were available. To the
left of the main thoroughfare of the Zone stand two giant toy soldiers.
Their size, as Figure 46 illustrates, was intended to impress from ground
level; from the perspective of the Aeroscope, they throw off the sense
of established scale, counterintuitively reducing the relative size of everything else. If "men" are that large, the entire exposition grounds come to
resemble nothing more than a scale model.

As the Aeroscope turns from a westward perspective to a northern one,
the Japanese Village comes into view, with its giant statue of the Buddha and
a miniature Mount Fuji in the background (Figure 47). Once again, exhibits
meant to be colossal from the ground are made miniature by the Aeroscope.
Such scale games are evidently not just built for the pedestrian, ground level
viewer, but for the Aeroscope rider, as well. This is a constructed aerial view,
which distinguishes it from the rest. The view from an airplane is in effect

FIGURE 46. The Zone, with Aeroscope in background. Glenn Koch postcard collection.

stolen from the unprepared Earth below; even the view from a skyscraper shows the back end of the city—all those chimneys, ducts, and other infrastructure placed "out of sight" on rooftops. I sometimes call these "Ed Ruscha aerials," for his photographic aerial views of parking lots in Los Angeles, which distill this sense of the "stolen" view that shows civic infrastructure not designed to be contemplated.[58] The PPIE, meanwhile, was built with an aerial view in mind; the fair required an aerial view to be classed properly as a fair. At any rate, these exhibits further miniaturize everything else in the scene, including the geographic features beyond the San Francisco Bay, which the postcard draws the viewer's attention to in the text running underneath the image: a bogus Mount Fuji comes to compete with a bona fide Mount Tamalpais. The text in Figure 48, continuing a panorama eastward, asks that we notice Alcatraz in the background, despite the scale model of Yellowstone Park that is in the foreground.

If the Aeroscope is, like Gullible's tour over the PPIE, at some level meant to present a global Wünderkammer, then its inclusion of monuments national and international, built and geographic, is a feature of this flyover. However, the radically shifting sense of scale, with mountains and toy soldiers on the same playing field, adds a mistrust of one's perception, a ludic emphasis on an already problematic component of all aerial vision. Even when an aerial view displays a location that we are familiar with, as

FIGURE 47.   Aeroscope
souvenir postcard.
Accompanying text
reads "Birdseye View of
U.S. Transport Dock and
Mt. Tamalpais as seen
from Aeroscope." Glenn
Koch postcard collection.

FIGURE 48.   Aeroscope
souvenir postcard.
Accompanying text reads
"Birdseye View of San
Francisco Bay, Alcatraz
Island, as seen from
Aeroscope." Glenn Koch
postcard collection.

the San Francisco Bay Area would have been for many visitors to the PPIE, there is a sense of geographic alienation alongside recognition. *Is that my neighborhood?*

"PANORAMIC WHEW"

The "giant's arm" of the Aeroscope, combined with the steroidal and shrunken exhibits in the Zone, made the colossal miniature, the plaything monumental.[59] Such upside-down reversals were made more vertiginous still by the languid helical twirl of the device's movement which, by perpetually shifting one's perspective and distance from the subjects of the view, further played with any appreciable scale markers. The Aeroscope was, in short, site specific, and its site was, like all world's fairs, ephemeral. It is thus unsurprising that its home in the media landscape beyond 1915 was never established. Reportedly, it went on to the Bronx International Exposition of 1918.[60] Another device of the same name was debuted at the

Santa Monica Pier. But the Aeroscope did not settle in any of these scenarios; it functioned only in concert with the design of the Zone. The itinerancy of the Aeroscope after the close of the PPIE reflects its site-specific utility—beyond, is it to be an art or a science, an attraction or a display? The question was never settled.

Why, today, do we not look out onto the Golden Gate to the Pacific from an Aeroscope's car, as expected in 1915? Because the Aeroscope was unclassifiable as an object: it was indeterminate, simultaneously too like and too unlike existing media. Because it had a strange and unfamiliar movement: a slow, helical turn that made it into a centrifugal monument, one that forbade a centripetal aerial perspective. Finally, because it was built upon the unfixed grounds of the PPIE, where standard cartographic proportions were gleefully thrown out of joint. These key elements of the Aeroscope—indeterminacy, centrifugality, disproportionality—push against the predominant theorization of the aerial view, which relies upon concepts of determinacy, centripetality, and fixed proportions. The Aeroscope, *rara avis* of the fair, is nevertheless typical of the devices I more generally refer to as "aeroscopic" in this work inasmuch as they too are beacons of an alternate lineage of aerial vision. This hermeneutic dizziness—this "panoramic whew"—is engineered directly into this observation ride.

5. The Aeroplane Gaze

Up to this point, the book's focus has been on the view from above, and the media infrastructure designed to offer this perspective. Panorama paintings, model cities, flight films, and observation rides provided proxy aerial experiences, and many period accounts detailed the perceptual surprises that such views afforded. The novelties of the bird's-eye view, alongside its eventual geopolitical ramifications, have resulted in an abundant corpus on this topic, a bookshelf's worth of analytic and historical work.[1] Here, however, I return to terra firma, arguing that to be faithful to the period that is this work's remit (the long nineteenth century, give or take a few years: 1792–1915) is to notice that the principal way that balloons, airships, and airplanes changed the direction or quality of a public's gaze was not by providing the view from above, but rather by necessitating the view from below. Early balloonists noted this as many took their inaugural flights in the 1800s. One such reflected, after launching and looking down at the assembled spectators below: "On first rising we seem amidst thousands of faces, to be central to the directed gaze of the oceans of human countenances, forming a crowd which seems to swell like the waves of the sea."[2]

Heavier-than-air flight, in particular, eventually guaranteed that people were looking up far more frequently than they had previously. Aviation still took place at the panoramic altitude during this period. The French aviator Louis Blériot's flight across the English Channel, for instance, took place at only 250 feet. Here was a new, vividly public science, impossible to confine to the laboratory, loudly announcing itself overhead. As film scholar Paula Amad has noted, the view from above is often tethered to the view from below.[3] Thus does the early aeronaut, above, note the land-locked

FIGURE 49. An early air show
audience at the Los Angeles
International Air Meet, 1910. Arthur
B. Dodge, *Los Angeles Times*, January
16, 1910, 2.

spectators' "directed gaze." Nevertheless, this upward glance has been over-shadowed in the history of the aerial view. In what follows, then, I offer the reverse-shot: a worm's-eye rebuttal to the focus on the bird's-eye view.[4]

The first public demonstration of the Wrights' invention in France was held in 1908; this year has often been heralded as the *annus mirabilis* of aviation.[5] But it was not until 1909 that this invention, and others like it, began to be seen and accounted for by a broader public. In 1909, the first air shows in France, England, Germany, and other nations were held, each landmark events (Figures 49 and 50).[6] Many aeronautical agencies, national and independent, were founded.[7] And everywhere, aeroplanes first began to be seen unannounced above city streets. As a result, pedestrians rubber-necked heavenward, an epiphenomenon of the arrival of the flying machine that was widely editorialized, fictionalized, and caricatured. This is the so-called "aeroplane gaze" of my title: a period term for this view from below—in particular, for the view of the rapt citizen looking up at the new machine.[8]

Almost all of the account that follows occurs between 1909 and 1911: there is a very tight date range during which the aeroplane gaze appears and then disappears. One of Gaumont studios' chase comedies of 1910, *Aeroplane Gaze*, provides in a series of sequences the clearest articulation of the meaning of the term at this moment in time.[9] Three vignettes from the film:

FIGURE 50.   Aeroplane gazers from an unidentified
airshow. *Aircraft* (March 1910), 1.

A group of workers are repairing a roof; suddenly, they begin pointing
upward and craning their necks—an aeroplane, implied offscreen but
never pictured in the film, is passing by overhead. In their distraction,
the workers fall from the roof; they dust themselves off and proceed
beyond the frame, still gesturing toward the plane, maintaining their
gaze, following its path.

A pair of robbers ensnare a man in a top hat; the policemen in the
background do not notice because they are too busy exclaiming over
the aeroplane flying above. Their gaze never settling into a horizontal
axis, they walk straight through the robbery without noticing the
crime.

A multitude of gazers collected from previous encounters are now
tracking the aeroplane, distractedly sowing chaos in their wake. The
pilot ultimately parachutes to the ground and lands in their path,
where the group harass and beat him about the head. The film ends.

Distraction, accident, and pursuit are the template, one that will be
familiar to the reader who has encountered any small number of early
chase films.[10] Here, the generic features of the chase film are put to work in
capturing the broader topos (an adaptable image or cliché) of the aeroplane
gaze.[11] The Gaumont film offers a snapshot of the gaze's perceived negative
effects, which I characterize as *civic disruption* (derelictions of duty, mob
violence) and *anatomical distortion* (the craned neck). Absent from
Gaumont's *Aeroplane Gaze* (either for budgetary reasons or as part of the
joke) is the object upon which the gaze rests, namely, the aeroplane. This

chapter correspondingly considers precisely *what* such gazers might have seen, arguing that their view newly mediated the sky as a blank canvas, one that must be filled by the colorful traffic of the aeroplane. As one period author framed it: "The Spectator is busily gazing at nothing whatever, except the sky"—then, like "a bolt from the blue," arrived the aeroplane.[12]

Premised upon several collections of aeronautica, as well as period accounts from essays and newspaper items, these widespread features of the aeroplane gaze will further be contextualized within the broader history of flight, as well as the history of aerial spectacles.[13] These histories are, I argue, one and the same. The spectacle of flight, here, is not in the lineage of trains or automobiles, but rather fireworks and astronomical displays. An important premise of this chapter is that we must look at human flight for its first 126 years (1783–1909) as, primarily, a form of spectacle, rather than a useful technology. Flight was a curiosity as a science, a failure as a means of transport, and a disaster as a weapon; it was successful only as a spectacle. Aeroscopics are one tributary of flight's success as a spectacle.[14]

By 1909, the tradition of heavenly spectacle that we call flight had coalesced into a medium that assembled in the skies overhead at unfixed occasions; a medium that determined a certain form of observer (in this case, gazer) and observation (gaze); a medium with only the potential, by no means guaranteed, of becoming a transportation technology. The arrival of the aeroplane prompted a series of unexpected contradictions: long-promised the fusion of man and bird, we receive instead the distorted anatomy of the aeroplane gazer; expecting fleeing, naive spectators, fearful of the new object, we find in their place pursuing lay scientists, citizen fans; witnessing a new mediation of the heavens by the aeroplane, we unearth a new skyscape populated by envisaged future traffic. This series of double looks—at medium and machine, gazer and gazed, earth and sky—form warped mirror images.

HEAVENLY SPECTACLES IN THE LONGUE DURÉE

Had you asked, say, a resident of Paris in 1809, "What is the use of the hot air balloon?" the response would have been negative. "Useless to mankind" says one; "of no certain use" says another.[15] Someone with the long view, such as Benjamin Franklin, who saw a demonstration of the Montgolfier in 1783, may have answered more generously: "Balloons may be said to resemble babies, insomuch as they are of no use at present, but may become of use in due time."[16] All, however, would have counted it, as Franklin did, "a most beautiful spectacle."[17]

The same would hold true had you asked such a citizen in 1909 the same question regarding the aeroplane. The prospects of travel and warfare, which we now take for granted (and which correspondingly color the historiography of human flight) were then still purely speculative; indeed, for most of the history of flight they were the domain of science fiction and failed experiment.[18] Of course, the history of technology is a necessary approach for understanding the developments that ultimately allowed for heavier-than-air flight, since it came to be, predominantly, a technological rather than aesthetic feat; however, it is out of step with virtually everything that happened prior to the Great War. To be true to our historical actors, we must look at balloons, airships, parachutes, and other such endeavors—in short, at all of eighteenth- and nineteenth-century flight—as instead, a history of entertainment.

Astronomy is likely the oldest science; all have looked up at the night's sky and marveled, and some aimed to intuit meaning (Figure 51). Others—aeromancers—even aimed to divine the future. The first manmade productions of heavenly spectacles aimed to recapitulate this wonder. Fireworks, as the historian of science Simon Werrett has shown, "amounted to a form of artificial nature, showing suns, stars, comets," and other atmospheric events.[19] This understanding of fireworks as an artificial nature reaches back to the early modern era, when they were a kind of sublime, spectacular astronomy. By the nineteenth century, when astronomy was being formalized as a science in observatories across the globe, "astronomical mania" set in and countless highly mediated versions of stargazing were introduced.[20] Popular lecturers toured with "orreries, 'telluria' (or Earth-Moon machines), and 'transparent scenes'" for magic lanterns.[21] Discoveries in the astronomical sciences and a thriving lecture circuit meant that the firmament newly required interpretation, and a robust media infrastructure developed to support this.[22] The night sky needed a hermeneutics, and the heavens were a flexible medium. There were numerous, if doomed, fin-de-siècle endeavors to use the sky as a medium for advertising or propaganda.[23]

The term *medium* is employed advisedly, here. Although media in our current, nontechnical sense of simple mass communication did not emerge until the end of the nineteenth century, prior to this and especially in the eighteenth century, the concept was intimately connected with *air*.[24] Air, as vehicle for sound, for flame—and here, for flying machine. This concept would be familiar to a media theorist like John Durham Peters, whose notion of "sky media" suggests that media technologies are the elements translated into artifacts—the clock, in this sense, is a terrestrial distillation of celestial movements.[25]

FIGURE 51. Broadsheet woodcut depicting citizens gazing at celestial phenomenon over Basel, 1566. Zürich Central Library.

Flight, meanwhile—specifically, hot air balloons—had since the Montgolfier Brothers' first ascent in 1783 served the function of public spectacle. Balloons often appeared before or after firework displays. Indeed, celebration was to be the balloon's abiding function, having never been used effectively in war or transportation; their limited useful purpose was to deliver mail (still unpredictably) beyond the blockade during the Paris Commune.[26] Inventors were full of prospective applications for flight, and indeed imagined all of those uses that we attribute to flight today (and more), but when trialed these endeavors were invariably failures. The issue, by and large, came down to a lack of navigability. Balloons in war were particularly dangerous and could easily drop bombs back on those who launched them; they also made large, slow-moving targets for gunfire. In transit, balloons invariably drifted out to sea. In science, a lack of pressurization technology made balloons dangerous for atmospheric study—beyond, that is, studying the effects of a lack of oxygen: Icarian echoes. In 1894, 101 years beyond the Montgolfiers, the great aviation entrepreneur Octave Chanute could write that flight "has hitherto been associated with failure," the province of the "eccentric" and the "crank."[27] And as late as 1902, the *Encyclopædia Britannica* began its entry on aeronautics with a caveat regarding "the prejudice consequent on past failures and upon premature assertion of impending success" in this field of science.[28]

The sole reliable use for the technology was as spectacle, and indeed there was a circuit of balloon celebrities, who would travel from country to country, rise for immense crowds in their tethered balloon, and perhaps perform a stunt. Some undertook acrobatic feats in the air. Others carried animals (presaging Laika the space dog by a century and more). The balloonist Charles Green was known in verse as follows:

The famous Mr. Green,
Whom almost all of us have seen
Quitting these grovelling realms below
For an aerial location,
Some miles above the clouds,
Came to the fixed determination —
That he might better please the crowds
Who came to gape and stare
At his exploits in air
Of carrying with him some animal aloft.
Should he give a goose an airy dance—
As once was done in France?
No! Mr. Green
Would make no mockery of the thing,
But would take up a beast of such a size
As might be worthy to be seen by all men's eyes.
He had a pony.[29]

Other stunts now seem obscure. Sophie Blanchard, the famed French aeronaut, would rise in a "tiny upholstered chair" and spend the night sleeping in the sky.[30] As the 1800s wore on, ballooning did not maintain its aristocratic pedigree; historian Richard Holmes has suggested that it accumulated an "end of the pier seediness," a commonplace status that is hard to envisage today.[31]

The aeroplane thus arrives in the context of technological failure and old-hat spectacle. When the aeroplane gaze is first haltingly launched as a topos in the 1890s, then, it is at the same moment pronounced a bust. The response was, in sum: "we have seen this before," or "it is a lie." Aviation's history of failure led to countless false reports; even the Wrights were disbelieved for many years, in many quarters. The public suffered from (as we call it today vis-à-vis hoverboards or flying cars) "rumor fatigue." On the occasion of yet another false report of the successful invention of yet another heavier-than-air craft, *The San Francisco Chronicle* wrote: "Public interest in the airship proposition has waned considerably.... People are tired of craning their necks and gazing into the sky on the invitation of any excitable person who takes it into his head that he sees something out of the common."[32] Accordingly, when citizens first met with a bona fide flying machine, unsought, in 1909, it was as an inutile spectacle, an art.[33]

HOMO AVIANS

The red herring of human flight was the bird. Tracing back to da Vinci, whose sketches for aeronautic inventions were premised upon avian

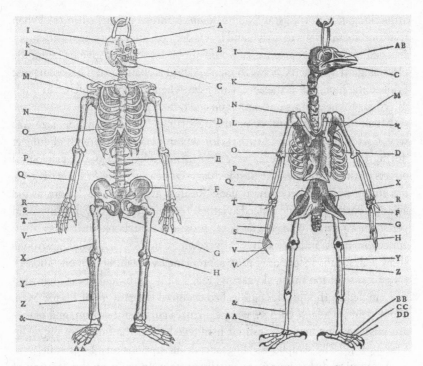

FIGURE 52. In 1909, *The Aero Manual* repurposed these images from Pierre Belon du Mans's *L'histoire de la nature des oyseaux* (1555) in order to demonstrate skeletal designs for flight. "Human Flight: The Solved Problem," *The Aero Manual* (London: Temple, 1909), 21.

anatomy, it was difficult to think beyond the temptation of flapping wings. (The *ornithopter*, a flying machine based on these principles, is named for the same Greek root as *ornithology*: *ornitho-*, "resembling birds.") If one could simply merge human and bird anatomies through some kind of apparatus, it was speculated, then an individual could take flight. This was the "ornithological school of aviation."[34] For those that assume that transportation was the ultimate goal of flight, the "bird template issue" was perceived to have misdirected flight research for centuries.[35] Just prior to heavier-than-air flight, aeronautic theoreticians began to doubt this premise. Journalist Sydney Hollands, writing in 1901: "If man were a butterfly, bug, beetle, or small bird, weighing a few ounces, he would have a good time of it, but his 100 lbs. (and more) avoirdupois effectively bars the way to any possibility of active flight derived solely from his physical exertions."[36]

Taking the long view of human flight, we see our physiology prospectively adapting itself, this way and that, to the possible technology. First, as fusion:

arms elongate into wings, and *homo avians* is foreseen (see Figure 52). When this combination fails to arrive, and it was decided, after centuries of attempts, that adding flapping apparatuses would not be sufficient to give us flight, the physiological symmetry between man and bird is abandoned. This occurs just prior to the moment of the aeroplane gaze, when the body stretches in other directions to meet this same desire: up and out.

Much of the commentary on the distortions of the aeroplane gaze was wry. Cartoonists and caricaturists, for whom aviation was a chief subject during the early comics era, were first to make light of the physiological effects of the aeroplane. The Sunday pages were especially full of aero gags, but so too was the daily newspaper.[37] Readers at the time took note, as did aviation enthusiasts, and indeed aviators. The pilot Howard Gill, who would perish in an aerial collision in 1912, produced scrapbooks full of aviation ephemera, news, and caricatures.[38] Everywhere in these scrapbooks, cartoons show pedestrians responding to the aeroplane by crashing into one another ("Just a case of too much skygazing, that's all"), limbs and necks elongated and tangled as though the nation had acquired the powers of Plastic Man. Women's hats adapt, with viewing apertures cut into the brim, and planes are mistaken for birds ("Gosh all fishhooks! Even the birds are bigger in Chicago!").[39] The scrapbooks suggest civic disruptions on a large scale.

Anatomical distortions were equally present. In 1910, on the occasion of the International Aviation Meet in Los Angeles, a local cartoonist pictured the "aeroplane face," contorted and unflattering to the bearer. Others imagined "aeroplanearis," a grotesque enlargement of the ears presumably caused by the noise of propellers. But most widely satirized was "aviation neck" (Figure 53).

A news item, "Insanity May Lurk in Aeroplane Gazing," which made the rounds widely in 1910, from Seattle to Pittsburgh, went further than the cartoonists and warned of the end result of this anatomical distortion:

> OVID, Mich., Dec. 10.—John B. Cross of this place, who died in the Kalamazoo insane asylum, was made insane, according to the doctors, by his peculiar occupation.
>
> Cross worked as a tree trimmer, and was compelled to be gazing upward most of the time. This unnatural position of his head strained certain spinal muscles and softening of the brain resulted.
>
> This case has caused speculation as to what will happen to those who gaze skyward at aeroplanes. The inference seems simple.[40]

Here are a cluster of media references, from only three years, pertaining to a new, and negatively perceived form of looking. It is a classic example of a media pathology, as introduced in chapter 3. New medium: new pathology.

THE NEW DISEASE, AVIATION NECK

FIGURE 53. Drawings from the scrapbooks of early aviator Howard Gill. Smithsonian National Air and Space Museum Archives, (NASM 2002-20957).

Similar questions apply: Does the aeroplane gaze describe an actual civic-spectatorial experience, or is it a joke ailment, another cooked-up media enthusiasm, humorously placed within the nomenclature of pathology, like "Kaleidoscomania" or the "Balloonatic"? (As a joke ailment, see Figure 54.) In the *Charlotte News*, they proposed, "The aeroplane gaze will probably succeed the 'automobile stare.'"[41] Is this another regrettably lost form of spectatorship, or are both of these audiences—the starers, the gazers—nonexistent?

GAZE, GAZER, GAZED

The history of film is instructive in this regard. This medium was, as Fernand Léger claimed, "born on the same day" as aviation.[42] One might give or take a few years; but certainly, one can imagine typical viewers who see their first film and first aeroplane in the same year. Both have their origin stories within a decade of each other (1895, 1903). Both created new categories of viewers, or even new publics altogether. It is wise to doubt the veracity of myths of origin, a point I return to in the conclusion, and to look instead for their longer utility, for the assumptions they make and the defining features of the medium that they implicitly claim. Take film

FIGURE 54. A mechanical postcard (one that changes images when a tab is pulled) demonstrates the perils of distraction caused by aeroplane gazing. N.d.

historian Tom Gunning's "aesthetic of astonishment," his account of initial spectator reaction to moving images, of, in particular, the credulous spectator who fled at the sight of the screened oncoming train. Gunning cautions against the existence of this spectator, against our tendency to, with end-of-history self-congratulation, imagine a more naive spectator than we would credit as extant today.[43] In film history, we call this naive historical actor "Uncle Josh," for the depiction of this rube in the Edwin S. Porter film, *Uncle Josh at the Moving Picture Show* (1902). In the film, Uncle Josh sees his first moving pictures, and variously dances with the characters onscreen, dashes away from a depicted train, and ultimately breaks through the screen to try to interrupt a romance. As film scholar Miriam Hansen argued in her well-known account of the character, even at this early stage of film history, "the childlike behavior of spectator figures was already a trope."[44]

The story of the aeroplane gaze recapitulates this origin myth of film reception. Gaumont's *Aeroplane Gaze* (1909) is, in effect, *Uncle Josh at the*

Moving Picture Show with flying machines, comically warning against a bumpkin response. But the accounts meaningfully differ. Uncle Josh willingly visits the new technology; for aeroplane gazers, the technology visits them, and indeed surprises them. When the encounter between viewer and technology occurs, Uncle Josh flees his; aeroplane gazers pursue theirs. The differences between these otherwise similar films are productive, for they are a reminder of the medial shaping of technology, and of the powerful messages that technological origin stories hold. Film's myth of first reception speaks to the medium's powers of verisimilitude and deceptive immersion; the aeroplane's myth of first reception speaks to its powers of surprise and distraction.

It is worth considering the unusual choice of the word *gaze* at this moment, and what it may contain. Although people had been looking up at hot air balloons since the 1780s, the unlikelihood of chancing upon these rare birds in flight, during an ordinary day in the city, prevented a specialized mode of looking from coalescing, let alone from claiming its own term, such as *gaze*. This was not to be the aeroplane "look" or the aeroplane "observation."[45] Bird watchers may watch; and train spotters spot; but aeroplane gazers gaze. These are not meaningless distinctions, especially considering that "the gazing multitude" was a broadly pejorative refrain that turns up repeatedly in eighteenth- and nineteenth-century literature, referring to the dim-witted audience who might be stunned and enthralled by a parade or an execution. The frequency of *gaze*'s use in derisive terms such as *star gazer*, a dismissive characterization for astronomers and daydreamers (historically, "too much stargazing could be a sin," as John Durham Peters reminds us), leaves the verb with negative undertones.[46] Indeed, in "navel-gazing," it signifies a "self-absorbed," perhaps "profitless" mode of looking.[47] (The use of the "gaze" in later psychoanalysis and film theory has its own long history, which would be anachronistic if applied here, but it is worth noting that similar connotations persist. Gazing is seldom desirable.) *Gaze*'s etymological relation to *gawk* and *gape* tells us more, for each of these terms implies a level of distraction that leaves mouths agape (*agape*, another lexical cousin). In short, to gaze at an aeroplane in 1909 is to be at the borderland of vacancy and wonder, bafflement and awe.

The aeroplane gaze differs from kaleidoscomania, to answer my question above, in that the aeroplane gaze does not imply the same type of preexisting devotion to a specific medium, but reflects rather an impromptu enthusiasm that can strike any pedestrian unbidden, whether or not they profess an interest in aviation. (There are films and other references to aeroplane fanaticism, such as *Mother-in-Law Would Fly*, also 1909, but these are a separate, if related, epiphenomenon.) The aeroplane gaze can afflict anybody; it is a form of attraction that turns a distributed mass public, spread over many city streets, into a momentarily unified audience. This is a medium that suddenly constructs itself out of thin air, in public, and produces a fixation where none existed before. One can imagine historical incidents that might have the same effect: great fires, perhaps, or a meteorological event. With the aeroplane gaze, however, what was once the rare event becomes commonplace. This disorderly, unsought form of vision attributes an amateur status to the gazer; they have no guide, no map, no instruments—no apparatus of knowledge—at hand to analyze what they see. *Observation*, discussed in chapter 1, is the more professional variation; the aeroplane gaze is a less professional, less ruminative, and less directed outlook.

In short, to dismiss the aeroplane gaze out of hand as a joke ailment or a media whim is a mistake. It is, rather, a revealing technological origin story with one foot in a long history of dumbfounded vision and the other in actual public response. One finds supplementary evidence in the writing of observant modernists. Le Corbusier, in his paean to the airplane, vividly describes his first sighting of such a machine above Paris, when he "craned his neck out of the window to catch sight of this unknown messenger. . . . In spring, 1909, men had captured the chimera and driven it above the city."[48] Others had their first sightings at the air show, still a nascent genre, and quite different from the one we may be familiar with today. The resemblance of the early airshow to the current iteration of air show is minimal, and the prestige and cultural standing of the event has been in steady decline since these early iterations. Flight was, recall, above all a spectacle; it was secondarily, at the air show, a demonstration of a technology; and finally, it was a daredevil sport for wealthy dilettantes and the poets who romanticized their daring.[49] Many dignitaries and artists attended, in addition to a mass public. Franz Kafka was one.

Kafka wrote about the aeroplane gaze in his first published work of journalism, "The Aeroplanes at Brescia," also in 1909. Kafka's account of French aviator Louis Blériot's flight at Brescia is in keeping with the aeroplane gaze:

> Enraptured, everyone looks up at him; there is no room for another in
> any heart. He flies a short lap, and then reappears above us, almost at a
> vertical. And craning their necks, everyone can see how the monoplane
> hesitates, how Blériot gets a grip on it, and it even rises higher. What is
> happening? Up there, twenty meters above the earth, is a man trapped
> in a wooden frame, defending himself against a freely undertaken,
> invisible peril. . . . For this fellow here, there is only the ocean.[50]

FIGURE 55. *Flight Weekly,* 1909.

Kafka captures, here, the neck-craning effects of the aeroplane gaze as well as the strangeness of this view, the strangeness of "the ocean" of the sky (Figure 55.) Hold onto this sense of spatial boundlessness, and we will use it as a turning point to discuss not *how* people gazed, how they were inattentive to their environment or craned their necks, but rather what it was they were looking *at*, precisely.

Just as when we look at planes flying by today—when we bother to do so—the biplanes that Le Corbusier and Kafka watched would often be minute in the expanse of the sky. Instead of a feature of the landscape, parallel to the mountain, or meeting the ocean, the sky becomes instead a kind of image, a background. The plane is a small subject on an immense, apparently empty screen. (And the screen of the sky was usually empty, cloudless, since pilots preferred a clear day to fly.) If the sky is to be an image, then it is overwhelmingly empty. This emptiness was noticed, as Kafka's representative account suggests. And humanity, like nature, abhors a vacuum.

Horror vacui may be too strong a term for what happened next, beyond the first sightings of the aeroplane gaze, as the 1910s went on—but it would not be inaccurate. In short, the newly empty canvas of the sky was imaginatively filled. Within a few years, skywriting was first developed in earnest. In chapter 4, I introduced Art Smith debuting a form of skywriting at the San Francisco World's Fair, flying loops in his biplane in the dark, as smoky, indecipherable curlicues in the sky were produced by flares attached to the vehicle (Figure 39).

Skywriting was one response to the transformation of the heavens into a screen; however, the more common response to this emptiness was to

FIGURE 56. The unusual premise of this illustration is that balloons, airships, and aeroplanes would become so popular that the ballast-sand they dropped would cover London. J. Foord, *Ballooning and Aeronautics*, 1908, 101.

imagine a sky peopled with aircrafts of all types, a mirror image of the heavily populated metropolises below, with their new automobile traffic. Indeed, these two traffics were often joined. As one newspaper asked: "Have you acquired the aeroplane gaze? Can you walk on Milwaukee streets, watch where you are going, and still be able to note the flight of the aeroplanes, as they dart hither and thither?"[51] There are clear parallels here with the framing of the jaywalker, who arrives not ten years after the construction of the aeroplane gazer.[52] Both aim to shame "hyper-stimulated" pedestrians, as Ben Singer might call them, into precautionary attentiveness.[53]

Aeronautic magazines frequently envisaged future aerial traffic, as did illustrations and postcards of the time (Figures 56 and 57).[54] However, it was the animated film that best delivered upon the crowded promise of the aeroplane gaze. Paintings did not capture movement in the sky; photographs made the object seem too distant. Only animation could remediate the strange physics of the view, and only animation could populate the image of the sky and give it life, transposing onto the sky the traffic and street life of the city.

FIGURE 57. One of a popular genre of postcard, usually titled "In the Future." The postcard was misleadingly noted to picture Wuppertal, Germany, because of the suspension railway that remains in use today. In fact, many "In the Future" postcards added suspension railways, so this could be any European city in the period. Not dated.

The best instance of this is found in the great French animator Émile Cohl's *En route*, (1910, Figure 58). *En route* offers, in a series of brief, cut-out segments, a potted history of transportation, from the horse and carriage to the automobile, the canoe to the ocean liner, the balloon to the aeroplane. It is this last lineage that is of most interest here. The action proceeds thus:

> *A caveman has a first encounter with a bird*; looking up, he falls over, stunned by its capacity for flight.

> *Time passes.* A single balloon makes its way across the sky; then, an airship; finally, an aeroplane. Then two. Then three. An intertitle reads: "Without a doubt, man is indefatigable, but his world had become very agitated."[55]

> *The final shot of the film pictures the globe* covered in fast-moving ocean liners and automobiles; the faces of the sun and moon are alarmed by the multitude of flying machines in the sky (at one point, eighteen in a single shot); the celestial bodies retreat offscreen. The technological momentum and speed continue until each machine comes crashing down and disappears. The film ends.

FIGURE 58. Images from Emile Cohl's *En route* (1910).

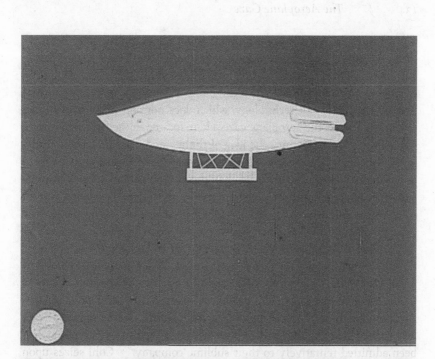

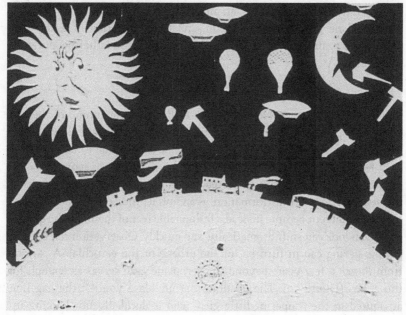

En route recapitulates an argument about the aeroplane gaze in filmic form, beginning with humankind's first gaze at the heavens, and ending with the tumult it creates on the ground. The empty sky of the beginning is noticed, mirrored, filled, and ultimately, abandoned. Cohl's pessimistic take on the history of technology, which does not end well for mankind, effectively judges the aeroplane gaze—here located in the first look up at a bird, which gives humanity the idea of flight—and finds this desire wanting. Cohl goes further than the suggestion that the aeroplane gaze is a form of urban distraction, further even than the idea of technological determinism, instead accusing these elaborate modes of transport of being part of some innate fatalistic drive, what Paul Virilio might call "dromology," the "science of speed."[56]

To place Cohl's narrative in the terms of this chapter: the aesthetic novelty of the airship provoked a new mode of spectatorship, the aeroplane gaze; this view turned the sky into a blank image; and this new tabula rasa, in turn, is to be occupied by the (also new) popular arts. As Hannah Arendt once wrote of Sputnik's launch, the aeroplane "dwelt and moved in the proximity of the heavenly bodies as though it had been admitted tentatively to their sublime company."[57] Cohl seizes upon this tentativeness, and offers an implied tertiary stage: the brevity of the aeroplane gaze epiphenomenon, and the restoration of a sky that offers once again, and however briefly, only the cosmic hermeneutics of astronomy.

· · ·

The image of the re-emptied sky is, in essence, the beginning of the end of the aeroplane gaze. Beyond the first aviation war that followed, this mode of looking, perhaps like the automobile stare, came to be attributed only to rubes and hayseeds. (As a reminder that these responses do not only flow in the direction of increasing familiarity, note that fireworks underwent a reverse transformation, as an initial proud nonchalance toward the entertainment became instead a fashionable fear of them.)[58] The quality of a given look can shift dramatically, and quickly. Observation can become gazing; gazing can in turn be for the urbane or the parochial. A cartoon from *Punch* a few years beyond the aeroplane gaze serves as epitaph for this topos (Figure 59). The headline is "our blasé youth"; the gag line, attributed to the "superior little girl" who is decidedly not looking up, reads, "Well, fancy you looking up at an aeroplane, auntie! Billie and I *never* do!"

Superior Little Girl: "Well, fancy you looking up at an aeroplane, auntie!
Billie and I *never* do."

FIGURE 59. A cartoon from *Punch*, June 19, 1918, 399.

AIR RAID GAZERS AND LOOKING DOWN, AGAIN

There is another, darker reading of the *Punch* cartoon, one given away by
its date: 1918. It was published in an England that had seen the first use of
flying machines in war—reconnaissance, bombings, dogfights.[59] All of this
was new. The worried look on auntie's face suggests fear of bombardment;
she is watching the skies not in wonder, but in alarm.

Footage exists from the Second World War of "air raid gazers" (to borrow
the title that British Pathé gives it): a public searching the skies for threat from
Trafalgar Square sometime in the early 1940s.[60] The crowd, one suspects, does
not wish to fill the sky with traffic. As a topos, the aeroplane gaze appears to
be flexible: first as novelty, then as war. For some decades thereafter, the aeroplane does not intrude on daily life as an entertainment, but as a harbinger of
war, its connotations of wonder drained and filled instead with fear.

This is a familiar trajectory.[61] In the twentieth century, we witnessed the
viewing techniques of birdwatchers become uneasily symmetrical with
those of wartime plane spotters during the Second World War.[62] In the Cold

War and beyond, amateur astronomers, so-called "moonwatchers," were summoned for enemy satellite spotting.[63] Aeroplane gazing was, if not expressly drafted, then transformed after the war. What was a technological fanaticism became instead "citizen vigilance."[64] Paul Virilio's argument that the view from above is per se a form of military reconnaissance (whatever its nominal intention) appears to have its on-the-ground mirror image, as innocuous hobbies are press-ganged into warfare.[65] The film historian Anton Kaes has, coincidentally, called this correspondence between vision, apparatus, and surveying the "cold gaze."[66]

While we may now routinely ignore airplanes and helicopters, the first glimpse of a drone, spontaneously, in the city sky, causes everyone to turn their head up and look. But the more familiar case study in our recent reception of technology is with smart phones. This will ring true to any who have encountered one of the innumerable newspaper items advising today's pedestrians that they are undertaking a dangerous, "distracted walking," and must stop looking down at their smartphones, lest they acquire the ailment "text neck" or indeed interrupt the flow of traffic.[67] ("How Smartphones Are Damaging Our Spines," *The Guardian* phrased it, stopping short of "softening of the brain.") The similarities between our present small-screen distraction and the big-screen, aeroplane distractions of a century ago are, evidently, closer than they may first appear.

Today's looking down is yesterday's looking up. The aeroplane gaze reminds us to examine not only the media enthusiasms and pathologies of our present moment, but also the long history of the aerial view. Which, as it was broadly experienced, had as much to do with the view from below as the view from above.

Conclusion

First Flights

This book began with vignettes of first encounters with aerial media. But firsts can be deceptive. When identifying historical first representations, first objects, or first experiences, one must be wary. For film historians, there is seldom a plausible case to be made that a given film contains the first documenting of a place, person, or thing, given that a large majority of the corpus of early film no longer exists.[1] The problem of survival and access—and so, the problem of firsts—bedevils media historians just as well. We are still discovering not only the forgotten products of dead media (think of the many luminaries still to be found on wax cylinders; or, in this book, the Aeroscope ride), but forgotten media tout court (such as the audible zoetrope; or, in this book, the panstereorama).[2] Book historians, of course, lay plausible etymological claim to that great destroyer of firsts: the idea of the lacuna.[3] If we do not know what we are missing, how can we claim a first? And as for historians of technology, who sometimes trade in a literature of invention and patent where we might expect plausible firsts to be found: they often wish to disassociate their method from this "unproductive" area of study and aim to focus on routine use instead.[4] To look at firsts with a skeptical eye is a good practice.

This is, nevertheless, advice that has been cumulatively challenged in this work, which is preoccupied with origins and firsts. Historians may not wish to speak of firsts, but people in history, reliably, do. Spectators will recount unforgettable experiences with, say, the physiological curiosity of a first ride in a balloon, the public excitement of a first glimpse of an airplane, the cosmopolitan appeals of a first visit to a world's fair. Moreover, events and ideas surrounding firsts that are accepted as facts gain a historical weight, whether or not they are true. Think again of the insightful myths that surround the earliest film screenings, and the apocryphal public that fled the oncoming train. False, maybe, but the tale speaks to something perceived to be essential about cinema—its enthralling capacity to *move* us—and aids in an understanding of cinema shared by historians and the public alike.[5]

In short, firsts are useful here as records of experience, and as formative stories. Indeed, the aeroscopic devices featured in this book were routine providers of firsts—during their respective reigns, they gave people their first glimpse of a range of unique viewing experiences. An astronomer's careful look back on the city from an observatory. A steady, solicitous view from a balloon, one that interprets anything below as the "whole." An accelerated, dissociative glance from the cockpit of an airplane. A playful, toytown map of a city. These media of the bird's-eye view—these paintings, models, films, and rides—helped to set the parameters for more than a century of cultural response to what we now call the aerial view. On account of the common sublimity of this view, and the nerves and giddiness that often arrive with it, such first "flights" are often deeply felt.[6]

The British filmmaker Humphrey Jennings was interested in such first encounters, and spent his later years collecting material for a book collection that came to be called *Pandaemonium: The Coming of the Machine as Seen by Contemporary Observers, 1660–1886.*[7] In nearly four hundred extracts, he captures moments of face-to-face insight with a range of new technologies, from the microscope to electric light. It is an industrial-revolution *Arcades Project*, just as inventorial, just as curated. Jennings argues in his introduction for the work of the poet (understood as an aesthete, not merely someone who writes poetry) as uniquely important in seeing these encounters clearly, in mediating the meetings of the machine and the observer, in making sure that our "means of vision kept pace with these alterations."[8] Jennings has been echoed in recent years by Tom Gunning. "Novelty," we know, "enacts a consistent scenario. Initial reactions express astonishment, which gradually gives way to an acceptance of the new technology as second nature."[9] This second nature can be troublesome; we cease to see the new technology clearly. We acclimatize to vertigo by habituation. Gunning, like Jennings, favors the poet, the avant-garde, for defamiliarizing this second nature, for making the machine appear once again strange.[10]

A first principle: *the aerial view is opaque.* We cease to see it clearly, too. This book is one attempt to clear the air, another investigation into "the coming of the machine as seen by contemporary observers"—an aerial update, to make even our own vision seem strange again. To this point the book has focused on popular visual spectacles, largely setting aside the avant-garde's immense but seldom discussed engagement with bird's-eye viewing.[11] But in the past few decades aeroscopic technologies have begun to inhabit not only historically popular sites (fairs, theaters, rotundas, etc.) but more rarefied settings (museums, galleries).[12] There, they have replayed and revivified moments of machinic intoxication in a form of experimental media archaeology.[13] At the end of chapter 5, I tracked the transformations of the aeroplane gaze after 1909; here, I turn to the afterlife of aeroscopics, in order to see how the alternate genealogy of the aerial that I have sketched plays out in the present, and how aeroscopics recur.

AEROSCOPICS TODAY

Contemporary artists have embraced the panorama painting and its immersive appeals. At the Velaslavasay Panorama in Los Angeles, housed in a historic movie theater, there is an art gallery and panorama rotunda. The curator, Sara Velas, runs the gallery like a nineteenth-century panorama rotunda showman, with a purpose-built viewing stage, pamphlet guides to the pictured panorama, and related exhibits. Subjects are scenic—desert and arctic scenes rather than bird's-eye views—but, stepping in off of the busy streets of Los Angeles, the panoramas carry a decidedly slow, ruminative mode.

The same is evident in the work of T.J. Wilcox, whose ten-projector panoramic film *In the Air*, which screened at the Whitney Museum in 2013–14, shows a day in New York City from his studio rooftop. Wilcox frames his film expressly in panoramic terms, directly referring to the medium and using terminology ("New York in the round") that is in keeping with the period lexicon. In video interviews regarding the exhibit, he notes the piecemeal logic of the panorama, that alternation between whole and detail described in chapter 1. So, too, does Wilcox devise strategies to combat the opacity of the elevated perspective, singling out individual stories from the city in six directions of the panorama; thus, he narrativizes what might otherwise have been a chaotic street scene.

The impact of panorama paintings on later immersive media, such as IMAX and virtual reality (VR), has been well documented, well enough that it does not demand a summary here.[14] My own experience with panoramas and VR, as a user and as a historian, simply confirms the existing account, that VR revives many of the appeals of the panorama. It also often trades in the same aeroscopic subject matter. Aerial games that simulate the bird's-eye view are ubiquitous, such as Ubisoft's *Eagle's Flight* (2016) for the PlayStation VR, in which players controls the flight of an eagle merely by tilting their heads. In it, the panoramic quality of VR is combined with the vertiginous appeals of aerial simulation films.

Contemporaneous technological developments in exploration continue to have an oblique influence on new media: just as the observatory played a key role in the panorama, airplane flight was vital for IMAX, views of Earth from space (the "blue marble".) catalyzed new cartographic developments, and the drone has profoundly impacted videogame aesthetics.

Today, as for the previous century, the primary vehicle for an aeroscopic experience is simply in the moving image. Phantom rides persist. There are many contemporary examples, including "D-Box" cinematic technology, which times the rumbling movements of the theater chairs precisely with the visuals and audio on screen; the so-called 4D cinema one finds today at museums and amusement parks that adds to the mix spritzes of scent or water; and the "Soarin'" rides of the Disney parks, which add to the previously described illusions by raising viewers off of the ground so that their feet dangle above the screen. This last aeroscopic ride even includes a warning sign at the entrance to the effect that those who have a fear of heights or are prone to motion sickness should not ride.

As discussed in chapter 2, many historical *plans-reliefs* remain on display and continue to communicate civic and historical knowledge to local citizens. World's fairs also continue to include model cities, and in a reconstructive mode. Expo Milano 2015, the most recent world's fair at the time of writing, included a model of Chicago as the city was in the "first half of the twentieth century" (Figure 60). Meanwhile in (actual) Chicago, the Architecture Foundation has on permanent display their Model of Chicago, a complete replica of The Loop that they promise to keep up to date with the city's changing skyline using 3D printing. Although presenting Chicago today, the model is likewise concerned with time and temporality, and provides an abbreviated, fifteen-minute approximation of the path of the sun on the summer solstice, making monuments cast long shadows across the miniature city.

The lighting selected for the model has the effect of further miniaturizing certain sections of the city, adding a tilt-shift effect. Tilt-shift photography, which adds the impression of miniaturization to photographs via the application of an out-of-focus blur, has boomed over the course of the writing of this work. Much of the inspiration for this technique comes from the work of Olivo Barbieri, the Italian photographer whose tilt-shift photographs of major American and European cities made models of them all— exaggerating their artifice, recasting them as though in plastic.[15] I am fortunate to include one of his photographs on this book's cover.

Model cities today continue to be made. But such models have lost their flight referent, and indeed they are made without the knowledge that there is a long-established medium of model cities, the panstereorama. Nevertheless,

FIGURE 60.   "Chicago, port area, first half of the twentieth century," Expo
Milano 2015, author's photograph.

they incidentally trade in certain of the same appeals as aeroscopics: they are
customarily crafted to be devoid of people, in line with the implied altitude of
the original models; and they are slow media, reflecting upon the history and
change of the given city, and decelerating the movement within the city. They
provide not the "annihilation of space and time," as was proverbially said
regarding the railway, but rather the preservation of space and time.[16]

Ferris wheels, those throwbacks to the era of observation rides, continue
to be made and included in carnivals and fairs, or made more monumental,
as in the case of the London Eye. These are the slow-moving exceptions;
seldom are these aerial viewing machines produced. The entire genre of the
observation ride has been forgotten, and only its greatest hit, the Ferris
wheel, is reproduced. Thrill rides, especially rollercoasters, are the dominant
form, and they receive most attention in the literature. When observation
rides are produced, once again there is seldom a generic memory of the
form; each time, ride engineers must reinvent the wheel. For instance, the
proposed "Skyspire" ride that the amusement company US Thrill Rides
has been promising in Philadelphia and San Diego, resembles an Aeroscope:
it includes a helix rotation, a height of two hundred feet or more, and

gondolas for small groups of people. The ride is currently unproduced; however, its makers hope to one day lead the "observation market"—a market that does not yet exist.[17]

These are by no means the extent of aeroscopics today. Nor has this book included all of those aeroscopic devices in the long nineteenth century— another volume might have dug into carnival "mug joint" photography, early panoramic photography, Great Globes, moving panorama backdrops in film, stereoscopic views, and many other technologies.[18] I leave such investigations into the breadth of the aeroscopics phenomenon to others. Aeroscopics are an abundant form of media, then and now, and it would be easy to generalize regarding the acceleration of our thrills when surveying their changes. Publics no longer have the patience for these slow machines of the aerial, one might speculate, mirroring arguments about new media and its speed that have been made for decades if not centuries. When looking at the aeroscopic in the long nineteenth century, however, it is evident that the slow, observational media of the panorama and the model city exist alongside the speed of the thrill ride. Nevertheless, there are meaningful historical shifts in aeroscopics, as group viewing and freedom of movement declined, and a change from an observational viewing to an intoxicated one transpired.

MECHANICAL SUBJECTIVITY

Aeroscopics technologically mediate the aerial view. Accordingly, they simulate the view from above according to the intrinsic properties of the given medium. They are medium specific. The urban panorama painting, requiring unimpeded views of 360 degrees, retreats to some of the few civic locations that can provide it: the observatory, the cathedral top. The model city plays upon the aerial effect of all miniaturization (e.g., a mere dollhouse turns a child into an airplane). Film adds the sense of movement through time that is its signature. And the observation ride, motor-driven, comes as close to flight as possible without flying: a leashed bird. They all do so with the aim of providing a group viewing experience.

Henri Giffard's captive balloon at the Exposition Universelle in Paris (1878) had a basket that carried 40 people. Grimon-Sanson's Cinéorama held 200. A panorama painting can have dozens of viewers, and the same number could circle a panstereorama. The Aeroscope held 120. By contrast, the new panoramas of the art world are much diminished in scale; a typical Ferris wheel holds only a couple per car; and VR presently serves only a handful of people at a time, and customarily only one. In the balloon era, these simulated group travel experiences, these "immersive views," as film historian Alison Griffiths called them, turned flight into a mass activity, not merely the province of small groups of balloonists. Inversely, now that flight actually *is* a mass activity, and the largest commercial aircrafts (the Boeings, the Airbuses) regularly seat 400–500 people, aeroscopics today offer more individual experiences.

The relationship of aeroscopics to travel and cartography was and remains pronounced. A visitor to Paris in 1803, having climbed Notre Dame, could claim that he had already "seen four panoramas of" the city—anticipatory mapping.[19] The aeroscopic is not the "view from nowhere," to borrow the phrase for the contested journalistic ethic; it is the *view from somewhere*, and somewhere specific: on top of the Friedrichswerder Church; riding the Wuppertaler Schwebebahn; 265 feet above San Francisco. When travel is constricted or rare, aeroscopics serve as a breed of immersive cartography. When travel is abundant and cheap, aeroscopics become niche—a part of contemporary art, a museum piece, an amusement park speculator's dream. Nevertheless, aeroscopics recur.

Aeroscopics offered freedom of movement, conceptual and physical, at a time when air travel was not able to do so. With this virtual travel, aeroscopics provided spatial and urban knowledge. But this knowledge arrived with a vertiginous frisson of intoxication. Reading the 1907 collection of aeronautic poetry, *A Short History of Balloons and Flying Machines*, quoted periodically in this book, one is struck above all that the bird's-eye view is the sight of freedom—stripped of worldly sounds, warping earthly sights, making the viewer giddy.

Jonathan Crary once argued for a model of human vision that transitioned from the objectivity of the portable camera obscura to the subjectivity of the stereoscope. The slow, careful movement of the viewer in a model city, for instance, gives way to the viewer who is more "fond of sensation."[20] While there is, of course, a vacillation within aeroscopic devices between those that center the viewer (the panorama, the plan-relief) and those that decenter (the film simulation, the observation ride) they all point toward the ludic. The panorama spectacularizes the astronomical observatory; the model city makes the balloon view into a game board; film simulations free the body from the confines of its seat; observation rides toy with the scale below.

Consider, as symbol of this playfulness, the predominant *shape* of the given apparatus; a useful cartographic measure that film scholar Teresa Castro has afforded us when discussing maps.[21] The panorama is circular, domed; the visitor is nominally in the center, but rotates to attempt to take in the whole. The panstereorama is rectangular, tabular, but ironically arrives without parallels, meridians, or any other accoutrements. The moving image simulation borrows the repetitive loop of the projected film stock. And the observation ride gives a spiral formation. These are all under the sign of *ilinx*; these shapes are emblems of intoxication. ·

The intoxication of aeroscopics definitionally "excites the mind," and does so "beyond the bounds of sobriety."[22] Intoxicants, especially psychedelics, have of course led humans on investigations into their own minds, on "trips" from which they nominally return with new insights. Aeroscopics intoxicate. The information that is gained in such a state—a singular state of special attention and openness to the aerial view—is a form of intoxicated knowledge. Not mechanical objectivity, but mechanical *subjectivity*.

. . .

In cartography, we are popularly under the sign of the automobile; road maps have been ubiquitous and inexpensive for almost one hundred years, from the gas companies of the early automobile to the Google Maps of today. The default use of maps in motordom is orientation. One must make an effort to think beyond wayfinding.[23] In the aerial, we are popularly under the sign of the bomber; perils from above have been chief in mind since the First World War, with 9/11 and the drone providing more recent motivations for such an understanding. One must make an effort to think beyond the hawk. Yet we must think beyond these signs to fill up the constellation of aerial viewing and cartographic spectacles with its more distant signals. This book has been an attempt to do so.

Aeroscopics carry within them an alternate telos from that which the drone, the end-goal of current aviation history, would suggest. Here is a history of aerial viewing that rejected or ignored warfare, that made a different promise, that slowed the pace of the thrill to allow for observation, that grabbed a map and twisted it into a vertiginous spiral. Instructive missives for the present, dropped from past balloons.

FIGURE 61.   "Leaflets Thrown from a Balloon," Gertrude Bacon, *The Record of an Aeronaut: Being the Life of John M. Bacon* (London: John Long, 1907), 339.

Notes

INTRODUCTION: SPOTTING THE SPOT

1. On cartography and wayfinding, see James R. Akerman, "Finding Our Way," in *Maps: Finding Our Place in the World* (Chicago: Chicago University Press, 2007), 19–63.

2. *Ballooning and Aeronautics* (London, 1907), 132.

3. Militaries widely used, for instance, stereoscopic viewers to better register relief and magnifying lenses to better register detail.

4. As an attempt at resurrecting overlooked theories of the aerial, certain abiding present-day accounts are purposefully neglected in these principles. The effects of *miniaturization* (a perennial observation regarding aerial views) and *ethical distance* (the reigning aerial principle of our time) are treated elsewhere in this book (in chapters 2 and 4, respectively).

5. Repurposing Steven Shapin and Simon Schaffer's "literary technology," from *Leviathan and the Air Pump: Hobbes, Boyle, and the Experimental Life* (Princeton, NJ: Princeton University Press, 1985), 25.

6. Christian Jacob, *The Sovereign Map: Theoretical Approaches in Cartography throughout History*, trans. Tom Conley (Chicago: University of Chicago Press, 2006), xiv.

7. Monck Mason, letter to *The Times* concerning "an ascent from Vauxhall," October 18, 1836, quoted in Hatton Turnor, ed., *Astra Castra: Experiments and Adventures in the Atmosphere* (London: Chapman and Hall, 1865), 138. "Like a baseless fabric of a vision" is a minor alteration of a line from *The Tempest*.

8. Michel de Certeau, "Walking in the City," in *The Practice of Everyday Life*, trans. Steven Rendall (Berkeley: University of California Press, 1984); Paul Virilio, *War and Cinema: The Logistics of Perception*, trans. Patrick Camiller (London: Verso, 1984); Roland Barthes, "The Eiffel Tower," in *The Eiffel Tower and Other Mythologies*, trans. Richard Howard (Berkeley: University of California Press, 1997 [1979]), 3–17; T.J. Clark, "The View from Notre Dame," in *The Painting of Modern Life: Paris in the Art of Manet and his Followers* (Princeton, NJ: Princeton University Press, 1999).

9. For two of the few who have discussed this plasticity, see Martyn Barber and Helen Wickstead, "'One Immense Black Spot': Aerial Views of London 1784–1918," *The London Journal* 35, no. 3 (2010), 237–38.

10. "A Balloon," in John Douglas-Scott-Montagu's *A Short History of Balloons and Flying Machines* (London: The Car Illustrated, 1907): 108, 110.

11. Le Corbusier, *Aircraft* (London, The Studio, 1935), 8.

12. The phenomenon parallels neatly, and not coincidentally, the acceleration of movement perceived through a microscope, when the heretofore static is suddenly filled with active life once we can examine it closely. "The erratic and frenetic motion constituted a perception that did not correspond to the given temporal relations either, as the movements appeared with a speed that they did not actually possess." Janina Wellmann, "Science and Cinema," *Science in Context* 24, no. 3 (2011), 314.

13. Thomas Guthrie, *The Parables Read in the Light of the Present Day* (New York: Robert Carter and Brothers, 1866), 170.

14. There is some record of this phenomenon from early train travelers, as in Wolfgang Schivelbusch's *The Railway Journey: The Industrialization and Perception of Time and Space* (Berkeley: University of California Press, 1987). I would speculate that by the time flight became widely available, riders had become so acclimatized to the feeling that it seemed scarcely worth mentioning.

15. See for instance Sarah Sharma, *In the Meantime: Temporality and Cultural Politics* (Durham, NC: Duke University Press, 2014); Eivind Røssaak, ed., *Between Stillness and Motion: Film, Photography, Algorithms* (Chicago: University of Chicago Press, 2011).

16. Anne Friedberg, *Window Shopping: Cinema and the Postmodern* (Berkeley: University of California Press, 1993).

17. To this day, many commercial balloon rides end with champagne. The supposed symmetry between balloon and alcohol intoxications provides a media-historical example of sponsorship that may help to explain some unusual present-day sponsorships, such as the caffeinated beverage Red Bull's support for a space free fall jump in 2012.

18. Thomas Hood, "Ode to Mr. Graham, the Aeronaut," *The Works of Thomas Hood: Comic and Serious, in Prose and Verse* (London: Edward Moxon, 1862), 149.

19. "*Vertige morale*" would better be translated as "moral vertigo," but here I defer to the period translation. Henri Lavedan, "Le vertige," *Petites fêtes* (Paris: Calmann Lévy, 1896): 177–92; English translation in *Ainslee's: A Magazine of Clever Fiction* 10, no. 5 (December 1902): 134.

20. Petran Kockelkoren, *Technology: Art, Fairground, and Theatre* (Rotterdam: NAi, 2003), 8.

21. Stephan Oettermann, *The Panorama: History of a Mass Medium*, trans. Deborah Lucas Schneider (New York: Zone, 1997).

22. In particular, it has been suggested that the various routes that make up the cross-country road map of the United States had to be imagined together by many local cartographers, piecemeal. See James R. Akerman, "Twentieth-Century

American Road Maps and the Making of a National Motorized Space," *Cartographies of Travel and Navigation* (Chicago: University of Chicago Press, 2006): 151–206.

23. Lewis Mumford places this date earlier, suggesting that "the social effects" of the airplane and automobile "did not begin to show themselves on any broad scale until around 1910." *Technics and Civilization* (Chicago: University of Chicago Press, 2010 [1934]), 236.

24. It is admittedly a long, slow decline, by most estimates petering out in the 1960s (and of course continuing, at a fraction of their historical prestige, today).

25. This is the period that Paul Virilio, the French theorist who has in large part determined the scholarly shorthand for thought on the aerial view, focuses on. Virilio's argument is treated in more detail in chapter 4. *War and Cinema: The Logistics of Perception*, trans. Patrick Camiller (London: Verso, 1984).

26. Tom Gunning, "Film History and Film Analysis: The Individual Film in the Course of Time," *Wide Angle* 12, no. 3 (July 1990), 5.

27. Donald Crafton, "The Veiled Genealogies of Animation and Cinema," *Animation: An Interdisciplinary Journal* 6, no. 2 (2011), 93–110.

28. Friedrich Kittler is usually credited as prompting the turn toward hardware in media theory. In English, see his *Gramophone, Film, Typewriter* (Stanford, CA: Stanford University Press, 1999 [1986]). On media metaphors, see for instance Stefan Andriopoulos's "Kant's Magic Lantern: Historical Epistemology and Media Archaeology," *Representations* 115, no. 1 (Summer 2011): 42–70; or Erkki Huhtamo, "Imagination in Motion: The Discursive Panorama," in *Illusions in Motion: Media Archaeology of the Moving Panorama and Related Spectacles* (Cambridge, MA: MIT Press, 2013).

29. Erkki Huhtamo, "Dismantling the Fairy Engine: Media Archaeology as Topos Study," *Media Archaeology: Approaches, Applications and Implications*, ed. Erkki Huhtamo and Jussi Parikka (Berkeley: University of California Press, 2011), 27–47.

30. At any rate, it has altered the discussion of film history, as demonstrated in Thomas Elsaesser's *Film History as Media Archaeology: Tracking Digital Cinema* (Amsterdam: Amsterdam University Press, 2016).

31. "Afterword," Erkki Huhtamo and Jussi Parikka, eds., *Media Archaeology* (Berkeley: University of California Press, 2011), 330.

32. *Oxford English Dictionary*, s.v. "bird's-eye view," oed.com. Walpole did not like balloons. See Richard Holmes, *The Age of Wonder* (Pantheon: New York, 2008), 135.

33. Oettermann, 37–38.

34. See, for instance, the film scholar Scott Curtis's call for film historians to take seriously the history of science, and the historian of medicine Jesse Olszynko-Gryn's reciprocal call. Curtis, "Science Lessons," *Film History* 25 (2013): 45–54; Olszynko-Gryn, "Film Lessons: Early Cinema for Historians of Science," *British Journal for the History of Science* 49 (2016): 279–86.

35. On "useful cinema," see Charles Acland and Haidee Wasson, eds., *Useful Cinema* (Durham, NC: Duke University Press, 2011). Kirsten Ostherr's

work on cinema and medicine takes on board many of Acland and Wasson's insights for the analysis of nontheatrical film in *Medical Visions: Producing the Patient through Film, Television, and Imaging* (Oxford: Oxford University Press, 2013).

36. See for instance Nick Hopwood's *Haeckel's Embryos: Images, Evolution, and Fraud* (Chicago: Chicago University Press, 2015).

37. Jimena Canales prompted this discussion in "Photogenic Venus: The 'Cinematographic Turn' and Its Alternatives in Nineteenth-Century France," *Isis* 93, no. 4 (2002): 585–613. It was continued in the special issue of *Science in Context*, "Cinematography, Seriality, and the Sciences," edited by Janina Wellmann, 24, no. 3 (2011).

38. What made this connection plain was the 2012 exhibit "Panoramas—Measured Worlds" (*"Vermessene Welten"*) at the Kunstmuseum Basel, which included panoramic landscape cartography alongside spectacular panoramas. Sadly, no catalog of the exhibit was produced. In any case, by the time of the origin of the panorama painting, it was routine for explorers to bring an artist to sketch the shoreline as a kind of panoramic map. See, for abundant examples of this form of cartography, the multivolume *Comprehensive Atlas of the Dutch United East India Company* (*Grote Atlas van de Verenigde Oost-Indische Compagnie*, Atlas Maior, 2006–present).

39. A bibliography for the *plan-relief* is provided in chapter 2; a lucid English summary may be found in David Buisseret's "Modeling Cities in Early Modern Europe," in *Envisioning the City: Six Studies in Urban Cartography*, ed. David Buisseret (Chicago: University of Chicago Press, 1998), 125–43.

40. See John W. Reps, *Bird's Eye Views: Historic Lithographs of North American Cities* (New York: Princeton Architectural Press, 1998). The Library of Congress' "Panoramic Maps" collection includes some fifteen hundred lithographs of this type.

41. On the possibility of maps as spectacle (not simply an art form, which has long been recognized), see Tom Conley, *Cartographic Cinema* (Minneapolis: Minnesota University Press, 2006); or Brooke Belisle, "Nature at a Glance: Immersive Maps from Panoramic to Digital," *Early Popular Visual Culture* 13, no. 4 (2016): 313–35.

1. THE PANORAMIC ALTITUDE

1. Percival Spencer, "Photography from Balloons," *Ballooning and Aeronautics* (1907), 84. Spencer wrote widely on ballooning and the view from this device. See also his "Ballooning," *Flying* (March 1902), 63–65 and "London from Aloft," *The Strand Magazine* (1891), 492–98.

2. Spencer's consideration of photography and flight was early, but hardly the first. Beyond the French balloonist Nadar's well-known accounts, see, for instance, John M. Bacon's "A Kodak in the Clouds" (*Cassell's Magazine*, June 1899); this was considered by Alan George Fielding in an essay of the same name in *History of Photography* 14, no. 3 (1990): 217–30.

3. Percival Spencer, "Photography from Balloons," *Ballooning and Aeronautics* (1907), 84.

4. Ibid.

5. Personal conversation. For examples of his photography, see Cris Benton, *Saltscapes: The Kite Aerial Photography of Cris Benton* (Berkeley, CA: Heydey, 2013).

6. H.G. Wells, *The War in the Air* (London: Penguin, 2005 [1908]), 64.

7. Ibid., 142.

8. For Siegfried Kracauer, the aerial includes the distance of a viewer to a showgirl routine; for Paul Virilio, Nadar's balloon photographs of Paris are on a par with satellite views of the same. Scholars today repeat this accordion logic, in which an iterative, expansive set of scales is reduced to only one. Rare is the scholar who attends to these differences; Edward Dimendberg and Paula Amad are two of the few. Edward Dimendberg, *Film Noir and the Spaces of Modernity* (Cambridge, MA: Harvard University Press, 2004); Paula Amad, "From God's-Eye to Camera-Eye: Aerial Photography's Post-humanist and Neo-humanist Visions of the World," *History of Photography* 36, no. 1 (February 2012): 66–86.

9. Mary Ann Doane, "The Close-Up: Scale and Detail in the Cinema," *differences: A Journal of Feminist Cultural Studies* 14, no. 3 (2003), 90; see also Noa Steimatski, "Of the Face: In Reticence," *A Museum without Walls: Film, Art, New Media*, ed. Angela Dalle Vacche (New York: Palgrave Macmillan, 2012).

10. This is not to say simply that the screening table in the camera obscura was merely circular, but that they were often (and sometimes still) made concave to better receive the projected image. "A greater sharpness of outline is also obtained by having the receiving surface hollowed out to the same curve as the lens; thus, the table at the Crystal Palace camera obscura is made of plaster of Paris, hollowed out to a concave form, the curvature being similar to the convexity of the lens." H.C. Standage, "The Camera Obscura: Its Uses, Action, and Construction," in *Amateur Work Illustrated* (London: Ward, Lock, 1881), 67.

11. "Space of knowledge" is from David Aubin, Charlotte Bigg, and H. Otto Sibum, "Introduction: Observatory Techniques in Nineteenth-Century Science and Society," *The Heavens on Earth: Observatories and Astronomy in Nineteenth-Century* (Durham, NC: Duke University Press, 2010), 7.

12. Roland Barthes, "The Eiffel Tower," *The Eiffel Tower and Other Mythologies*, trans. Richard Howard (New York: Hill and Wang, 1979), 10. In fact, he then answered the question simply, if inadequately: "An image we attempt to decipher, in which we try to recognize known sites, to identify landmarks."

13. Panoramas continue to be made sporadically to this day, by contemporary artists such as Yadegar Asisi, whose panoramas have shown across Germany, and Sara Velas at the Velaslavasay Panorama in Los Angeles. North Korea also has a panorama culture today, via a circuitous route from Russia. For a recent account of this, see Amy Qin, "An Art Powerhouse from North Korea," *New York Times*, January 25, 2016, C1.

14. I leave aside a third contemporary understanding of the panoramic, one inspired by Wolfgang Schivelbusch's account in *The Railway Journey: The*

Industrialization of Time and Space in the 19th Century (Berkeley: University of California Press, 1987). His "panoramic vision" or "panoramic perception" refers to the new view from the train window, a view that offers a synoptic glimpse of the landscape beyond, which is simultaneously removed from the viewer's actual experience and reified. Schivelbusch's account accurately grasps the perceptual effects of the railway, and his panoramic media metaphor is warranted and inspired by period reference; however, he clearly means to refer to the *moving* panorama, a medium with an almost completely different history, cultural standing, and operation from the immense circular panoramas discussed here.

15. Ralph sadly passed away during the writing of this book. I am grateful to have had his guidance. The anecdote above was relayed in person, at his home, when he generously shared from his personal archive on model cities. The obituary written by Erkki Huhtamo in *The Guardian* (July 14, 2015) does justice to Ralph's remarkable career.

16. The panorama effect can also upset one's equilibrium, according to Alison Griffiths, who in her *Shivers Down Your Spine: Cinema, Museums, and the Immersive View* (New York: Columbia University Press, 2008) notes the story of visitors to a maritime panorama who experience seasickness (57).

17. Vanessa Schwartz, *Spectacular Realities: Early Mass Culture in Fin-de-Siècle Paris* (Berkeley: University of California Press, 1999), 151.

18. Dolph Sternberger, *Panorama of the Nineteenth Century* (New York: Urizen, 1977), 8.

19. Jonathan Crary, "Géricault, the Panorama, and Sites of Reality in the Early Nineteenth Century." *Grey Room* 9 (Fall 2002), 21.

20. Stephan Oettermann, *The Panorama: History of a Mass Medium*, trans. Deborah Lucas Schneider (New York: Zone, 1997), 7; Crary, "Géricault, the Panorama, Sites of Reality," 18.

21. Michel Foucault, *Discipline and Punish: The Birth of the Prison* (New York: Vintage, 1995 [1975]), 317n4.

22. William Uricchio untangles the nominal equivalence of the panorama and the panopticon in "A 'Proper Point of View': The Panorama and Some of Its Early Media Iterations," *Early Popular Visual Culture* 9, no. 3 (2011): 225–38.

23. Bruno Latour, *Reassembling the Social: An Introduction to Actor-Network-Theory* (Oxford: Oxford University Press, 2005), 197.

24. Above all: Alison Griffiths' *Shivers Down Your Spine*.

25. Oettermann, *The Panorama*, 40.

26. Ibid., 18.

27. Alison Griffiths has productively noted the similarly sublime interior space of the panorama rotunda and the cathedral. See *Shivers Down Your Spine*, 60.

28. A clarification concerning the italicization of panorama painting titles. A number of the surviving panorama paintings that have long-standing displays are known colloquially and in the literature not by the original title of the painting but by other key features. For instance, the *Panorama of Scheveningen* is typically referred to as the Panorama Mesdag, for its artist Hendrik Willem

Mesdag and the museum of that name in The Hague. I have deferred to the existing naming norms of panoramas in this text; as a result, there is some variability in italicization.

29. On *Wimmelbilds* and their relation to certain kinds of contemporary children's puzzle books, which encourage the same kind of playful detail finding, see Cornelia Rémi, "Wimmelbuchs," in *The Routledge Companion to Picture Books*, ed. Bettina Kümmerling-Meibauer (London: Routledge, 2018): 158–68.

30. Bernard Comment's well-illustrated, non-scholarly book on panoramas emphasizes this, the dual "from near/from far away" pleasure of the panorama. *The Panorama* (London: Reaktion, 1999).

31. Oettermann, *The Panorama*, 21.

32. See Ralph Hyde's catalog of the Barbican exhibit, *Panoramania: The Art and Entertainment of the 'All-Embracing' View* (London: Trefoil, 1988), and Schwartz, *Spectacular Realities*, 177. See also Andy Newman, "A Panorama of the Use of the Suffix '-Rama'," unpublished paper, 20th International Panorama Conference.

33. "Exposition Sideshows," *New York Times*, September 9, 1900.

34. Charlotte Bigg, "The Panorama, or La Nature A Coup d'Œil," in Erna Fiorentini, ed., *Observing Nature—Representing Experience: The Osmotic Dynamics of Romanticism, 1800–1850* (Berlin: Dietrich Reimer, 2007), 95.

35. Samuel Johnson, *Johnson on Shakespeare* (London: Harry Frowde, 1908), 158.

36. David Aubin provides an excellent overview of this period in "A History of Observatory Sciences and Techniques," in *Astronomy at the Frontiers of Science*, ed. Jean-Pierre Lasota (Dordrecht: Springer, 2011), 109–21.

37. David Aubin, Charlotte Bigg, and H. Otto Sibum, "Introduction: Observatory Techniques in Nineteenth-Century Science and Society," in *The Heavens on Earth: Observatories and Astronomy in Nineteenth-Century* (Durham, NC: Duke University Press, 2010), 2.

38. Ibid., 22.

39. Aubin, "A History of Observatory Sciences," 112.

40. Ibid.

41. Ibid., 114–15.

42. My use of this term, *observation*, will likely cause some readers to recall Jonathan Crary's *Techniques of the Observer*, a volume that has done so much for the history of "pre-cinematic" technologies, specifically the portable camera obscura and the stereoscope. There, Crary provides a now well-known account of the construction of the "observer"—that rule-bound, realist, normative viewer of the seventeenth and eighteenth centuries, whose paradigmatic optical device is the camera obscura. Crary uses *observation* by and large as a Foucauldian condemnation, tying it to a deceptive concept of objectivity. I have no quarrel with Crary's account—on the contrary, I owe his historical work a debt and return to it in the conclusion—however, since the publication of his book, historians have subsequently detailed the historical construction of concepts such as "observation" and "objectivity," and I follow their lead. Jonathan

Crary, *Techniques of the Observer: On Vision and Modernity in the Nineteenth Century* (Cambridge, MA: MIT Press, 1990).

43. Aubin et al., "Observatory Techniques," 2.

44. Ibid., 6.

45. Ibid., 20.

46. For further bibliography on the transits of Venus see Jimena Canales, "Photogenic Venus: The 'Cinematographic Turn' and Its Alternatives in Nineteenth-Century France," *Isis* 93, no. 4 (2002): 586n1.

47. Ludwik Fleck, quoted in Aubin et al., "Observatory Techniques," 6.

48. Lorraine Daston, "Aperspectival Objectivity: Objectivity and the Escape from Perspective," *Social Studies of Science* 22 (1992): 599. The article is premised upon her book with Peter Galison, *Objectivity* (Cambridge, MA: Zone, 2010), which historicizes objectivity as a scientific value.

49. Simon Schaffer, "Astronomers Mark Time: Discipline and the Personal Equation," *Science in Context* 2, no. 1 (Spring 1988): 115–45.

50. So Daston titles the essay: "Aperspectival Objectivity: Objectivity and the Escape from Perspective."

51. Daston subsequently contrasted the piecemeal approach of aperspectival objectivity with the coup d'oeil, the singular glance that can take in an entire system intuitively. The panorama painting was, as she rightly notes, advertised using this term at the time; but as I propose in this chapter, this facet of the panorama does not take into account panoramic practice and use. Indeed, coup d'oeil vision has more in line with a medium like the panstereorama, characterized in the next chapter. See Lorraine Daston, "The Coup d'Oeil: On a Mode of Understanding," *Critical Inquiry* 45 (Winter 2019): 307–31.

52. The French historian of science Charlotte Bigg has usefully tied observation (unconnected from the observatory) as a practice important to the emergence of the panorama, claiming that the "growing emphasis placed on observation is clearly part of the transformation of investigative practices in the eighteenth century." Bigg, "The Panorama," 76, 86.

53. As well as, in a similar vein, the reproduction of Louis Lumière's *Photorama* of 1900 in Lyon.

54. Albert Smith, "Albert Smith's First Ascent," in *Astra Castra: Experiments and Adventures in the Atmosphere*, ed. Hatton Turnor (London: Chapman and Hall, 1865), 212.

55. Lorraine Daston, Elizabeth Lunbec, eds., *Histories of Scientific Observation* (Chicago: University of Chicago Press, 2011), epigraph for part four, table of contents.

56. Robert Burford, "A View of the City of New York" (London: T. Brettell, 1834), n.p.

57. Robert Barker and Robert Burford, "Description of the View of Venice" (London: Adler, 1819), 3.

58. Ibid., 4.

59. Ibid., 4. The view from St. Mark's Campanile, although very fine, would likely have been too constrained by its narrow windows to produce the

desired frameless view. Besides, the tower is a key monument to have *within* the view.

60. Ralph Hyde, "Thomas Hornor: Pictural Land Surveyor," *Imago Mundi* 29 (1977), 29.

61. Thomas Hornor, "Prospectus. View of London" (London: Hornor, 1823), 23.

62. Robert Barker, "La Nature à Coup d'Œil," Patent, June 19, 1787.

63. Hyde, "Thomas Hornor," 28.

64. Hornor, "Prospectus," 13.

65. *The Mirror of Literature, Amusement, and Instruction* 8 (1829), 35.

66. James Elmes, *Metropolitan Improvements; or, London in the Nineteenth Century* (London: Jones, 1828), 78.

67. Gerard L'E Turner, *Nineteenth-Century Scientific Instruments* (London: Sotheby; Berkeley: University of California Press, 1983).

68. Scottish physician Neil Arnott, for instance, recommended glass instruments for production as well as exhibition. *Elements of Physics, or Natural Philosophy, General and Medical* (Philadelphia: Blanchard and Lea, 1853), 376.

69. "Notes on Current Events," *The British Architect*, June 3, 1881, 278.

70. *Description of a View of the North Coast of Spitzbergen* (London, Adler, 1819), 8.

71. Oettermann, *The Panorama*, 297.

72. "Panoramas," *Chambers's Journal*, January 21, 1861, 35.

73. *Description of a View of the City of Edinburgh, and Surrounding Country* (London: J. and C. Adlard, 1825), 5. Reprinted in Laurie Garrison, Anne Anderson, Sibylle Erle, Verity Hunter, Phoebe Putnam, and Peter West, eds., *Panoramas 1787–1900: Texts and Contexts, Volume 1* (London: Routledge, 2012).

74. Robert Barker, "La Nature à Coup d'Œil," Patent, June 19, 1787.

75. Oettermann, *The Panorama*, 100.

76. *Oxford English Dictionary*, s.v. "observation," oed.com.

77. Henry Aston Barker, *View of the City of St. Petersburg* (1818).

78. Robert Burford, *Description of a View of the City of Lima* (London: T. Brettell, 1836).

79. For the camera obscura in art, see Philip Steadman, *Vermeer's Camera* (Oxford: Oxford University Press, 2001); for its use in the observatory sciences, see Wolfgang Lefèvre, ed., *Inside the Camera Obscura: Optics and Art under the Spell of the Projected Image* (Berlin: Max Planck Institute for the History of Science, 2007).

80. These small, portable camera obscuras are also the focus of Jonathan Crary's *Techniques of the Observer*. See note 42.

81. John H. Hammond, *The Camera Obscura, A Chronicle* (Boca Raton, FL: CRC Press; 1981),161.

82. The one onsite today opened in the 1990s, but camera obscuras have been present at the Greenwich Observatory since the late seventeenth century.

83. Alison Reiko Loader, "A Rational and Entertaining Species of Amusement to Bipeds of All Ages: The Splendid Camera Obscura," in *Corporeality in Early*

Cinema: Viscera, Skin, and Physical Form, ed. Marina Dahlquist et al. (Bloomington: Indiana University Press, 2018): 289–300.

84. This was said in reference to the camera obscura in Dumfries, which I treat elsewhere in this section. Henry Thomas Cockburn, *Circuit Journeys* (Edinburgh: David Douglas, 1888), 57.

85. The Edinburgh camera obscura has likely the largest published history of any, due to its fascinating use beginning in the 1890s by the town planner Patrick Geddes. See for instance Pierre Chabard, "Towers and Globes: Architectural and Epistemological Differences between Patrick Geddes' Outlook Towers and Paul Otlet's Mundaneums," in *European Modernism and the Information Society: Informing the Present*, ed, W. Boyd Rayward (London: Routledge, 2016): 105–25.

86. This camera obscura is in the Dumfries Museum. The museum does not have a record of how high the tower is, so this cautious estimate is made with the assistance of their Museums Officer and Ordnance Survey maps.

87. As well as a contemporary land art camera obscura in Durham: Chris Drury's "Cloud Chamber" (2003) at the North Carolina Museum of Art.

88. Neil Harris defined this useful concept, in which the mechanism of creation (the *how* of the spectacle) is as much of a draw as the spectacle itself. *Humbug: The Art of P. T. Barnum* (Chicago: University of Chicago Press, 1981).

89. For a discussion of object lessons and optical toys, see Patrick Ellis and Colin Williamson, "Object Lessons, Old and New: Experimental Media Archaeology in the Classroom," *Early Popular Visual Culture* 18, no. 1 (2020).

90. Robert Hunt, *A Manual of Photography* (London: R. Griffin, 1857), 40–42.

91. Quoted in Mary Coward, *Clifton Observatory* (Bristol: J Publishing, n.d.), 35.

92. Cook was describing the view from the camera obscura in Portmeirion, Wales. Olive Cook, *Movement in Two Dimensions: A Study of the Animated and Projected Pictures Which Preceded the Invention of Cinematography* (London: Hutchinson, 1963), 24.

93. At the Coney Island camera obscura, "our attention is attracted by a middle-aged lady calling the attention of her spouse to a certain point in the picture, and exclaiming, 'while I never!'" *Coney Island and What Is to Be Seen There* (New York: C. J. Macdonald, 1879), 36.

94. *Ward & Lock's (Late Shaw's) Illustrated Guide to, and Popular History of the Land of Burns, Including Ayr, Arran, and Dumfries* (London: Ward, Lock, and Co., 1888), 38.

95. See Arnaud Maillet, *The Claude Glass: Use and Meaning of the Black Mirror in Western Art* (Brooklyn, NY: Zone, 2004).

96. Anna Jameson, *The Diary of an Ennuyée* (Paris: Baudry: 1836), 108.

97. John Christopher Draper, *A Text-book of Medical Physics* (London: J. & A. Churchill, 1885), 461. For another expressly panoramic account of a camera obscura, see *Doidge's Western Counties' Illustrated Annual* (Plymouth, UK: Doidge, 1886), 266.

98. Isaac Chillcott, *Chillcott's Descriptive History of Bristol* (Bristol: Chillcott, 1857), 397.

99. Jan Golinski, "Sublime Astronomy: The Eidouranion of Adam Walker and His Sons," *Huntington Library Quarterly* 80, no. 1 (Spring 2017): 135–57.

100. Griffiths, *Shivers Down Your Spine*, 132.

101. Lisa Parks, *Cultures in Orbit* (Durham, NC: Duke University Press, 2005), 141.

102. Here, I acknowledge the contested use of the term *popular science* in the history of science. Whipple Museum curator Josh Nall has provided a historicized defense of the term vis-à-vis the observatory sciences. Astronomers spoke in the nineteenth century in terms of "popularization." *News from Mars: Transatlantic Mass Media and the Forging of a New Astronomy, 1860–1910* (Pittsburgh: University of Pittsburgh Press, 2019), 13.

103. Ibid., 28.

104. Garrett P. Serviss, "Telescope for the People," *The Herald* (July 21, 1909), 3.

105. Daston and Galison, *Objectivity*, 335.

106. Aubin et al., "Observatory Techniques," 22.

2. THE PANSTEREORAMA

1. On the Maltese model, see Catherine Delano-Smith, "Cartography in the Prehistoric Period in the Old World: Europe, the Middle East, and North Africa," in *The History of Cartography, Volume One*, ed. J. B. Harley and David Woodward (Chicago: Chicago University Press, 1987), 81. Pfyffer's relief of the Alps, built between 1762 and 1786, remains on display at the Glacier Garden Museum in Lucerne; see Andreas Bürgi, *Relief der Urschweiz: Entstehung und Bedeutung des Landschaftsmodells von Franz Ludwig Pfyffer* (Zurich: Neue Zürcher Zeitung, 2007). The Chicago Model, first put on view in 2009, is on permanent display at the Chicago Architecture Foundation and its structures are updated yearly.

2. Nevertheless, the history of cartography has brought such models into its repertoire. See, most recently, Gabriel Granado-Castro and Andrés Martín-Pastor, "An Unsuccessful Spanish Cartographical Project of the Eighteenth Century: New Data on the *Plan-Relief* Ministry of Charles III," *Imago Mundi* 68, no. 2 (2016): 183–95. I am leaving out of this list analogous, quasi-cartographic miniatures such as dollhouses, model train sets, or indeed model villages such as Bekonscot, outside of London.

3. Shannon Mattern, *Deep Mapping the Digital City* (Minneapolis: Minnesota University Press, 2015), 47.

4. Charles F. Partington, *The British Cyclopedia of the Arts and Sciences*, Vol. 2 (London: Orr & Smith, 1835): 116.

5. The latter figure comes from David Buisseret, "Modeling Cities in Early Modern Europe," in *Envisioning the City: Six Studies in Urban Cartography*, ed. David Buisseret (Chicago: University of Chicago Press, 1998), 150.

6. Although specialized cartographic computer programs exist for balloon-ists today, in the long history of aviation cartography balloon maps are curi-ously absent. See Walter W. Ristow, *Aviation Cartography: A Historico-bibliographic Study of Aeronautical Charts* (Washington, DC: Library of Congress Map Division, 1960), 2. For an interesting exception, see Lily Ford, "'For the Sake of the Prospect': Experiencing the World from Above in the Late 18th Century," *The Public Domain Review*, July 20, 2016.

7. Instances of "the whole" vis-à-vis panstereoramas will be shown through-out. For one of many possible ballooning examples, consider Percival Spencer's essay "Photography from Balloons," where "the whole" is a continual refrain. *Ballooning and Aeronautics* (1907), 84.

8. Most accounts of ballooning in this period mention the uncanny quiet of the air, as described in chapter 1. For example: "All sounds from the earth having ceased, we sailed silently along enjoying the wonderful panorama." Alfred E. Moore, "Amateur Ballooning," *The Century Illustrated Monthly Magazine* 32, no.10 (1886), 674.

9. Quatremère de Quincy, "Panstéréorama," in *Encyclopédie méthodique: Architecture, vol. 3* (Paris, 1825), 75.

10. The literature on the panorama painting is surveyed in chapter 1.

11. Most authors that treat the panorama painting discuss the "o-rama craze" in some form. See Vanessa Schwartz, "Representing Reality and the O-rama Craze," *Spectacular Realities: Early Mass Culture in Fin-de-Siècle Paris* (Berkeley: University of California Press, 1999). On the cinéorama, see Jacques Meusy, "L'énigme du Cinéorama," *Archives* 37 (January 1991), 1–16; on the cosmorama, see John Plunkett, "Optical Recreations, Transparencies, and the Invention of the Screen," *Visual Delights Two: Exhibition and Reception*, Vanessa Toulmin and Simon Popple, eds. (Eastleigh, UK: John Libbey, 2005), 187; on the georama, see Jean-Marc Besse, *Face au monde: Atlas, jardins, géo-ramas* (Paris: Desclée de Brouwer, 2003); on the myriorama, see Ralph Hyde, "Myrioramas, Endless Landscapes: The Story of a Craze," *Print Quarterly* 31, no. 4 (December 2004): 403–21.

12. *Saturday Review* 115, April 12, 1913, 450. It is worth noting here that the panstereorama predates and is unrelated to, in terms of technique, the later *stereorama*.

13. Walter Benjamin, "Panorama," in *The Arcades Project*, trans. Howard Eiland and Kevin McLaughlin (Cambridge, MA: Harvard University Press, 2002), 536. See also his account of the abundance of -oramic devices in the nineteenth century: "In our time so rich in pano-, cosmo-, neo-, myrio-, kigo-, and dio-ramas" (527).

14. In one of the only works that has compared the model city (in its mili-tary, *plan-relief* variant) and the panorama, Bruno Weber argues that they share a desire for mastery of the world, one that is "Unabhängig und unberührt von den Imponderabilien der Tages- und Jahreszeiten, von Witterung und Verwitterung" ("independent and unaffected by the imponderables of the day and the seasons, by weather and decay"). Bruno Weber, "Von oben herab:

Gelände in Relief und Panorama als wissenschaftliche und künstlerische Ausdrucksform der Erdoberfläche," in *Europa Miniature: Die kulturelle Bedeutung des Reliefs, 16.–21 Jahrhundert*, ed. Andreas Bürgi (Zurich: Neue Zürcher Zeitung, 2007), 36. Stephan Oettermann briefly compared the panstereorama and the panorama, in his volume on the latter, arguing that they are connected by more "than just name. Both stem from the same desire to reproduce a particular region as precisely as possible, to create an exact duplicate. The panorama uses perspective to achieve this, the panstereorama uses miniaturization. For the average person whose eye was untrained in art, the three-dimensional form of the relief required less sophistication and abstraction." See Stephan Oettermann, *The Panorama: History of a Mass Medium*, trans. Deborah Lucas Schneider (New York: Zone, 1997), 147.

15. There is one exception to this absence of miniature inhabitants, the "panstereomachia," addressed on pages 62–63.

16. Malcolm Baker, "Representing Invention, Viewing Models," in *Models: The Third Dimension of Science*, ed. Soroya de Chadarevian and Nick Hopwood (Stanford, CA: Stanford University Press, 2004): 32. For other uses of civic models, see Richard Dennis, *Cities in Modernity: Representations and Productions of Metropolitan Space, 1840–1930* (Cambridge: Cambridge University Press, 2008).

17. de Chadarevian and Hopwood, *Models*.

18. James A. Secord, "Monsters at the Crystal Palace," in de Chadarevian and Hopwood, eds., *Models*, 138–69.

19. Simon Schaffer, "Fish and Ships: Models in the Age of Reason," in de Chadarevian and Hopwood, eds., *Models*, 86.

20. The brief survey of the *plan-relief* phenomenon here is indebted (beyond visits to the important collections themselves, with their attendant literature) to the following texts. The most substantive treatment of France's collection is found in Antoine De Roux et al., *Les plans en relief des places du roy* (Paris: Adam Biro, 1989), which includes a map of extant *plans en relief* circa 1989 (6). A colloquium held one year after the publication of this landmark book likewise produced a helpful anthology of commentary on individual models: André Corvisier, ed., *Actes du colloque international sur les plans-reliefs au passé et au present* (Paris: Sedes, 1993). In English, Buisseret's "Modeling Cities" is indispensable.

21. Bernard Rouleau, "Les plans reliefs et la cartographie au XVIIe siècle: Palliatif ou object de prestige?" in *Actes du colloque international sur les plans-reliefs au passé et au present*, ed. André Corvisier (Paris: Sedes, 1993): 71–73.

22. De Roux et al., *Les Plans en relief des places du roy*, 18.

23. A date range determined by the literature on *plans-reliefs*, detailed above.

24. de Quincy, "Panstéréorama," 75.

25. David Buisseret writes of the fragility of *plans-reliefs*, many of which were destroyed simply in attempts to transport them. See Buisseret, "Modeling Cities."

26. France's extant *plans-reliefs* also form a bridge between the oldest model city records and present mapping concerns. In 2013, Google digitized a small number of France's collection (Bergen op Zoom, Saint Tropez, Strasbourg, etc.) and adapted this information to function within their Google Earth mapping program. These add-ons are, at the time of writing, still available for download, and they allow the user to explore, instead of a present-day, satellite Strasbourg, the version from that city's Musée historique.

27. *York Chronicle*, August 23, 1773.

28. *An Account of the Model in Relievo of the Great and Magnificent City and Suburbs of Paris* (London: H. Hart, 1771), iii–iv. At least three different editions of this guide survive; I have been able to consult two of them: the earliest, held at Harvard University (1768), and a later version from the British Library (1771). The differences between the two are minimal, except for a note in the Harvard guide disparaging the former owners of the model—"the then Proprietor meeting with some Misfortune, we shall not mention from what Cause" (vii)—and attesting to improvements made since 1760. It may thus be estimated that Le Quoy's model showed in England for some eleven years at minimum. After notices of its sale in 1777, mentions of it appear to cease.

29. Ibid., v.

30. *Public Advertiser*, January 1777.

31. *An Account of the Model in Relievo*, 25.

32. Ibid., 25–26.

33. *York Chronicle*, August 23, 1773. Remarkably, while trading in very similar attractions, Le Quoy's model was exhibited twelve years prior to Barker's original attempt at a panorama painting in 1792, and further precedes the Montgolfiers' original flight over Paris in 1783.

34. *An Account of the Model in Relievo*, 10.

35. *Panstéréorama Ville de Londres* (Paris, 1802).

36. Indeed, the information and presentation are so similar, it would not be surprising if the text of the panstereorama guide was taken from a guidebook. See, for instance, Philippe-Denis Langlois, *Les rues et les environs de Paris* (Paris: Langlois, 1777).

37. The one at the Pavillon de Hanovre is likely the same one described in the *Gazette de France* (June 26, 1810) as near the Porte Maillot.

38. The Musée des Arts Forain in Paris best documents this period of fairground amusement, with many preserved rides. In the 1810s, there were as many as ten such roller coasters operating in Paris; see Jeff Horn, "What Is Old Is New Again," *Historical Reflections/Réflexions Historiques* 44, no. 3 (2018), 1.

39. *The Theatrical Inquisitor, or, Monthly Mirror*, "Account of the Theatres at Paris" (London: E. Hildyard, 1814), 169.

40. Peter Hervé. *How to Enjoy Paris: Being a Complete Guide to the French Metropolis* (London, 1818), 323–24.

41. August von Kotzebue, *Travels from Berlin through Switzerland to Paris in the Year 1804*, vol. 2 (London, 1804), 262. Stephan Oettermann quotes this extract in his section on the panstereorama.

42. *La Vie Parisienne*, May 15, 1875, 275.

43. Stéphanie Félicité, *Voyages poetiques d'Eugène et d'Antonine* (Paris: Maradan, 1818), 189.

44. William Wordsworth, *The Prelude* (London: Edward Moxon, 1850), book seven, 181. The report of a visit to a panorama painting that Wordsworth offers in *The Prelude* is oft and justly quoted in the literature on the subject. Richard Altick's *Shows of London* first contextualized Wordsworth's stanzas on models. See Altick, *The Shows of London: A Panoramic History of Exhibitions, 1600–1862* (London: Belknap, 1978), 116. Altick also offers a survey of some of the later models in London not treated here, including, from 1843, models of Venice and Edinburgh (394).

45. Journalists searched for this model in the 1990s to no avail. Rostislav Nikolayev, "Where Is the Lost Model of St. Petersburg?" *Neva News*, April 15–30, 1992.

46. *Scientific Gazette*, May 18, 1831.

47. *Morning Post*, April 13, 1826, 1.

48. Ibid., 1.

49. "Model of Paris," *Atheneum; or, Spirit of English Magazines* (April–October 1826), 368.

50. "The Model of Paris," *Times of London*, February 24, 1825, 3.

51. Charles Bullock, "An Historical and Descriptive Account of the Battle of Poitiers, Compiled from the Best Authorities; Explanatory of Mr. Charles Bullock's Panstereomachia" (London: James Bullock, 1826), 1.

52. One interesting article relates the panstereomachia instead to popular displays of the medieval past, using Madame Tussaud's as another example. See Barbara Gribling, "The Panstereomachia, Madame Tussaud's and the Heraldic Exhibition: The Art and Science of Displaying the Medieval Past in Nineteenth-Century London," *Science Museum Group Journal* 10 (Autumn 2018).

53. Ibid., 5.

54. *The Theatrical Observer* 1447 (July 26, 1826), 3.

55. On the Great Globe, see Besse, *Face au monde*; on Wyld's model of the Siege of Sebastopol, see Ulrich Keller, *The Ultimate Spectacle: A Visual History of the Crimean War* (New York: Routledge, 2001), 64.

56. Eziekiel Porter Belden, *New-York—As It Is* (New York: John P. Prall, 1849), 7–8.

57. Ibid. 7–8.

58. Belden, *New-York—As It Is*, 9.

59. Outside of the ride named the Aeroscope in chapter 4, this is one of the only uses of the term "aeroscopic" that I have come across in the historical record—it predates the ride by almost seventy years. *American Whig Review* 4, no. 2 (August 1846), 246.

60. Belden, *New-York—As It Is*, 23.

61. Lorraine Daston, "The Coup d'Oeil: On a Mode of Understanding," *Critical Inquiry* 45 (Winter 2019): 307–31.

62. Belden, *New-York—As It Is*, 5

63. Ibid., 20.

64. For instance, Kellog's panstereorama depicting the Great Chicago Fire of 1871, which toured the United States in that decade, was rather some kind of moving panorama with theatrical staging. So, too, were *Hamilton's Excursions and Panstereorama of Current Events*, which showed in London in the 1870s and '80s. By the early 1900s, the panstereorama was in the American context understood as any miniature structure. These, however, are exceptions; on the whole, the panstereorama referred to model cities. See "Kellog's Panstereorama," *Buffalo Evening Courier*, February 17, 1872; or, for *Hamilton's Excursions*, Erkki Huhtamo, *Illusions in Motion: Media Archaeology of the Moving Panorama and Related Spectacles* (Cambridge, MA: MIT Press, 2013). 293–94; . on American diffusion of the concept, see Dr. Judd, "The Old Panorama," *Billboard* (December 3, 1904), 23.

65. *Great Exhibition of the Works of Industry of All Nations, 1851: Official Descriptive and Illustrated Catalog* (London: Royal Commission, 1851), 1229.

66. For recent scholarship on world's fairs, see Alexander Geppert, *Fleeting Cities: Imperial Expositions in Fin-de-Siècle Europe* (London: Palgrave, 2010).

67. There are two other nineteenth-century reconstructive model cities on permanent display in the Wien Museum, picturing Viennas of years past. There are exceptions to this reflective/anticipatory purpose, including perhaps the most well-known twentieth-century model city in this country, showing the boroughs of New York City as they were during that city's 1964 World's Fair. This model is still on exhibit at the Queens Museum of Art, accounting for its familiarity. It is, moreover, named a "Panorama of New York," giving some indication of the lasting similitude between the panoramic and the panstereoramic.

68. Ralph Hyde, "Naples, Rome, London, etc. as Portrayed in Panoramas *Al Fresco*," *L'Europa Moderna: Cartografia urbana e vedutismo*, ed. Cesare de Seta and Daniela Stroffolino (Naples: Electa Napoli 2001), 4. See also Anders Ekström, who connects the alfresco panorama, although not named such, to a longer tradition of "disaster shows." "Exhibiting Disasters: Mediation, Historicity, and Spectatorship," *Media, Culture & Society*, 34, no. 4 (2012): 472–87.

69. There were also pyrotechnic exhibits at amusement parks of this period that had many of the same objectives. See, for instance, John Kasson, *Amusing the Million: Coney Island at the Turn of the Century*. (New York: Hill and Wang, 1978).

70. "San Francisco," *Biograph Bulletin* 68 (May 16, 1906).

71. David S. Hulfish, *The Cyclopedia of Motion Picture Work* (Chicago: American Technical Society, 1914); Lee Royal, *The Romance of Motion Picture Production* (Los Angeles: Royal, 1920).

72. For more on "modeling urban destruction," see Helmut Puff, *Miniature Monuments: Modeling German History* (Berlin: de Gruyter, 2014), which provides case studies of postwar models of ruined German cities.

73. "San Francisco Scale Model Finally Home after 77-Year Absence," *San Francisco Chronicle*, January 14, 2019.

74. William Bryant, "The Re-vision of Planet Earth: Space Flight and Environmentalism in Postmodern America," *American Studies* 36, no. 2 (Fall 1995): 43–63.

75. Friedrich Kittler, "The City Is a Medium," trans. Matthew Griffen, *New Literary History* 27 (1996): 721.

76. James Glaisher, *Travels in the Air* (London: Richard Bentley, 1871), 126.

77. For summary accounts of balloonists' metaphors, see Alison Byerly, *Are We There Yet? Virtual Travel and Victorian Realism* (Ann Arbor: University of Michigan Press, 2012): 59–62; Sonja Dümpelmann, *Flights of Imagination: Aviation, Landscape, Design* (Charlottesville: University of Virginia Press, 2014), 78–79.

3. VERTIGO EFFECTS

1. Dan Auiler, *Vertigo: The Making of a Hitchcock Classic* (New York: St. Martin's, 1998), 66.

2. For example, to take two of many possible instances, *Dizzy Heights and Daring Hearts* (1915) and *Le mystère de la tour Eiffel* (1927).

3. "You'll Go Blind: Does Watching Television Close-Up Really Harm Eyesight?" *Scientific American*, January 27, 2010.

4. William Wordsworth, "Expostulation and Reply," *Lyrical Ballads* (Oxford: Oxford University Press, 2013 [1798]), 117.

5. David A. Gallo, "The Power of a Musical Instrument: Franklin, the Mozarts, Mesmer, and the Glass Armonica," *History of Psychology*, 3, no. 4 (November 2000): 326–43.

6. They had such a combination at the 2018 exhibit *Phantasmagoria!* that was held at the Museum of Fine Arts in Boston and premised upon the Richard Balzer collection.

7. José Ingenieros, *Le langage musical et ses troubles hsytériques* [sic] (Paris: Félix Alcan, 1907).

8. Johannes Maria Verweyen, "Radioitis! Gedanken zum Radiohören," *Werag* 1 (1930): 8, in *Medientheorie 1888–1933: Texte und Kommentare*, ed. Albert Kümmel and Petra Löffler (Frankfurt am Main: Suhrkamp, 2002), 454. I use the translation from Erik Born, "Sparks to Signals: Literature, Science, and Wireless Technology, 1800–1930," PhD diss., University of California at Berkeley, 2016, 48.

9. "TV Blamed for Kids' 'Frogitis' (Frog Knees)," *Variety*, October 7, 1953, 27. See also the related ailment, "TV Bottom," compared in Ted Okuda and Jack Mulqueen, *The Golden Age of Chicago Children's Television* (Carbondale: Southern Illinois University Press, 2016 [2004]), 4.

10. Also called "nintenditis." See Maarten Jalink et al., "Nintendo Related Injuries and Other Problems: Review," *BMJ* 349 (2014), 7267.

11. Gareth Branwyn, "Jargon Watch," *Wired*, January 1, 1997.

12. Martin Amis, *Invasion of the Space Invaders* (Millbrae, CA: Celestial Arts, 1982), 13.

13. Erkki Huhtamo, "From Kaleidoscomaniac to Cybernerd: Notes toward an Archaeology of the Media," *Leonardo* 30, no. 3 (1997): 221–24; Patrick Ellis, "What Made the Mechanicals Move? Postcards in Transit," in *Provenance and Early Cinema*, ed. Joanne Bernardi et al. (Bloomington: Indiana University Press), 179–90.

14. *Oxford English Dictionary*, s.v. "-itis," oed.com.

15. Quoted in John Harley Warner, "The Aesthetic Grounding of Modern Medicine," *Bulletin of the History of Medicine* 88, no. 1 (Spring 2014), 20.

16. Yuri Tsivian, *Early Cinema in Russia and Its Cultural Reception* (Chicago: University of Chicago Press, 1998 [1994]), 32.

17. Friedrich Kittler, *Gramophone, Film, Typewriter* (Stanford, CA: Stanford University Press, 1999 [1986]).

18. Marshal McLuhan and Quentin Fiore, *The Medium Is the Massage: An Inventory of Effects* (Corte Madera, CA: Gingko Press, 2001 [1967]).

19. Jonathan Crary, *Techniques of the Observer: On Vision and Modernity in the Nineteenth Century* (Cambridge, MA: MIT Press, 1990); Thomas Gold, "Hearing II. The Physical Basis of the Action of the Cochlea," *Proceedings of the Royal Society of London. Series B, Biological Sciences* 135, no. 881 (1948): 492–98.

20. Lev Manovich, "Visual Technologies as Cognitive Prostheses: A Short History of the Externalization of the Mind," in *The Prosthetic Impulse: From a Posthuman Present to a Biocultural Future*, ed. Marquard Smith and Joanne Morra (Cambridge, MA: MIT Press, 2007), 204. Here I am interested in media metaphors for various body parts and senses, but scholars have traditionally focused on the many media analogues for mind—Manovich, above, notes the clock and the motor; and Trevor Owens, the phonograph, in *The Theory and Craft of Digital Preservation* (Baltimore: Johns Hopkins University Press, 2018), 24.

21. Timothy Lenoir, "Helmholtz and the Materialities of Communication," *Osiris* 9 (Instruments, 1994): 184–207.

22. George Wald, "Eye and Camera," *Scientific American* 183, no. 2 (August 1950), 38.

23. On optograms, see Bernd Stiegler, *Belichtete Augen: Optogramme oder das Versprechen der Retina* (Frankfurt am Main: Fischer, 2001).

24. See Arthur B. Evans, "Optograms and Fiction: Photo in a Dead Man's Eye," *Science-Fiction Studies* 20, no. 3 (January 1993): 341–61.

25. See also Christian Quendler, *The Camera-Eye Metaphor in Cinema* (New York: Routledge, 2017).

26. Linda Williams, "Film Bodies: Gender, Genre, and Excess," *Film Quarterly* 44, no. 4 (Summer 1991): 2–13.

27. In its earliest years—roughly, its first decade—the cinema was still too novel, and not widely enough used, to have a diagnosable effect. The medical journal *The Lancet*, for instance, did not consider the impact of the medium on the eye until 1906 when Dr. Edwin Magennis of Dublin described what may well have been an instance of *mal de débarquement*, a phenomenon characterized later in this chapter. "Blindness and the Kinematograph," *The Lancet*, 167, no 4315 (1906): 1349.

28. *The Auckland Star*, July 1, 1909. For more on "picturitis," its origins in 1908, and its fascinating rise and fall through the 1920s, see Gary D. Rhodes, *The Perils of Moviegoing in America: 1896–1950* (New York: Continuum, 2012).

29. "Cinematopthalmia," *Scientific American* 101, no. 12 (September 18, 1909), 193. See also discussion of cinematopthalmia and color in Joshua Yumibe, *Moving Color: Early Film, Mass Culture, Modernism* (New Brunswick, NJ: Rutgers University Press, 2012), 114–15.

30. Aaron E. Singer, *The Visual Fatigue of Motion Pictures: A World-Wide Summary and Survey* (New York: Amusement Age, 1933), 17.

31. "Eye-Strain in Kinemas," *The Lancet*, 196, no. 5063 (1920), 565.

32. Singer, *The Visual Fatigue of Motion Pictures*, 16.

33. George Gould, "Acute Reflex Disorders Caused by the Cinematograph," *JAMA* 59, no. 25 (1912): 2254.

34. "Cinematopthalmia," *Scientific American* 101, no. 12 (September 18, 1909), 19; J. C. Elvy, "Kinematograph Illumination: The Use and Abuse of Light in Studios for Kinema Film Production," *The Lancet*, 197, no. 5086 (1921):413–14; Singer, *The Visual Fatigue of Motion Pictures*, 32.

35. A. Ray Irvine and M.F. Weymann, The Effect on Visual Acuity of Viewing Motion Pictures," *JAMA* 87, no. 14 (1926), 1123.

36. Thomas Elsaesser, "The 'Return' of 3-D: On Some of the Logics and Genealogies of the Image in the Twenty-First Century," *Critical Inquiry* 39, no. 2 (Winter 2013), 220.

37. Albert Brown, "Klieg Eyes," *JAMA* 86, no. 6 (1926): 436–37.

38. "Don't Blame the Specs," *Film Bulletin*, May 18, 1953, 37; for a contemporary instance see Daisuke Danno et al., "Clinical Features of 16 Cases of Headache Which Were Provoked after Watching 3-D Videos," *Internal Medecine* 51, no. 10 (2012):1195–98.

39. Frank Schmäl, "Neuronal Mechanisms and the Treatment of Motion Sickness," *Pharmacology* 2013 (91), 231. To be distinguished from *film sickness*, an excessive viewing habit among children diagnosed in the Soviet Union in the 1930s, and with accompanying withdrawal symptoms. See Anna Toropova, "Science, Medicine, and the Creation of a 'Healthy' Soviet Cinema," *Journal of Contemporary History*, prepress.

40. Alison Griffiths, *Shivers Down Your Spine: Cinema, Museums, and the Immersive View* (New York: Columbia University Press, 2008), 57.

41. Scott C. Richmond, *Cinema's Bodily Illusions: Flying, Floating, and Hallucinating* (Minneapolis: Minnesota University Press, 2016); Lauren Rabinovitz, "More Than the Movies: A History of Somatic Visual Culture through Hale's Tours, Imax, and Motion Simulation Rides," in *Memory Bytes: History, Technology and Digital Culture*, ed. Lauren Rabinovitz and Abraham Geil (Durham, NC: Duke University Press, 2004).

42. Percy Fridenberg, "Visual Factors in Equilibration and Vertigo," *International Journal of Surgery* 31, no. 4 (April 1918), 117.

43. Raymond Fielding, "Hale's Tours: Ultrarealism in the Pre-1910 Motion Picture," *Cinema Journal* 10, no. 1 (Autumn 1970), 34–47.

44. Ibid., 42. This motion was sometimes dealt with euphemistically, for example, "the rocking has caused the women to remain away after the first visit" (46).

45. Eileen Whitfield, *Pickford: The Woman Who Made Hollywood* (Lexington: University of Kentucky Press, 2007), 65.

46. Sergei Eisenstein, "Montage of Attractions," trans Daniel Gerould, *The Drama Review* 18, no. 1 (March 1974 [1923]), 84.

47. And sometimes, even less. In recent years, the response to the unsteady handheld camerawork of *The Blair Witch Project* (1999) was widely accused of causing nausea and headaches.

48. Phantom rides were one of any number of illusory "Phantom" amusements, including the Phantom Swing, a theme park ride still in use today that gives the sensation of movement (of "swinging") by rotating a fixed room around a stable seat.

49. Charles Musser, *Before the Nickelodeon: Edwin S. Porter and the Edison Manufacturing Company* (Berkeley: University of California Press, 1991), 160.

50. Indeed, the first record of a Hale's Tour provided the experience of an "imaginary sky voyage" over New York City. See Lauren Rabinowitz, "Bells and Whistles," in *The Sounds of Early Cinema*, ed. Richard Abel and Rick Altman (Bloomington: Indiana University Press, 2001), 178n2.

51. The parenthetical English subtitle of Méliès' *A Balloon Ascension* is "(Very Comical)." Almost all of Méliès' balloon films suggest a characteristic sense of malfunction: from *The Ballonist's Mishap* (1900) to *The Catastrophe of the Balloon* (1902) to *The Inventor Crazybrains and His Wonderful Airship* (1906).

52. For an interesting analysis of *Panorama pris d'un ballon captif* see Teresa Castro, "Aerial Views and Cinematism," in *Seeing from Above: The Aerial View in Visual Culture*, ed. Mark Dorrian and Frédéric Pousin (London: I.B. Taurus, 2013), 118–33.

53. Raoul Grimoin-Sanson, *Le film de ma vie* (Paris: Henry-Parville, 1926), 126.

54. Jacques Meusy, "L'énigme du Cinéorama," *Archives* 37 (January 1991), 1–16.

55. Elizabeth L. Stocking, "Motion Picture Possibilities," *American Motherhood* 35, no. 6 (December 1912), 360.

56. Robert Smithson, *The Collected Writings* (Berkeley: University of California Press, 1996), 152.

57. Leonard Keene Hirschbirg, "Dizziness and Vertigo Have Causes Which Lie Behind Mind and Muscle," *Washington Times*, March 15, 1915.

58. "Aviation and Surgery," *The Boston Medical and Surgical Journal*, September 7, 1911, 380.

59. Ibid., quoting the University of Bordeaux pathologists René Cruchet and René Moulinier, who would author *Air Sickness: Its Nature and Treatment* (London: John Bale, 1920).

60. "Defects in Flying That Spell Death," *New York Times*, June 30, 1918.

61. Rudolf Arnheim, for instance, characterized this in the 1930s, although the quote is from John F. Golding, "Motion Sickness Susceptibility," *Autonomic Neuroscience: Basic and Clinical* 129 (2006), 68.

62. Robert Wohl, *A Passion for Wings: Aviation and the Western Imagination, 1908–1918* (New Haven, CT: Yale University Press, 1996), 257.

63. On the debt to McCay, see Musser, *Before the Nickelodeon*, 342.

64. Contemporary film theorists have paid just as much attention to the body, typically attentive to the subtler physiological responses of affect. I have preferred the categories that classical film theorists and historians of medicine cumulatively provide—of physiological response, intoxication, pathology, treatment, patient.

65. Patrick Ellis, "A Cinema for the Unborn: Moving Pictures, Mental Pictures, and Electra Sparks' New Thought Film Theory," *British Journal for the History of Science* 50, no. 3 (2017): 411–28.

66. Ibid., 415.

67. Arno Arndt, "Sports on Film," trans. Sara Hall, in *The Promise of Cinema: German Film Theory 1907–1933*, ed. Anton Kaes, Nicholas Baer, and Michael Cowan (Oakland: University of California Press, 2016), 35.

68. Rudolf Arnheim, *Film as Art* (Berkeley: University of California Press, 1957), 34, 112.

69. Paul Virilio, *The Aesthetics of Disappearance*, trans. Philip Beitchman (New York: Semiotext(e), 1991), 12.

70. Roger Caillois, *Man, Play, and Games*, trans. Mayer Barash (New York: The Free Press, 1961), 23.

71. Ben Singer, *Melodrama and Modernity: Early Sensational Cinema and Its Contexts* (New York: Columbia University Press, 2001).

72. Ben Singer, "Modernity, Hyperstimulus, and the Rise of Popular Sensationalism," in *Cinema and the Invention of Modern Life*, ed. Leo Charney and Vanessa Schwartz (Berkeley: University of California Press, 1995), 72.

73. Often associated with Karl Marx (for good if erroneous reason), the origin of the formulation "the annihilation of space and time" was investigated by Leo Marx in *The Machine in the Garden: Technology and the Pastoral Idea in America*. He proposes that the original construction is from an Alexander Pope couplet: "Ye Gods! annihilate but space and time / And make two lovers happy." It is a fine reminder that the phrase has a history beyond that which we are acclimatized to, since Pope's line dates to 1728 and is a plea *for* annihilation rather than a commentary on, or bemoaning of, its arrival. Quoted in Leo Marx, *The Machine in the Garden* (Oxford: Oxford University Press, 1964), 194.

74. See for a sample, Noel Carroll, "Modernity and the Plasticity of Vision," *Journal of Aesthetics and Art Criticism* 59, no. 1 (2001): 11–17; Tom Gunning, "An Aesthetic of Astonishment: Early Film and the (In)Credulous Spectator," *Art and Text* 34 (Spring 1989); Charlie Keil, "'To Here from Modernity': Style, Historiography, and Transitional Cinema," in *American Cinema's Transitional Era: Audiences, Institutions, Practices*, ed. Charlie Keil and Shelley Stamp, (Berkeley: University of California Press, 2006), 51–65; Frank Kessler, "Viewing

Change, Changing Views: The 'History of Vision'-Debate," in *Film 1900: Technology, Perception, Culture*, ed. Annemone Ligensa, Klaus Kreimeier (New Barnet, UK: John Libbey, 2009): 23–35.

75. Ben Singer, "Making Sense of the Modernity Thesis," *Melodrama and Modernity: Early Sensational Cinema and Its Contexts* (New York: Columbia University Press, 2001): 101–30.

76. Williams, "Film Bodies," 4. For a similar line of inquiry, see Martin Barnier, "The Viewer's Body in Motion: Physical and Virtual Effects of Three-Dimensional Spectacles," in *Viscera, Skin, and Physical Form: Corporeality and Early Cinema*, ed. Marina Dahlquist et al. (Bloomington: Indiana University Press, 2018), 263–74.

77. Guenter Risse, "The History of Therapeutics," *Clio Medica* 22 (1991), 6.

78. J.M. Rolfe and K.J. Staples, *Flight Simulation* (Cambridge: Cambridge University Press, 1986).

79. David M. Parker, "A Psychophysiological Test for Motion Sickness Susceptibility," *Journal of General Psychology* 84 (1971): 87–92; with Marthe Howard, "Effects of Repeated Administration of the Psychophysiological Test for Motion Sickness Susceptibility," *Journal of General Psychology* 91 (1974): 273–76.

80. Parker, "A Psychophysiological Test," 88.

81. Ibid.

82. I was able to speak with Professor Marthe Howard, coauthor of the second paper. If Parker's aerial tests were ever undertaken, the results were not published.

83. Parker and Howard, "Effects of Repeated Administration," 276.

84. Ibid., 274.

85. Golding, "Motion Sickness Susceptibility," 71.

86. "Aviation and Surgery," 381.

87. Roland Barthes, "Leaving the Movie Theater," in *The Rustle of Language*, trans. Richard Howard (New York: Hill and Wang, 1986), 345.

88. The quoted line is from the title of Jeremy Greene's talk at the History of Science Society meeting in 2017. For good evidence of his approach in practice, see "When Television Was a Medical Device: On Technology and Health Care," *Humanities* 38, no. 2 (Spring 2017).

89. Miriam Bratu Hansen, "Room-for-Play: Benjamin's Gamble with Cinema," *October* 109 (Summer 2004), 29.

4. OBSERVATION RIDES

1. Wolfgang Schivelbusch, *Disenchanted Night: The Industrialization of Light in the Nineteenth Century* (Berkeley: University of California Press, 1988), 127.

2. "Air Demons or the Holy War 1912," Panama Pacific International Exposition Records, BANC MSS C-A 190, The Bancroft Library, University of California, Berkeley.

3. Jonathan Crary, *Techniques of the Observer: On Vision and Modernity in the Nineteenth Century* (Cambridge, MA: MIT Press, 1990), 5–6.

4. Charles Musser, *Before the Nickelodeon: Edwin S. Porter and the Edison Manufacturing Company* (Berkeley: University of California Press, 1991), 160; Erkki Huhtamo, *Illusions in Motion: Media Archaeology of the Moving Panorama and Related Spectacles* (Cambridge, MA: MIT, 2013).

5. *Cinemaniac* and *balloonatic* share in a wry pathologization of fan culture. The term *cinemaniac* dates at least to the 1910s, when it was employed to characterize those who were excessively interested in cinema; a documentary film about such devoted film viewers was released in 2002, *Cinemania*. The term *balloonatic*, meanwhile, reserved for the balloon enthusiast (or, sometimes, the reckless balloon pilot) in the nineteenth century, would be immortalized by Buster Keaton in his film of that title in 1923.

6. In March of 1915, a couple even wed there—"Here's a chance to start at the top of the ladder," the news item read. "Couple to Marry in Joy Zone Aeroscope," *San Francisco Chronicle*, 13 March 1915, 4.

7. *San Francisco Chronicle*, 7 April 1915.

8. There were many films screened at the exposition, as described in Marina Dahlquist, "Health on Display: The Panama-Pacific International Exposition as Sanitary Venue," in *Performing New Media, 1890–1915*, ed. Kaveh Askari et al. (London: John Libbey, 2015): 174–85. However, the only recording of the Aeroscope besides the Fatty Arbuckle picture that I have located is in *The Opening of the Panama Pacific International Exposition, Feb 20, 1915*. This newsreel is available from the Prelinger Archives, San Francisco. The paucity of representations of the Aeroscope on film (versus a comparably prominent exposition viewing tower) may be partially explained by the rights required to film it. Straus registered his unhappiness about the scenario in a letter held in the Panama Pacific International Exposition Records at The Bancroft Library, University of California, Berkeley (BANC MSS C-A 190).

9. The "captive airplane," or "captive flying machine" was a type of thrill ride ordinarily attributed to amateur cinematographer and inventor of the Maxim machine gun, Hiram Maxim, who debuted the invention at London's Crystal Palace in 1904. The ride, consisting of aircraft-shaped gondolas attached to steel wires, spinning from long mechanical arms, was intended to be a profitable public experiment in flight dynamics. It found a home in emergent amusement parks including both Coney Island and Blackpool (where an original remains, albeit updated for the rocket age). Maxim's machine, however, was less intended to provide an aerial view (its airplanes did not "fly" high enough) than to provoke a thrill, and the mention of the "captive aeroplane" in *Mabel and Fatty Visiting the World's Fair at San Francisco* was thus only a misleading point of reference. See Alan Kattelle, "The Amateur Cinema League and Its Films," *Film History* 15, no. 2 (2003): 238–51; Hiram Maxim, *Artificial and Natural Flight* (London: Whitaker, 1909).

10. "A method of incandescent light design . . . in which the lines of a pencil sketch of a building serve as a guide for the placement of incandescent bulbs."

Kristen Whissel, *Picturing American Modernity: Traffic, Technology, and the Silent Cinema* (Durham, NC: Duke University Press, 2008): 127.

11. John Henry Goldfrap published all his works with New York publisher Hurst: *The Boy Scouts on the Range*, 1911; *The Boy Scouts at the Panama Canal*, 1913; *The Boy Scouts under Fire in Mexico*, 1914; *The Boy Scouts on Belgian Battlefields*, 1915; *The Boy Scouts at the Panama Pacific Exposition*, 1915; *The Boy Scouts with the Allies in France*, 1915.

12. Popular children's works such as The Boy Scouts series are rich resources and underused by media scholars. For evidence of their good utility, see Doron Galili, "Tom Swift's Three Inventions of Television: Technological Imaginary and Media History," *VIEW Journal of European Television History and Culture* 4, no. 7 (2015): 54–67.

13. Goldfrap, *The Boy Scouts at the Panama Pacific Exposition*, 149.

14. Ibid., 150.

15. Ibid., 150.

16. Ibid., 154.

17. Ibid., 163.

18. Thomas Elsaesser, "Media Archaeology as Symptom," *New Review of Film and Television Studies* 14, no. 2 (2016): 205.

19. Bill Brown, "Science Fiction, the World's Fair, and the Prosthetics of Empire, 1910–1915," in *Cultures of United States Imperialism* (Durham, NC: Duke, 1993).

20. Paul Virilio, *War and Cinema: The Logistics of Perception*, trans. Patrick Cammiler (London: Verso, 1989).

21. Walter Benjamin, "Theses on the Philosophy of History," in *Illuminations* (New York: Schocken, 1968 [1955]), 256.

22. See, for a small sample, James C. Scott, *Seeing Like a State: How Certain Schemes to Improve the Human Condition Have Failed* (New Haven, CT: Yale University Press, 1998); Brown, "The Prosthetics of Empire"; Paul Saint-Amour, "Modernist Reconnaissance," *Modernism/Modernity* 10, no. 2 (2003): 349–80; Davide Deriu, "Picturing Ruinscapes: The Aerial Photograph as Image of Historical Trauma," *The Image and the Witness: Trauma, Memory and Visual Culture*, ed. Frances Guerin and Roger Hallas (London: Wallflower Press, 2007), 189–206; Benjamin Fraser, "The Ills of Aerial Photography: Latin America from Above," *Chasqui* 39, no. 2 (November 2010): 70–84; Caren Kaplan, *Aerial Aftermaths* (Durham, NC: Duke University Press, 2018). One might add to this bibliographic list Harun Farocki's film, *Images of the World and the Inscription of War* (1989).

23. Richard P. Hallion, *Taking Flight: Inventing the Aerial Age, from Antiquity through the First World War* (Oxford: Oxford University Press, 2003).

24. John Belton, *American Cinema / American Culture* (New York: McGraw-Hill, 2013), 48.

25. Paula Amad, "From God's-Eye to Camera-Eye: Aerial Photography's Post-humanist and Neo-humanist Visions of the World," *History of Photography* 36, no. 1 (February 2012): 66–86; Anders Ekström, "Seeing from Above: A Particular History of the General Observer," *Nineteenth-Century*

Contexts 31, no. 3 (2009): 185–207; Jason Weems, "Aerial Views and Farm Security Administration Photography," *History of Photography* 28, no. 3 (2004): 266–82. Tom Conley, in his classic *Cartographic Cinema* (Minneapolis: Minnesota University Press, 2006), anticipated and inspired much of this reconsideration of the aerial, including my own.

26. Le Corbusier, *Aircraft* (London: Trefoil, 1987 [1935]), 8.

27. Peter Demetz, *The Air Show at Brescia, 1909* (New York: Farrar, Straus and Giroux, 2002).

28. Charles McClellan Stevens, *Uncle Jeremiah at the Panama-Pacific Exposition* (New York: Grosset & Dunlap, 1915), 260.

29. This has understandably been the most frequent object of scholarly attention at the PPIE. However, as Anders Ekström notes, there has been a tendency to accept the face-value aims of the world's fairs and expositions ("Seeing from Above"). In this instance, widely distributed PPIE images depicting, for instance, Hercules' "thirteenth labor" as parting the Isthmus of Panama have pointed research into the fair toward its "official" "imperialist" purpose while ignoring the experience of visitors and the variety of that experience. The notion that the fair was essentially a chauvinist rally is further belied by, for instance, anarchist Emma Goldman's lecture on "The Philosophy of Atheism" at the Hall of Religion (23 July 1915), or the well-attended and apparently sanctioned parade by the Industrial Workers of the World, documented in exposition newsreels. Furthermore, the imagined extent to which the average visitor to the fair felt the desired propaganda amid an abundance of distractions does not correspond to the historical record nor indeed to contemporary experiences with world's fairs.

30. Frank Morton Todd, *The Story of the Exposition, Vol. 2* (New York: Knickerbocker, 1921), 131.

31. "Patrons ride in a cage on a tall steel spider leg, the trip through the air giving an illusion of an aeroplane ride," *Municipal Record*, 28 January 1915, 55.

32. Ekström, "Seeing from Above," 186.

33. Mollie Slater Merrill, *Gullible's Travels to the Panama Pacific International Exposition* (San Francisco: Self-published, 1915), 5.

34. Daniel J. Boorstin, *The Image: A Guide to Pseudo-Events in America* (New York: Harper & Row, 1961), 107.

35. Tom Gunning has discussed the world-in-miniature logic of the world's fairs in "The World as Object Lesson: Cinema Audiences, Visual Culture and the St. Louis World's Fair, 1904," *Film History* 6, no. 4 (1994): 422–44.

36. Merrill, *Gullible's Travels*, 21.

37. Elizabeth Gordon, *What We Saw at Madame's World's Fair* (San Francisco: Samuel Levinson, 1915), 85.

38. Alexander Geppert, *Fleeting Cities: Imperial Expositions in Fin-de-Siècle Europe* (London: Palgrave, 2010), 95.

39. And, later, to offer "the" view of Paris: "To visit the [Eiffel] Tower is to get oneself up onto the balcony in order to conceive, comprehend, and savor a certain essence of Paris," Roland Barthes, "The Eiffel Tower," *The Eiffel Tower*

and Other Mythologies, trans. Richard Howard (Berkeley: University of California Press, 1997 [1979]), 8.

40. "The Ferris Wheel," *Scientific American Supplement* 916 (July 22, 1893), 14633–34. It is worth noting that not all observation rides reminiscent of the Ferris wheel were met with such enthusiasm. Nashville's Giant See-Saw, which debuted during the Tennessee Centennial and International Exposition of 1897, received comparatively little fanfare.

41. Naomi Schor, "'Cartes Postales': Representing Paris 1900," *Critical Inquiry* 18 (1992): 188–244.

42. *Edison Monthly*, May 1916, 469.

43. *New York Tribune*, 5 September 1915.

44. These citations are from, respectively, the *New York Tribune*, 12 September 1915; *Engineering News* 73, 18 February 1915, 354; *Popular Mechanics*, April 1915; the *New York Tribune* (again), 12 September 1915; and Hamilton Wright, *Overland Monthly* 66, 4 October 1915, 297.

45. Mark Dorrian, "Cityscape with Ferris Wheel: Chicago, 1893." in *Urban Space and Cityscapes: Perspectives from Modern and Contemporary Culture*, ed. Christopher Lindner (London: Routledge, 2006), 17–37.

46. *Popular Electricity Magazine*, May 1913, 65.

47. Anne Friedberg, *Window Shopping: Cinema and the Postmodern* (Berkeley: University of California Press, 1993), 82.

48. "The feeling as one rises with it is similar to that experienced in the ascent of a captive balloon." Herman Whitaker, "Aeroscope of the Panama Fair Takes 120 People 265 Feet in Air," *New York Tribune*, 5 September 1915.

49. Todd, *The Story of the Exposition*, 151.

50. One might profitably compare its movement with the revolving restaurant, another world's fair innovation. See Synne Tollerud Bull, "Kinetic Architecture and Aerial Rides: Towards a Media Archaeology of the Revolving Restaurant View," *Journal of Contemporary Archaeology* 2, no. 1 (2015): 1–147.

51. *Popular Mechanics*, April 1915, 515.

52. Descriptions noting the Aeroscope's spiral were common, and included here are only a few among many representative accounts. Another that focuses on the *sensation* of the spiral is to be found in the *San Francisco Chronicle*'s report, "Aeroscope Juggles Gravity: Novel Sensations Afforded": "To operate the Aeroscope, motors are started simultaneously for the circular and gradual tilting movements, the tower revolving and the end of the long crane rising, the cage rising by a spiral motion." *San Francisco Chronicle*, 12 January 1913, 40.

53. Theodore Cooke, *Curves of Life: Being an Account of Spiral Formations and Their Application to Growth in Nature, to Science and to Art* (London: Constable, 1914), xiv.

54. The earliest designation of *spurl*—presumably some form of onomatopoeic abbreviation of *spiral*—appears to be Mort Walker's definition in *What's Funny about That? A Cartoon Carnival from This Week Magazine* (Boston: E.P. Dutton, 1954), 109, although the use of the iconographic spiral predates

this naming by at least seventy years. See David Kunzle, who notes that such "patterns of oscillation" precede filmic shorthand for movement and speed by several decades. *The History of the Comic Strip* (Berkeley: University of California Press, 1990), 356.

55. Roger Caillois, *Man, Play, and Games* (New York: Macmillan, 1961), 23.

56. Ibid., 23–26.

57. Identical versions of this photograph were distributed as separate postcards that did not mention the fact that it was shot from the Aeroscope, but was rather labeled generically as "Bird's Eye View of Exposition Grounds, Pan.-Pac. Int. Exposition, San Francisco, 1915," Cardinelli-Vincent Postcards.

58. Ed Ruscha, *Thirtyfour Parking Lots in Los Angeles* (artist book), 1967.

59. *Los Angeles Times*, 1 January 1915.

60. *New York Tribune*, 14 October 1917, 7. Strauss later made a reconnoitering apparatus and a spotlight observation tower (not dissimilar to a lighthouse) along the same principles. See William A. Finke, "Joseph B. Strauss: His Life and Achievements," Thesis, University of Cincinnati, 1960, 54.

5. THE AEROPLANE GAZE

1. The contemporary literature on this topic—the aerial view as such, rather than adjacent literature on cartography, panorama painting, aviation, or what have you—has been documented in the chapters above. Other key texts that it would be remiss to omit would include Beaumont Newhall's *Airborne Camera: World from the Air and Outer Space* (Waltham, MA: Focal, 1969); Richard Muir's *History from the Air* (London: Michael Joseph, 1983); Jeanne Haffner's *The View from Above: The Science of Social Space* (Cambridge, MA: MIT, 2013); and the catalog accompanying the Centre Pompidou-Metz' exhibit on the topic, *Vues d'en haut* (Metz: Centre Pompidou-Metz, 2013).

2. Thomas Forster, *Annals of Some Remarkable Aerial and Alpine Voyages* (London: Keating and Brown, 1832), xiv.

3. Paula Amad, "From God's-Eye to Camera-Eye: Aerial Photography's Post-humanist and Neo-humanist Visions of the World," *History of Photography* 36, no. 1 (February 2012): 66–86.

4. Note here that the implied spectator vulnerability in the phrase the "worm's-eye view"—suggesting that the bird of the "bird's-eye view" may swoop in for breakfast—is not present in 1909. That arrives later.

5. Which *annus* in particular was unclear at the time—some thought perhaps 1911—but the secondary literature has settled upon 1908. See, for instance, Charles Harvard Gibbs-Smith, *The Invention of the Aeroplane, 1799–1909* (New York: Taplinger, 1966), 55.

6. La Grande Semaine d'Aviation de la Champagne, Reims; The Olympia Aero Show, London; Die Internationalen Luftschiffahrt-Ausstellung, Frankfurt: all 1909. The air show, like the aeroplane gaze, is at this time largely a Western European and American phenomenon, because that is where flight was overwhelmingly debuted (with the Brazilian Alberto Santos-Dumont's efforts being a

notable exception). Despite its continued relevance, there are next to no scholarly treatments of the air show; Peter Demetz's *The Air Show at Brescia, 1909* is one of the best popular books on the topic (New York: Farrar, Straus and Giroux, 2002).

7. David Edgerton discusses the Aerial League of the British Empire, founded in 1909, in *England and the Aeroplane: Militarism, Modernity and Machines* (London: Penguin, 2013), 20–21.

8. A note on terminology. Overwhelmingly, usage in the period under discussion is to the *aeroplane*, rather than to the *airplane* familiar to us. I have been careful to adapt spelling according to period and user.

9. Usually titled *Aeroplane Gaze*, it was sometimes rendered *Airship Gaze*—or, in the original French, *Voila Aeroplane!* (In German, *Ah! Da fliegt ein Aeroplan!*) The film was distributed by Essanay in the United States.

10. For closely related parallels, see *La course à la perruque* (Pathé, 1906), which features a runaway wig attached to a helium balloon; or *Erste Ausfahrt einer Radlerin* (1907), which instead of an aeroplane has a mob following an erratic bicyclist.

11. See Erkki Huhtamo, "Dismantling the Fairy Engine: Media Archaeology as Topos Study," in *Media Archaeology: Approaches, Applications and Implications*, ed. Erkki Huhtamo and Jussi Parikka (Berkeley: University of California Press, 2011), 27–47.

12. From "The Spectator," a pseudonymous column in *The Outlook*, August 1, 1908, 745.

13. I am especially indebted to the aeronautica collections at the Smithsonian National Air and Space Museum and the Anderson Aeronautical History Collection at the Woodson Research Center at Rice University.

14. We find another holdover of this spectacular era of flight in the stylish, grandiose early days of commercial aviation, and in the Jet Age that many seem to be nostalgic for today. For some time now, the spectacle of flight has been confined to the screens onboard. On the Jet Age, see Vanessa Schwartz, "Dimanche à Orly: The Jet-Age Airport and the Spectacle of Technology between Sky and Earth," *French Politics, Culture & Society*, 32, no. 3 (Winter 2014): 24–44; on inflight entertainment, see Stephen Groening, "Aerial Screens," *History and Technology* 29, no. 3 (December 2013): 281–303.

15. "Institutes of Hydrostatics," *The Monthly Review* (December 1787), 449; Mary Elliot, *Early Seeds to Produce Young Flowers* (London: William Darton, 1820), 14.

16. Readers may be familiar with the more well-known, pithier version of this line: "What is the use of a new-born baby?" This instance is drawn from a period text, John Douglas-Scott-Montagu's *A Short History of Balloons and Flying Machines* (London: The Car Illustrated, 1907), 119. In any case, the line is likely apocryphal.

17. Benjamin Franklin to Joseph Banks, December 1, 1783, in *The Complete Works of Benjamin Franklin, vol. 8* (New York: G. P. Putnam, 1888), 382.

18. Any history of aviation and ballooning is a history of failed experiment and few successes. For speculative travel and warfare accounts, 1908 was the key

year; both H.G. Wells's novel *The War in the Air* and Albert Robida's illustrated *La guerre infernale* were published, as discussed in chapter 4.

19. Simon Werrett, "Watching the Fireworks: Early Modern Observation of Natural and Artificial Spectacles," *Science in Context* 24, no. 2 (June 2011), 170. See also Werrett's *Fireworks: Pyrotechnic Arts and Sciences in European History* (Chicago: University of Chicago Press, 2010).

20. Allan Chapman, *The Victorian Amateur Astronomer: Independent Astronomical Research in Britain, 1820–1920* (Chichester: Wiley, 1998), 167. See also Charlotte Bigg, "Staging the Heavens: Astrophysics and Popular Astronomy in the Late Nineteenth Century," in *The Heavens on Earth: Observatories and Astronomy in Nineteenth-Century Science and Culture* (Durham, NC: Duke University Press, 2010): 305–24.

21. Chapman, *The Victorian Amateur Astronomer*, 167.

22. We might count, today, the planetarium space show in this same tradition. See Alison Griffiths, "'A Moving Picture of the Heavens': Planetarium Space Shows as Useful Cinema," in *Useful Cinema*, ed. Charles Acland and Haidee Wasson (Durham, NC: Duke University Press, 2011), 230–59.

23. Erkki Huhtamo, "The Sky Is (Not) the Limit: Envisioning the Ultimate Public Media Display," *Journal of Visual Culture* 8, no. 3 (2010): 329–47.

24. Paula McDowell, "Media and Mediation in the Eighteenth Century," *Oxford Handbooks* (Cambridge: Cambridge University Press, 2017).

25. John Durham Peters, *The Marvelous Clouds: Toward a Philosophy of Elemental Media* (Chicago: University of Chicago Press, 2015), 165.

26. For a full account of the Paris Commune and balloons, see Richard Holmes's "Paris Airborne," *Falling Upwards: How We Took to the Air* (London: William Collins, 2013).

27. Octave Chanute, "Opening Address," *Proceedings of the International Conference on Aerial Navigation* (New York: The American Engineer and Railroad Journal, 1894), 8–9. Richard P. Hallion's indispensable *Taking Flight: Inventing the Aerial Age, from Antiquity through the First World War* (Oxford: Oxford University Press, 2003) alerted me to this document.

28. "Aeronautics," *The New Volumes of the Encyclopædia Britannica, Volume 25* (Edinburgh: Adam & Charles Black, 1902).

29. The poem continues: "The great day came, and all was ready: / Crowds of spectators at Vauxhall were gazing, / And to the spot. Rose from his quiet grazing / Forthwith was brought. / Into the car by ropes kept steady / The pony went. / And to prevent his tumbling into the street / A lock was put on each of Rose's feet— / Or rather, his fetlocks were locked. / Now Mr. Green mounts on the back of Rose, / The ropes are cut, and away in a crack she goes! / Ten minutes more, and this aërial tour was over. / And at some place in Kent, / To his unspeakable content / Our pony was quietly regaling in a field of clover." Douglas-Scott-Montagu, *A Short History of Balloons and Flying Machines*, 116–17.

30. Richard Holmes, *Falling Upwards: How We Took to the Air* (London: William Collins, 2013), 42.

31. Ibid., 195.

32. "The Airship Craze Fast Fading Away: Star-Gazing has Ceased," *San Francisco Chronicle*, November 26, 1896, 14.

33. Readers may wonder, at this stage, where the Italian Futurists figure in this reception, given that they are perhaps the most well-known group to aestheticize flight. Their enthusiasm for aviation is by and large beyond the historical purview of this chapter; with few exceptions, they became most interested in flight in the 1920s, with the development of *aeropittura*. In any case, the trajectory traced here has the effect of normalizing their evaluation of aviation into a typical *nineteenth-century* response, rather than one of avant-garde, technophilic rupture. That is to say, an aesthetic appreciation of aviation that we (rightly) associate with modernists was once a pedestrian enthusiasm.

34. Anson Rabinbach, *The Human Motor: Energy, Fatigue, and the Origins of Modernity* (Berkeley: University of California Press, 1992), 99.

35. Hallion, *Taking Flight*, 26. Avian aerodynamics did inspire successful aviation in other domains, but the flapping wings of the ornithopter were a dead end.

36. Quoted in Sydney Hollands, "Motor Aviation of To-day and of Recent Years," *Flight*, March 1902, 53.

37. For many examples of aviation satire in the Sunday pages, see the reprint volumes edited by Peter Maresca, *Forgotten Fantasy: Sunday Comics 1900–1915* (Palo Alto, CA: Sunday Press, 2011), and *Society Is Nix: Gleeful Anarchy at the Dawn of the American Comic Strip, 1895–1915* (Palo Alto, CA: Sunday Press, 2014).

38. The examples in this paragraph come from the clippings of the Gill scrapbooks, which survive in the archives of the Smithsonian National Air and Space Museum. The images are from unidentified and undated period newspapers, but at least one gives an indication of the general date range, as it depicts the Harvard–Boston Aero Meet of 1910. See the Howard Gill Early Aviation Scrapbooks Collection, NASM.XXXX.025.

39. It is no wonder that the hat adapted to the airplane at this time in comic form. Women's large hats were a frequent source for comic gags at the time, and often materialize in the work of Winsor McCay. They were a source of complaint at the movie theater. See Maggie Hennefeld, "Women's Hats and Silent Film Spectatorship: Between Ostrich Plume and Moving Image," *Film History* 28, no. 3 (2016): 24–53.

40. The prose varied slightly from newspaper to newspaper. This version is from the *Spokane Press*, December 10, 1910, in an unpaginated section for humor and unusual news.

41. Anticipated in the *Charlotte News*, September 17, 1908, 4.

42. The entire quote runs as follows: "Le cinéma et l'aviation vont bras-dessus, bras-dessus dans la vie, ils sont nés le même jour." Fernand Léger, "A propos du cinema," *Intelligence du cinématographe*, ed. Marcel L'Herbier (Parris: Corrêa, 1946), 337.

43. Tom Gunning, "An Aesthetic of Astonishment: Early Film and the (In)Credulous Spectator," *Art and Text*, 34 (Spring 1989), 115.

44. Miriam Hansen, *Babel & Babylon: Spectatorship in American Silent Film* (Cambridge, MA: Harvard University Press, 1991): 57.

45. In French, it was the catch-all *regard*, as in Nadar's account of a crowd of balloon watchers: "the people who look from below to above—eyes half-closed, mouth wide open" ("des gens qui regardent de bas en haut—les yeux mi-clos, la bouche grande ouverte"). Nadar, "Le dessus et le dessous de Paris," *Paris Guide: Par les principaux écrivains et artistes de la France* (Paris: Internationale, 1867), 1580.

46. Peters, *The Marvelous Clouds*, 190; contrariwise, in his history of American aviation, Joseph Corn compares the view to "rapture." *The Winged Gospel: America's Romance with Aviation* (Baltimore: Johns Hopkins University Press, 2001 [1983]), 3.

47. *Oxford English Dictionary*, s.v. "navel-gazing," oed.com.

48. Le Corbusier, *Aircraft* (London: Trefoil, 1987 [1935]), 6.

49. Treatment of aviation as a novel sport has largely been forgotten. See, for instance, the journalist and anarchist James Huneker, who considered flying to be "the sport of the gods." "Riding the Whirlwind," in *Unicorns* (New York: Scribner, 1921), 349.

50. Franz Kafka, "The Aeroplanes at Brescia," *A Hunger Artist and Other Stories*, trans. Joyce Crick (Oxford, Oxford University Press, 2012 [1909]), 9. Kafka's account is remarkably similar to some of the promotional literature that circulated with air shows at the time. Take, for instance, the promoter of the Blackpool Aviation Week, explaining why it is thrilling to view aeroplanes in flight: "What is it that makes one's sensations, as one watches these flying men, so exciting and ecstatic? Why is it that, when the wheels of their machines leave the ground, when they rise with throbbing movement in to the air, one experiences such a vivid sense of triumph and of joy, such an irresistible need of working off emotion by shouting and running and cheering the exploit on? You have seen a child's glee as a kite mounts up and up. It gives little delighted cries, and claps its hands and jumps about." *Blackpool Aviation Week Official Program-Souvenir*, 1909.

51. "Aeroplane Gaze," *Milwaukee Journal*, October 31, 1911, 3.

52. The term was coined in 1917 according to the OED. *Oxford English Dictionary*, s.v. "jay-walker," oed.com. For more on the social construction of jaywalking, see Peter D. Norton, *Fighting Traffic: The Dawn of the Motor Age in the American City* (Cambridge, MA: MIT Press, 2008).

53. Ben Singer, "Modernity, Hyperstimulus, and the Rise of Popular Sensationalism," in *Cinema and the Invention of Modern Life*, ed. Leo Charney and Vanessa Schwartz (Berkeley: University of California Press, 1995), 72–99.

54. Of course, crowded skies had been pictured prior to this time, and indeed beyond, but having consulted numerous collections of aeronautica, I can say with confidence that there is a particular boom of such imagery in this moment.

55. "*L'Homme, sans doute, ne se fatiguait plus mais son monde était devenu vraiment très agité.*"

56. Paul Virilio, *Speed and Politics: An Essay on Dromology* (New York: Columbia University Press, 1986).

57. Hannah Arendt, *The Human Condition* (Chicago: Chicago University Press, 1958), 1.

58. "Once knowledge of fireworks was widespread, making them familiar, it became fashionable to act as if one was afraid of them." Simon Werrett "Watching the Fireworks: Early Modern Observation of Natural and Artificial Spectacles," *Science in Context* 24, no. 2 (June 2011), 172. Media historian Artemis Willis notes a potentially similar shift in astronomy as such, moving from sublimity to wonder, in "'What the Moon Is Like': Technology, Modernity, and Experience in a Late-Nineteenth-Century Astronomical Entertainment," *Early Popular Visual Culture* 15, no. 2 (2017): 175–203.

59. On aviation during the First World War, see John H. Morrow, *The Great War in the Air: Military Aviation from 1909 to 1921* (Tuscaloosa: University of Alabama Press, 1993); on how this was rendered in art, see Jon Mogul, "The Art of Aerial Warfare," in *Myth + Machine: Art and Aviation in the First World War* (Miami: The Wolfsonian–Florida International University, 2014).

60. There is no date on the film, but British Pathé provides this estimate.

61. However, the militarization of aerial viewing witnessed in the aeroplane gaze is by no means a given—and indeed two important "demilitarizations" have been tracked in this book, in the form of the formerly military panstereorama and the rejection of the "Air Demons or the Holy War 1912" exhibit.

62. Helen Macdonald, "'What Makes You a Scientist Is the Way You Look at Things': Ornithology and the Observer, 1930–1955," *Studies in History and Philosophy of Science Part C: Studies in History and Philosophy of Biological and Biomedical Sciences* 33, no. 1 (March 2002), 56.

63. W. Patrick McCray, *And Keep Watching the Skies! The Story of Operation Moonwatch and the Dawn of the Space Age* (Princeton, NJ: Princeton University Press, 2008).

64. Ibid., 26.

65. Paul Virilio, *War and Cinema: The Logistics of Perception*, trans. Patrick Cammiler (London: Verso, 1989).

66. Anton Kaes, "The Cold Gaze: Notes on Mobilization and Modernity," *New German Critique* 59, (Spring–Summer, 1993): 105–17.

67. Such cautions number in the hundreds. Within weeks of the time of writing this note, three have crossed my path (a small sample of an editorial cottage industry): Katherine Shaver, "Safety Experts to Pedestrians: Put the Smartphones Down and Pay Attention," *Washington Post*, September 20, 2014 (washingtonpost.com); Homa Khaleeli "Text Neck: How Smartphones Are Damaging Our Spines," *The Guardian*, November 24, 2014 (theguardian.com); Nick Bilton, "Message to Self: In 2015, Stop Texting while Walking," *New York Times*, December 24, 2014, E1.

CONCLUSION: FIRST FLIGHTS

1. The exact percentage of lost films is unknown, ranging between 75 percent (Library of Congress) and 90 percent (American Film Institute). For a discussion of the institutional politics around the issue, see Caroline Frick, *Saving Cinema: The Politics of Preservation* (Oxford: Oxford University Press, 2011), 65.

2. For wax cylinders, see the UC Santa Barbara Cylinder Audio Archive; and on the audible zoetrope, see Machiko Kusahara, "The Baby Talkie, Domestic Media, and the Japanese Modern," in *Media Archaeology: Approaches, Applications and Implications*, ed. Erkki Huhtamo and Jussi Parikka (Berkeley: University of California Press, 2011), 123–47.

3. Although much used in art history, the term *lacuna* originally referred to a "hiatus, blank, missing portion" of a manuscript. *Oxford English Dictionary*, s.v. "lacuna," oed.com.

4. "The discussion of 'firsts' does not frequently arrive in discussion as a historiographic problem—most historians agree it is not the most productive area of focus." George E. Smith and David Mindell, "The Emergence of the Turbofan Engine," in *Atmospheric Flight in the Twentieth Century*, ed. Peter Galison and Alex Roland (Dordrecht: Kluwer, 2000), 145. See also David Edgerton's critique of the firsts presented by science and technology museums in *The Shock of the Old: Technology and Global History since 1900* (Oxford: Oxford University Press, 2007), 29.

5. Tom Gunning, "An Aesthetic of Astonishment: Early Film and the (In)Credulous Spectator," *Art and Text*, 34 (Spring 1989), 115.

6. An anthology collecting accounts of people's first actual flights would be a document of vivid, well-remembered moments.

7. Humphrey Jennings, *Pandaemonium: The Coming of the Machine as Seen by Contemporary Observers, 1660–1886* (New York: Free Press, 1985).

8. Ibid., xxxviii.

9. Tom Gunning, "Re-newing Old Technologies: Astonishment, Second Nature, and the Uncanny in Technology from the Previous Turn-of-the-Century," in *Rethinking Media Change: The Aesthetics of Transition*, ed. David Thorburn and Henry Jenkins (Cambridge, MA: MIT Press, 2004), 40.

10. See also Gunning's later reflections on these ideas with Annie van den Oever in "Viktor Shklovsky's Ostrannenie and the 'Hermeneutics of Wonder,'" *Early Popular Visual Culture* 18, no. 1 (Feb 2020): 1–14.

11. Another book—call it *The Aeroscopic Avant Garde*—might have focused on interwar art; on precisionist work such as Charles Sheeler's emblematic painting, *Church St El* (1920); Dadaist collage such as Hannah Hoch's *From Above* (1926–27); surrealist ersatz aerials such as Man Ray's *Dust Breeding* (1920); not to mention the Futurists. As it stands, this footnote will have to suffice.

12. I have also considered contemporary aeroscopics in a series of non-scholarly articles on model cities, aerial photography, and world's fairs. See Patrick Ellis, "Cities in Miniature: Ahmet Öğüt's 'Exploded City,'" *Rhizome*,

February 10, 2010; "The Centurion in the Parking Lot," *Paper Monument*, July 8, 2010; "Coca-Cola Milanese," *n+1*, August 28, 2015.

13. On experimental media archaeology, see Andreas Fickers and Annie van den Oever, "Experimental Media Archaeology: A Plea for New Directions," in *Techné / Technology: Researching Cinema and Media Technologies—Their Development, Use, and Impact*, ed. Annie Van den Oever (Amsterdam: Amsterdam University Press, 2013): 272–78; Patrick Ellis and Colin Williamson, "Object Lessons, Now and Then: Experimental Media Archaeology in the Classroom," *Early Popular Visual Culture* 18, no. 1 (2020): 2–14.

14. See Alison Griffiths, *Shivers Down Your Spine: Cinema, Museums, and the Immersive View* (New York: Columbia, 2008); Brooke Belisle, "Nature at a Glance: Immersive Maps from Panoramic to Digital," *Early Popular Visual Culture* 13, no. 4 (2016): 313–35.

15. Olivo Barbieri, *Site Specific* (New York: Aperture, 2013).

16. Cf. chapter 3, note 73.

17. "US Thrill Rides and Bill Kitchen Announce a New and Innovative 'Twist' in Observation Attractions," *PRWeb*, October 27, 2011.

18. I am also leaping over the many aeroscopic technologies of the twentieth century. Take Norman Bel Geddes's "Futurama" model for an interesting midcentury example that has been discussed in a similar context. See Adnan Morshed, *Impossible Heights: Skyscrapers, Flight, and the Master Builder* (Minneapolis: Minnesota University Press, 2014).

19. *The European Magazine and London Review*, vol. 44 (1803), 185.

20. See film of the same name discussed on page 86.

21. Teresa Castro, "Cinema's Mapping Impulse: Questioning Visual Culture," *The Cartographic Journal*, 46, no. 1 (2009): 9–15.

22. *Oxford English Dictionary*, s.v. "intoxication," oed.com.

23. This last note bookends this volume's first note: evidence of the intellectual debt that I owe to James R. Akerman's magisterial "Finding Our Way," in *Maps: Finding Our Place in the World* (Chicago: Chicago University Press, 2007), 19–63.

Index

Founded in 1893,
UNIVERSITY OF CALIFORNIA PRESS
publishes bold, progressive books and journals
on topics in the arts, humanities, social sciences,
and natural sciences—with a focus on social
justice issues—that inspire thought and action
among readers worldwide.

The UC PRESS FOUNDATION
raises funds to uphold the press's vital role
as an independent, nonprofit publisher, and
receives philanthropic support from a wide
range of individuals and institutions—and from
committed readers like you. To learn more, visit
ucpress.edu/supportus.